MODIFIED
BODIES
MATERIAL
SELVES

Julie E. Starr

MODIFIED
BODIES
MATERIAL
SELVES

Beauty Ideals

in Post-Reform Shanghai

UNIVERSITY OF WASHINGTON PRESS SEATTLE ●

Modified Bodies, Material Selves was made possible in part by a grant from the Association for Asian Studies First Book Subvention Program.

UNIVERSITY OF WASHINGTON PRESS *uwapress.uw.edu*

LIBRARY OF CONGRESS CATALOGING-IN-PUBLICATION DATA
Names: Starr, Julie E., author.
Title: Modified bodies, material selves : beauty ideals in post-reform Shanghai / Julie E. Starr.
Description: Seattle : University of Washington Press, 2023. | Includes bibliographical references and index.
Identifiers: LCCN 2023010377 | ISBN 9780295751757 (hardcover) | ISBN 9780295751764 (paperback) | ISBN 9780295751771 (ebook)
Subjects: LCSH: Feminine beauty (Aesthetics)—China—Shanghai. | Beauty, Personal—Social aspects—China—Shanghai. | Women—China—Shanghai—Social conditions—21st century. | Middle class women—China—Shanghai. | Shanghai (China)—Social conditions—21st century.
Classification: LCC HQ1220.C6 S73 2023 | DDC 305.40951/132—dc23/eng/20230414
LC record available at https://lccn.loc.gov/2023010377

●

FOR MY MENTORS

Lindsay Jones and John R. Shepherd,

whose support and guidance

made this book possible

CONTENTS

ACKNOWLEDGMENTS

The completion of this book relied on the support, vision, and insight of many caring, discerning, and wonderful people. To all of my friends, family, and colleagues who have supported me during this long journey, you have made me and my scholarship better and I thank you.

There is no doubt that my greatest debt is to the women I got to know and became friends with in Shanghai, on whom this research is based. I cannot thank you enough for letting me into your lives, sharing with me your personal experiences, and growing with me throughout our time together. My hope is that my ethnographic descriptions do justice to your experiences in Shanghai and my analysis keeps alive the conversations that were important to us in the city. I would also like to thank my friends at Shanghai Normal University for providing an intellectual home for me during my fieldwork for this book, including Deng Yanyan, Liu Yunhua, and Wenyuan Shao. Finally, a big thank you to Jian Xiaobing for helping me procure a research relationship with Shanghai Normal University, a last-minute arrangement that had lasting implications for this project.

It is with sincere gratitude that I extend my thanks to my mentors and teachers who have provided me with intellectual and personal support. I owe a special debt to John R. Shepherd, who has been tireless in his commitment to my work, reading every iteration of the chapters I produced. Through your comments and critical engagement, you have helped mold me into a scholar who cares about the details as much as the larger theoretical issues. To Richard Handler, I offer many thanks for your continuing encouragement. From piquing my interest in the history of anthropology to continuing to read and engage with my scholarship, you are always generous with your time and ideas. I would also like to extend my gratitude to Eve Danziger, whose insights and friendship helped shape my intellectual curiosities. Your ability to render and then articulate the logic internal to a document is truly astounding and has no doubt made me a better thinker and writer. Fred Damon provided opportunity upon opportunity for me to socialize with great minds and helped me see that the ability to "be a person," however defined in a particular context, is what makes for great anthropology. In addition, I would like to extend my thanks to Ira Bashkow and Susan McKinnon, whose classes and scholarship laid the foundation for my theoretical orientation to anthropology. I am deeply grateful to Chaise LaDousa and Bonnie Urciuoli, who provided insightful feedback and much-needed moral support throughout the revision process and have made Hamilton feel like home. I would also like to thank the many wonderful students I've had the opportunity to teach at Hamilton College who have helped me work through and clarify my thoughts in this book.

My development as an anthropologist is no doubt indebted to the many hours of discussions with my friends and colleagues, including Beth Hart, Nathan Hedges, Viktoryia Kalesnikava, Dionisios Kavadias, Kristin LaHatte, Melissa Maceyko, Colin Quinn, and Chenyu Wang. In addition, I would like to extend special thanks to David Flood, Roberto Armengol, Arsalan Kahn, Rose Wellman, and Grace Reynolds. Your friendships, intellectual sparring sessions, and feedback on early versions of the chapters helped me solidify my ideas for this book as well as my engagement with anthropology (and the wider world) more generally.

To my friends, teachers, and mentors at The Ohio State University and in Qingdao, China, especially Galal Walker, Cao Ana, and Liu Shitong, thank you for believing in me and supporting me as I began my studies of Chinese language.

Generous financial support for this research, at various stages, was provided by the Mellon Foundation, the Wenner-Gren Foundation, the Foreign Language Area Studies (FLAS) program, the Buckner W. Clay Endowment for the Humanities, and the Department of Anthropology and the East Asia Center at the University of Virginia.

Many thanks to my editor, Lorri Hagman, and her colleagues at University of Washington Press for their support and guidance bringing my first book to fruition.

My family has been a much relied-on source of encouragement throughout this process. To my parents, grandparents, aunts, uncles, and siblings, thank you for being a steady source of comfort and inspiration. I was able to turn to you when I needed those things the most. Appreciations to my dad, for reading multiple drafts of the manuscript and helping me check references at the very end of the process; to my mom for being a wonderful Grammy and loving and playing with my children while I wrote; to Grandma Woolf and Aunt Jamie Woolf for always encouraging and championing my intellectual pursuits. And finally, I must thank my amazing husband and partner in life, Adam, for his truly remarkable support and generosity, and our two children, Ellie and Ziggy, for teaching me about love and how to see the world anew.

MODIFIED
BODIES
MATERIAL
SELVES

INTRODUCTION

On a blustery Tuesday evening, my good friend Mei met me to help with my research. We chose to meet at the mall adjoined to the Shanghai Stadium subway station, centrally located between her apartment and mine—for our purposes, we might have chosen any mall in the city. Mei knew about my interest in beautification and body modifying practices and suggested we go together to one of the salons specializing in weight loss, which are prevalent in malls throughout the city.

The mall where we met had two of these salons, owned by competing Hong Kong companies offering almost identical services. It was late winter of 2012, the year after Marie France Bodyline opened dozens of weight-loss clinics in Shanghai to launch its "New Body, New Life" campaign. In no time at all, in a pattern familiar to those living in this dizzyingly fast-changing city, there were "copycat" versions of the salons all over Shanghai, most advertising that they were "successful" companies from Hong Kong. So we picked one of the salons and walked in.

The lobby was dimly lit, with furniture reminiscent of a waiting room at a doctor's office. The receptionist greeted us warmly and handed me a small questionnaire to fill out. Mei and I decided that I would be the client and she would act as my friend and translator, if needed. Once I finished the paperwork, the receptionist led us back to a small private room, where we met with one of the salon's specialists. She asked me about my daily habits—what I typically ate for breakfast, lunch, and dinner; what kind of job I had; how much I worked, and so forth—and my desired weight. She then asked me to take off my clothes, down to my underwear and bra. As

I stood almost naked in front of a large mirror, she took measurements of my waist, hips, thighs, calves, arms, and bust. Along the way, she made comments: "oh, that's good" (my waist), "very nice" (my bust), and "oh, not good at all" (my thighs). Mei nodded in agreement at her assessments.

After recording my measurements, she showed me—by using her hands to twist and pull my thighs into what they should look like—what the program could do for me. She described the technique used: bandages are soaked in a special solution for twenty-four hours and then wrapped, mummy-style, for thirty minutes around the problematic parts of the body (she again pointed to my thighs). The special solution works by activating a certain property of cells, causing them to consume the fat surrounding them. So, her pitch went, all I would have to do is sit, wrapped up like a mummy, and I could lose weight and slim my thighs.

As we were chatting about the process, I asked her about the advantage of using the bandages instead of dieting and exercising. She said, first, dieting could be dangerous if you are not paying attention to your *tizhi* (bodily disposition). At this point Mei excitedly jumped in and said, "She's absolutely right. I went on a horrible diet when I was younger and messed up my *tizhi* so badly that I got very ill. Three years later, I'm still recovering." The woman nodded in agreement. "Unless you're very careful, making sure you're not eating too many cold foods, dieting isn't a good idea." She then went on to explain that the problem with exercising is that it makes you lose weight all over your body. You have much less control over where you lose weight and where you don't. By using the bandages, you can target certain areas, so you can slim your legs while retaining a nice round butt. Moreover, exercising takes a lot of time, and when you do too much, it can make you really tired, depleting the energy you need for other essential tasks.

When we finished talking to the specialist, I got dressed and Mei and I explored the menu of treatment options. The salon was running a special: for ¥888 (approximately US$150), I could get eight sessions, two a week for a month, and lose up to ten *jin* (about eleven pounds). We decided to think it over (since it was such a big investment) and left the salon to go have dinner.

Upstairs, in the same mall, was a fabulous Sichuan restaurant, and over a pot of spicy fish we chatted about the experience. Mei acknowledged that the treatment was expensive but thought I should consider it. Slimming my thighs would improve my look, she said, which might make me a more effective researcher. She went on to say that she was my friend and wanted to help me be successful. "You need to be both healthy and beautiful to influence others," she reminded me as we said our good-byes for the night.

The next evening, my husband, Adam, and his local musician partner had a show at a bar in town. I gathered with some of our Western friends for a few drinks and we listened to the performance. As we were chatting and catching up on our week, I described my experience in the salon. Somewhat to my surprise, my friends could not contain their horror: "Holy shit, that sounds like a hazing stunt at a sorority or something," my friend Sarah exclaimed. The other women shook their heads. Emily leaned across the table and asked, sympathetically, how I was doing. "You OK after that? I mean, I know you're doing research, but just make sure you aren't internalizing that stuff. You're beautiful, just as you are, you know." They went on to talk about how "sad" it made them feel that women in China (anywhere, really) would feel the need to change themselves to meet other people's standards. Everyone is beautiful, they said, and as empowered women, they rejected the need for beauty ideals at all.

● Set against the backdrop of the post-reform era, this book compares the radically different attitudes the middle-class "Chinese" and "Western" women I knew in Shanghai had toward pursuing beauty. As such, the book joins an ongoing conversation about the impact of recent economic reforms on social life in China, focusing specifically on the ways that late capitalism interacts with different notions and experiences of bodies to inform culturally particular body politics. A consideration of theories of embodiment, culturally variant experiences of selfhood, and the politics of beauty shows how, in the highly consumerist context of Shanghai, Chinese and Western professional women had strikingly different ideas about the relationship between the materiality of selfhood and embodied identities. These differences directly informed the extent to which the Chinese women were untroubled by the pursuit of beauty, while the Western women were highly critical of the ideals they encountered in Shanghai. Rather than viewing the Chinese women's willingness to pursue beauty ideals as an indication of their internalizing Western ideals of beauty (as the Western professional women suspected and an older literature assumes) or a neoliberal ethic of self-cultivation and individual responsibility (as much work on beautification tends to do), this book extends the analysis of body modifications to include the ways that understandings of bodies, and the politics ascribed to them, are culturally produced—for both groups of women in Shanghai.

Women's bodies, sexuality, and appearances are being commodified in current-day China. Many scholars view this as part of the shift to a consumer-based society, in which new forms of gendered labor and the pursuit of beauty are highly entangled with discourses about "the market" and naturalized or biologically based bodily differences. Yet, other scholars have shown, building on and contributing to the insights of medical anthropology that challenge the hegemony of biomedicine and the universality of biology (see, for example, Lock 1993; Lock and Farquhar 2007; Lock and Nguyen 2010), that notions of "the body" in China are fundamentally different from bodies as conceptualized and experienced in "the West." When these literatures are read alongside each other, the juxtaposition is striking: the body is either a naturalized site ripe for exploitation by consumer-based late capitalism or a culturally variable entity that can contest Western assumptions about bodies and the material world. This book's ethnographic comparison of Chinese and Western women in Shanghai brings the literatures together to contend that far from producing a universalized commodifiable "body," consumerism—and the identities constructed through it—is inevitably a culturally enabled process (Yanagisako 2002) that reflects diverse understandings of bodies and selves. Building on the anthropologist Susan Brownell's (1995) work on "body culture," and extending it to the realm of beauty and body politics, I show that for the women I knew in Shanghai different understandings about the materiality of self informed the kinds of political importance they attached to modifying certain traits of their bodies and the actions of bodily consumerism they deemed agentive. These different notions of embodied selfhood also informed their more general commentary about the gendered and racialized differences in the city and the ways their own bodies implicated them in local hierarchies.

For example, most of the Chinese women I knew were committed to improving their bodily appearance and were not at all troubled by such pursuits. It became clear through our discussions that many of them saw the body as a legitimate site for personal, social, and career advancement and thought beauty ideals were a necessary road map for improvement. To these women, the body was but *one among many* aspects of self that could and should be improved on in the pursuit of success.[1] They were adamant that the body was not "special" in any sense: it should not be given too little or too much attention. They were critical of the women in China who focused too much on their appearance. They were also critical of Western women who were "too sensitive" about their bodies, and they were displeased with Western media's critical accounts of beauty in China. In fact, they thought it was a Western trait to attach overtly political implications to appearance or bodies, and they attributed their own willingness to pursue the beauty ideals in Shanghai to a *Chinese* way of doing things.

The Western women I knew, by contrast, were deeply troubled by the moral implications of modifying their bodies on the basis of "society's" ideals. They were caught in an unending tension between wanting to "look good" and being adamant that bodies "shouldn't matter." They associated an authentic self with an unmodified body, and thus, for them, working on "the body" was quite distinct from other kinds of "self-discovering" that they saw as central to their pursuit of happiness or contentment in life. As such, they typically couched the pursuit of beauty ideals as a form of self-betrayal that should be actively guarded against. Many of their discussions sought to critique, undermine, or downplay the significance of the beauty ideals they encountered in Shanghai, which they viewed as patriarchal and racist.

The comparison of the body politics of these two groups of women is not meant to be representative of Chinese and Western approaches to beauty. For example, there are plenty of Chinese women in China who are highly critical of the beauty ideals described in this book, especially the way they are linked to gender inequality in China.[2] There are also celebrities in China who represent or are pushing for alternative ideals.[3] The Shanghai Chinese women I knew were familiar with these counternarratives. However, they mostly dismissed the critiques as "too Western" (that is, as internalizing the Western propensity to take the body too seriously) and thought that the alternative ideals might work for others (such as minorities in China) but were unacceptable for themselves, as Han women. Similarly, plenty of women in the Western world pursue beauty ideals. It is well documented, however, that they typically do so in order to align their appearance with how they view themselves, sharing with the Shanghai Western women a cultural orientation that prioritizes an authentic self. Such comparisons demonstrate how bodily politics emerge in particular ways for particularly situated professional women and how those politics cannot be disentangled from experiences of selfhood and the pursuit of consumer-based agency.

The explicit comparison of these two groups unsettles some of the political-ethical sureties of contemporary academic understandings of the body. In the well-worn critiques of beautification, for example, scholars typically assume that the "natural" body—the unadorned, unmodified body—makes a more authentic statement about agency and empowerment than the altered body. These critiques, however, rely on a culturally particular default understanding of bodies, one shared by the Western women I knew in Shanghai, as the interface between an external world that seeks to impose unjust standards and an authentic interiority where some true self resides. It also smuggles in a preference for a particular kind of white-collar labor, "corporate" in nature, that shelters the body from daily modifications. An alternate way of thinking about bodies, body modification, and the relationship of the self to external regimes of power enables a reconsideration of the all too often taken-for-granted notion, central to critiques of the role of the body in social life, that what is "cultural" is easier to change than what is "natural."

CONSUMERISM, BODIES, AND BEAUTY IN "THE WEST"

Given the critical attitude of Western scholarly (and many popular) accounts of the beauty industry and body modification practices, dating at least as far back as the feminist author Naomi Wolf's (1990) account of the "beauty myth," it is no surprise that the Western women I knew were uncomfortable with the ideals they encountered in Shanghai. Indeed, in the Western context, many scholars have shown how in late capitalism the aesthetics of bodies has assumed central importance in our understanding of identity, inducing acute anxiety about bodily appearance and the need to be beautiful (Giddens 1991; Shilling 2005). Many trace this anxiety to the emergence of a consumer-based economy in the second half of the twentieth century, which they theorize produced new ways by which people understood, experienced, and engaged with bodies. In this line of argument, late-capitalist technologies of consumption and self-making, by bombarding people with images of ideal bodies and myriad products that promise to transform their bodies into the ideal type, promote a new understanding of the body as "plastic"; it becomes a "project" that people can transform into an aesthetically pleasing entity.[4] This, some suggest, gave rise to placing "greater emphasis on appearance, display and the management of impressions" (Featherstone 1982, 27; see also Featherstone 1991, 187; Csordas 1999, 179) and shifted conspicuous consumption to the body; it was no longer enough to be surrounded by nice things, there was now the desire *to be* a nice thing (Carolan 2005).

Within this narrative, scholars demonstrate that these shifts created difficulties for individuals (mostly women) in the West as they became responsible for managing their "plastic" bodies. For the anthropologist Rebecca Popenoe (2005), the extent to which women in the West feel threatened by beauty ideals is somewhat of a "paradox": most have the freedom to choose their own careers, partners, and styles, yet they are tormented by the beauty standards by which they are judged. According to Popenoe, the problem stems from a "culture of individualism," where not meeting the ideals is seen as an individual failure (2005, 24–25). Thus women in the West, as they navigate their freedoms, must contend with having their character assessed by their ability to attain (mostly unattainable) standards. The most recent iteration of this dynamic can be found in the relentless pursuit of "wellness" by the white upper-middle class in the United States, what has been termed the "wellness syndrome" (Cederström and Spicer

2015). It is deemed a syndrome because of the anxiety, self-blame, and guilt that it induces for anyone who is not "well" (more on this phenomenon in chapter 3). In addition, the "aesthetic labor" necessary for pursuing beauty is another illustration of neoliberalism producing an "enterprising self," whereby "preoccupations with appearance, beauty and the body are turned into yet another project to be planned, managed and regulated in a way that is calculative and seemingly self-directed" (Elias, Gill, and Scharff 2017, 39).

In addition to this anxiety-producing responsibility for managing and maintaining their bodies, women in the West also must struggle to navigate competing ideals in consumer-based capitalism. On the one hand, they are expected to embody the ideal of a worker, including self-restraint and discipline. They should be thin and fit. But, on the other hand, much advertising—especially for decadent cuisine and desserts—is geared toward satiating women's individual desires, and they are expected to embody the ethos of consumerism: self-indulgence (see, for example, Counihan 1999; Reischer and Koo 2004). Navigating these competing ideals creates irresolvable conflicts for women in how to live right and be beautiful. In short, for women, "the central contradiction of the system inscribes itself on our bodies" (Bordo 1993, 201).

The relationship posited in this literature between consumerism, bodies, and the pursuit of beauty in the West has a threefold significance for this book. First, it provides the foundation for making sense of why the Western women I knew in Shanghai were deeply troubled by the pressure to pursue certain kinds of beauty. But focusing ethnographically on their commentary about the specific ideals of being thin and having light skin and big eyes in the context of Shanghai demonstrates that what created turmoil for the women had less to do with when to indulge and when to restrain the self, or about the burden of taking personal responsibility for their bodies, and more to do with how they understood "body" as a site of the tension they felt between an authentic "self" and an imposing and oppressive "society." Depending on the topic at hand, they either conflated self with body or denied any correlation between the two. This tension was amplified by the consumer context in which the women understood "self" to be vulnerable to desires created through advertising but thought "body" was an impermeable site of authenticity.

Second, the literature sets the stage for thinking about the recent economic changes in China and their relationship to the emerging discourse about beauty. What is particularly interesting is that two of the most often cited changes in contemporary China—the emergence of consumerism and a shift toward a neoliberal emphasis on individual responsibility—align almost perfectly with the reasons given for why women in the West struggle with body image. In reading the descriptions of these transformations in China alongside writings about bodies, consumer culture, and beauty, one might expect to find that Chinese women (like their American counterparts) are struggling with selfhood as they modify bodies in pursuit of beautification (see, for example, Otis 2012). But the Chinese women I knew in Shanghai were not at all troubled by pursuing better bodies and instead saw bodily aesthetics as a legitimate means for improving their social and economic standing in the world; moreover, they ascribed the bodily anxiety of their Western peers to a Western problem of overpoliticizing bodies. When I socialized with the Chinese women, for example, they would often make fun of me for being "too Western" when I chose a boring nail color at a salon or dressed too plainly. They would roll their eyes and urge me not to take my body or appearance too seriously, a flaw they saw as all too common with Westerners. These were playful critiques done in the presence of friends for the purpose of getting a good laugh. But, as the argument here will show, these jokes were part of a larger project of the women to "push back" against the hegemony of the Western world by rejecting body-based politics and pursuing what they saw as authentically Chinese beauty ideals. Unlike the Western women who were navigating the tension between self and body, these women wanted China to be taken seriously as a nation that was inherently *different* from "the West." The tensions for both groups were embodied, amplified by the consumer context of Shanghai, and inextricably linked to the politics of bodily appearances.

Third, this project is indebted to the way previous scholars sought to highlight how bodies are not just "natural" entities on which culture is inscribed but are actually produced in particular ways by particular social contexts. Their work demonstrated, among other things, how understandings of and problems with the body in the Western context were informed by capitalism and consumer desires. And while they sometimes hinted at the ways in which the economic context articulated with other Western (that is, medical) notions of the body—especially the way that some of the contradictions of capitalism map nicely onto the Cartesian legacy of a mind/body duality—the cultural variability of bodies in relation to selfhood has rarely been brought into discussions about beauty in consumer China.

CONSUMERISM, BEAUTY, AND GENDER IN POST-REFORM-ERA CHINA

China has undergone tremendous changes since the reform period began in the 1980s. One of the most visible and drastic changes noted between revolutionary China and reform-era China was the shift in emphasis from production and the comrade-worker to consumption and the consumer, spawning what some called a "consumer revolution" (see D. Davis 2000; see also Croll 2006). Indeed, against the backdrop of the drab clothing, strict distribution of goods through one's work unit, and a complete absence of time or money for apolitical "leisure" activities in revolutionary China, the explosion of goods, products, and state incentives encouraging citizens to shop in reform China was truly striking. An important element of this shift was the way consumer products and images shaped new forms of femininity, which stood in stark contrast to the gender-neutral politically oriented woman of Maoist China (see, for example, Evans 1997). A welcomed response to the gender denial of Maoist times (see Zhong, Zheng, and Di 2001), the newly available fashion and beauty-related products made possible individualized choice associated with femininity. However, scholars soon noted the ways this idealized notion of femininity was based on the ability to live a certain lifestyle, in effect creating class-based hierarchies that denigrated other (more rural or poor) forms of being a woman (see, for example, Evans 2006). Thus in the reform era, a particular kind of femininity, spawned by consumerism and the pursuit of beauty (see J. Yang

2011), emerged simultaneously with class-based status rankings (see, for example, Hanser and Li 2015).

Now, four decades later, China has moved into what some are calling the "post-reform" era in which consumer-based lifestyles—and the identities constructed through them—are a taken-for-granted part of life, especially in urban centers like Shanghai. There has been an explosion of the beauty industry, with beauty products and cosmetic procedures mushrooming into billion-dollar businesses that employ tens of millions of workers (see Y. Liu 2012, as cited in J. Yang 2017). In most urban areas, there is a seemingly endless supply of options available to those seeking to improve their bodies, from skin-whitening agents to double eyelid surgery, from gyms and dieting advice to complete facial reconstruction. These bodily "improvements," although much more integrated into the fabric of daily life now than they were forty years ago, are still very much entangled with notions of social mobility and femininity.

For example, in conjunction with the rise of consumer products dedicated to enhancing one's appearance, ample evidence suggests that women's bodies and sexuality are being commodified in the post-reform era as women's status is further marginalized in the political economy and in the workplace (see, for example, J. Liu 2017). The commodification of bodies and sexuality is perhaps most visible in the burgeoning feminine beauty economy (*meinü jingji*), an extensive marketplace in which young, beautiful saleswomen are used to promote commercial products and services.[5] Many of the women who work in the so-called beauty economy are also part of a category the Chinese feminist He Qinglian (2005) labels "gray women" (*huise nüren*): the mistresses and second wives (*ernai*) of wealthy and powerful businessmen and officials and the hostesses and massage girls who entertain them (He 2005, as cited in Osburg 2013, 143). These recognized social positions are "gray" in that their structural status is caught between the morally upright women in the official (white) economy and the prostitutes of the illegal (black) economy. A growing industry of hostesses in KTV (Karaoke TV) parlors help entertain businessmen and officials, often including sexual services (see X. Liu 2002; T. Zheng 2009). These women are, for the most part, rural migrants in search of better lives, and the kinds of jobs and positions they pursue offer them a chance to gain access to luxurious apartments, cars, and other goods, often quite quickly, by finding a powerful businessman or official who provides the funds for their daily living expenses in exchange for sexual and romantic relationships.

As the anthropologist John Osburg (2013) explains, there is a rather rigid divide in the ways that women of different social positions understand these phenomena. On the one hand, successful female entrepreneurs (Osburg's main informants) align with Chinese media and social critics to view the gray women as troublesome and an indication of "the general loss of belief and values" in Chinese culture—they break up families and "trade feminine sexuality for money" (145). On the other hand, in response to this critical narrative, the gray women Osburg interviewed defended themselves by arguing that all women, even women in marriages and legitimate careers, trade their sexuality for material comfort provided by men. Moreover, they saw their desirability as a form of ability (167).[6]

My work, by focusing on professional or "white-collar" women working outside the masculinized and sexualized world of entrepreneurs, brings into this conversation yet another perspective.[7] In contrast to the successful entrepreneurial women Osburg quotes, who see the beauty economy and gray women as a threat to their achievements (as they use their bodies and sexuality rather than their business acumen to get ahead), the successful white-collar women I knew saw their bodies as a perfectly legitimate site for personal and economic cultivation. Moreover, whereas Osburg's informants worked to maintain the boundary between using their ability and using their sexuality in order to legitimize their business success, the white-collar women I knew saw a strict boundary between non-material "ability" and material "bodies" as an imposition of Western values on Chinese ways of viewing "sociality."

Furthermore, while most scholarship on the topic understandably concentrates on the poorest (that is, rural) women, who are the most vulnerable to the pressures for bodily commodification—and the ones typically doing the aesthetic labor in salons (see J. Yang 2017)—this often leads to a form of economic determinism, where marginalized status is seen as a starting and ending point for making sense of how (and why) people might "use" their bodies for social or economic gain (although for an account of how women from a variety of economic backgrounds are undergoing cosmetic surgery, see Wen 2013).[8] Many of the middle-class or professional Chinese women I knew in Shanghai were also actively pursuing beautification. Since they were not economically marginalized, did not intend to sell sex to get ahead, and did not view gender inequality as preventing their successes, it is worth asking: When middle-class women pursue bodily beauty in China, what kind of project do they envision it to be, and how do they understand the personal, social, cultural, and moral implications of that project?

Instead of assuming that in the context of late capitalism only one concept of body is operating, then, this work explores culturally different notions of bodies and bodily improvements, *as they shape and are shaped by consumerism and individuality*. Although economic status, too, plays a serious role for many of these women, I observed that attitudes about bodily cultivation were influenced as much by "cultural" factors as by "economic" ones. However, far from being an apolitical or amaterialistic domain of social life, "culture" in this analysis is taken to be particular entanglements of social and material factors that serve as a framework through which (certain kinds of) politics become possible.[9] A central question is, What bundling of concepts, embodied experiences, and historical legacies make bodies seem (to some but not others) inherently political and the modification of them inherently problematic?

BEAUTY, AGENCY, AND POWER

Beauty is an especially fraught topic in much (feminist) literature, as there is an unmistakable tension between "informants," who often feel agentive in their decisions to pursue beauty, and scholars, who understand such practices as reproducing and reinscribing existing gender and racial hierarchies (see also Elias, Gill, and Scharff 2017, 5–10). Indeed, for many, beauty has been and continues to be an explicit tool of patriarchal oppression, which makes resistance strategies based on the body seem to have limited validity (see Morgan 1991; Hunter 2005). At the same time, those who reject the idea that all women who pursue beauty are victims of false consciousness (see, for example, K. Davis 1995; Banet-Weiser 1999) still recognize that women's bodies have been central to their marginalization, making "individual choices about the body become laden with political meanings" (Weitz 2001, 668).

While there has been ample discussion about the limitations of either/or models that presuppose false consciousness (victimization) or free choice (empowerment), of concern here are theorizations of power and agency regarding the body that integrate the binary models into unified approaches. Explicating three approaches scholars have taken, I rethink resistance in relation to the body and grapple with how power is assumed to operate through naturalized desires that make women *want* to pursue beauty. Each of these models relies on the problematic premise that there is a universal (acultural) way in which power operates on or through bodies/selves that makes bodies inherently political. This assumption universalizes what is actually a culturally particular model of what a body/self is and thus hinders the possibility of understanding the ways that various kinds of power operate in relation to bodies in the contemporary world.

The first approach attempts to identify whose interests beauty ideals serve and redefines concepts such as resistance and accommodation to better understand how they operate together in daily life. This Foucauldian approach to bodily discipline argues that it is no surprise that the body is an important site of power struggles in the modern world. Bodies have become political because "docile bodies" are necessary for a properly working modern economic system: "In turn, these disciplinary practices have made the body a site for power struggles and, potentially, for resistance" (Weitz 2001, 668).

In this view, given the body's central role in the marginalization of women, in order to understand its potential for resistance a more accurate definition is needed of what it means to resist. In an article about women's hair, the sociologist Rose Weitz defines resistance as "actions that not only reject subordination but do so by *challenging the ideologies that support that subordination*" (2001, 670; italics in the original). Thus, adopting hairstyles that challenge the norm (for example, short "butch" hairstyles) can be seen as "individual acts of resistance [that] offer the potential to spark social change"

(670). By comparison, the actions that accept, or at least do not actively challenge, norms of subordination constitute accommodation. Women who adopt more "traditional" hairstyles to pursue their own empowerment are thus considered to be accommodating the norms of subordination rather than resisting them.

Far from being opposites, however, Weitz argues that resistance and accommodation coexist in most daily practices, and thus focusing on the details of women's choices can lead to a better understanding how resistance operates in daily life. In the end, though, she contends that modifying the body has limited political effect because using the body as a political tool only serves to reproduce the ideology of women's inferiority, as all choices rely on some engagement with hegemonic beauty norms. Therefore, "although some of the strategies women use to gain power through their hair contain elements of resistance, *all* contain elements of accommodation" (Weitz 2001, 683).

In the second approach, grappling with the contradictory nature of false consciousness versus free choice in beauty necessitates a more drastic theoretical shift. The sociologist Patricia Gagné and English professor Deanna McGaughey, for example, are interested in why women would want to undergo cosmetic surgery. They suggest that the problem is not one of definitions but the very way in which power is assumed to operate as a zero-sum entity (men have it, women don't) and how the body is treated as a passive object that is "either inscribed by hegemonic norms constructed by men or used by women as a tool in their social construction of a gendered self" (Gagné and McGaughey 2002, 817). As they describe it, following Michel Foucault, a theory of power needs to be incorporated that is more complete (that is, concerned not with who "has" it but with how it operates). They suggest this is possible by employing Antonio Gramsci's notion of hegemony, which focuses on how capitalist ideas are accepted as common sense, and shifting our attention to *desire*.[10]

This notion of hegemony is deemed useful because it grants insight into how wants are produced, especially those that align with cultural norms that work to marginalize the very people who pursue them. Such wants are described as emerging through a process of "internalization," which is a part of self-formation where, rather than being "coerced" to embody norms, individuals are "guided in their willing obedience" (Gagné and McGaughey 2002, 819). This "guiding" is done through an invisible and insidious mechanism that "naturalizes" certain wants as part of the self: "Women are not forced to undergo cosmetic surgery or most of the other practices in their beauty regimens. Rather, they internalize as natural and normal the standards of beauty that are pervasive in the hegemonic culture" (819). Thus, in important ways, although employing different theoretical devices, they echo Weitz's point that modifying the body has limited political impact: "Cosmetic surgery can both contest and reify hegemonic culture, although it is more often a tool for creating and maintaining cultural hegemony" (Gagné and McGaughey 2002, 818). Moreover, tacitly, they assume that power operates on embodied selves everywhere the same way, through an invisible process of internalization that creates certain desires that are experienced as natural. Notice how this is a direct result of Foucault's theorizing that assumes a certain economic system (regardless of the political or cultural context in which it operates) produces selfhood through the mechanism of disciplinary practices.

The third approach is focused on *affect*, or, according to the women's studies scholar L. Ayu Saraswati (2010; 2013, 10), "bodily reactions to experiences."[11] Examining the historical continuity over thousands of years and throughout a variety of colonial periods of a preference for whiteness in Indonesia, Saraswati argues that to understand why women have wanted whiter skin in Indonesia throughout all those periods one needs to examine the way that emotions are inherently entangled with the production of hegemonic norms that justify gendered, racial, and national hierarchies. She writes, "Understanding when, how, and why bodies feel certain affects toward specific bodies allows us to understand the larger social structures within which the meanings of these bodies and their responses make *sense*" (2013, 2; italics in original).

Saraswati's discussion—and assumptions about power—has a twofold relevance for this book. First, unpacking her use of affect reveals ways in which it overlaps but also contrasts with theories of desire, which is typically seen as the *outcome* of processes of internalizing cultural norms. For Saraswati affect is the "apparatus" through which naturalization occurs: "Affect functions as an apparatus of power that does the work of naturalizing various social hierarchies including racial, gender, and skin color hierarchies, in a transnational context. As such . . . power enters the domain of the emotions" (2013, 4). Although she leaves it unexplained, she appears to use "naturalization" in a Gramscian sense, as a substitute for "hegemony," where one way of doing things is taken for granted and no alternatives seem possible (or they are degrading). Thus, rather than seeing processes of internalization as invisible aspects of self-making that become embodied (such as desire), Saraswati argues that the body is the very *mechanism* through which processes of naturalization take place. Or, put another way, it is through "the body" that certain norms become hegemonic.

But what is the body? Eschewing all the work that scholars of embodiment have done to demonstrate that bodies are themselves cultural (that is, not just the site where culture is transposed), Saraswati contends that there is a divide between a body-as-affect and a cultural interpretation of that body, what she calls emotions. As she describes, affect, or the way "the body" responds to a given situation, is the basis on which cultural interpretation takes place. In some ways affect, then, is akin to "internalization" in that it is a precultural (or at least acultural) mechanism through which certain naturalizations occur. And, similar to desire, emotions are the embodied and culturally specific content that those acultural mechanisms of power produce. However, Saraswati's theory of affect relies on the assumption that there is a precultural body, which theorists of desire and embodiment reject. Thus she is able to apply the same model of power regardless of when and where the subjectivities—or hegemonic norms—were formed.

In all of these models, then, attempting to make sense of why women *want* to pursue and embody certain hegemonic beauty norms leads scholars to theorize power as an acultural process that works on or through a universalized notion of the body or an embodied self. In response, building on the anthropologist Alexander Edmonds's call to modify the framework of seeing beauty practices as just "exercises in patriarchal power that disciplines, normalizes, and medicalizes [the body]" (2007, 365), I draw attention to the way that culturally specific bodies and selves necessitate culturally specific approaches to power. Indeed, if bodies themselves (not just the interpretation of them) are products of cultural contexts, as much work on embodiment has convincingly illustrated, then one must be open to the fact that power operates on and through them in varying and unique ways. Moreover, if "self" varies culturally, then the mechanism through which norms become embodied, and how such norms are understood and experienced in relation to such selves, perhaps varies as well.

● Scholars have convincingly demonstrated, oftentimes in separate literatures, that there are two "kinds" of bodies informing social life in current-day China: bodies-as-naturalized-difference and bodily-persons-in-flux. The way the literatures employ notions of "the West" as a comparative framework reveals long-standing epistemological problems in anthropology of how to theorize the relationship between "the West" and "Other" places, particularly when focusing on emerging inequalities that are implicated in the current world order and globalizing economy. For example, in these literatures there is a strict divide between being critical of local practices when they are assumed to originate from deleterious influences from the West and being sympathetic when they are different enough (and in the right ways) to critique the hegemony of Western notions about the body. Setting up an explicit comparison of the two groups of women in Shanghai enables this tension to be rectified by drawing attention to "cultural" difference without implying an untheorized sympathetic stance toward "local" practices of either group.

BODIES-AS-NATURALIZED-DIFFERENCE

As scholars describe emerging body-based inequalities in China, including the commodification of certain kinds of labor and sexuality, they point to the way that imported ideas about biology are working in conjunction with notions about "the market" and "nature" to solidify hierarchical orderings in the post-reform era. According to their historical narrative of *displacement*, as Western notions of biology came to China they created a new understanding of nature—it could be objectively studied, produces bodily differences, and is linked conceptually with a logic of self-interest in neoliberalism or late capitalism—which superseded conceptualizations of bodies and nature in flux in imperial China. When employed in strategic ways, this can have dangerous implications for women: "Just as Adam Smith discovered the 'natural' and immutable laws of economics, laws that overturned the old moral order in the name of natural law, biological determinism frees men to act with impunity regardless of the consequences. If it is natural, it is right" (T. Zheng 2009, 126). Parallel to the way bodily difference is used to produce gender and racial discrimination in the West, biology is now employed as a trope in China to produce a similar body-based hierarchy.

This biological determinism of body-based difference is relatively new in China—its historical roots are typically traced to the pivotal time of republican China (1912–49). When the Qing Empire fell, and Sun Yat-sen established the Republic of China in 1912, it ended four thousand years of imperial rule. It also ushered in (or was symptomatic of) a period of "unprecedented openness" (Dikötter 2008) in which all levels of Chinese society sought engagement with the rest of the world. Part of this "engagement" included drawing on discourses of gender and sexuality from the West, which produced a conceptual shift concerning the idea of "nature" and its relationship to human bodies: "Previously imagined as a purposeful whole, a benevolent structure which could not exist independently from ethical forces, 'nature' was now conceptualized as a set of impersonal forces which could be objectively investigated" (Dikötter 1995, 8).

Within this new framework, physical bodies were no longer linked to the cosmology of the universe (making harmonizing the body with nature unnecessary) but were instead understood as being *produced* by "nature" (Dikötter 1995, 8). The use of medical science, and an "objective" point of view, legitimized this new way of thinking and solidified the dichotomy between "nature" and "culture," a radical departure from an ideology that stressed a socially produced harmony of Confucian ethics and a moralized nature. Thus, whereas Confucians moralized nature (they saw filial duty as reflecting the natural order of things), moderns naturalized ethics, putting biology in control. Republican intellectuals, then, began to see human biology, as opposed to imperial cosmology, as the basis for social order (Dikötter 1995, 180). A major consequence of this new understanding of nature and biology was linking gender difference to physical bodies in a new, more deterministic way (Dikötter 1995; but see also Evans 1997; Barlow 1994).[12]

For some, this new paradigm held liberating possibilities—Chinese feminists mobilized the imported notion of "woman" to contest gender discrimination in relational Confucian ethics (Barlow 1994). By comparison, as in the West, biological difference provided a powerful platform for justifying new gender-based hierarchies. This was readily apparent in literature produced in the 1920s and 1930s, where discussions of gender in textbooks, childbirth manuals, popular magazines, and marriage guides illustrated a shift to biological determinism (Dikötter 1995, 14). Since the social roles of men and women were now thought to be determined by biology, it was assumed that their differences (such as male superiority) could be found in all aspects of their bodies. For example, as illustrated in a biology textbook, the female's skeleton was smaller than the male's: this was taken to be empirical evidence that she was less intelligent. Or, proper social roles were assumed to be a natural extension of the biology of bodies. For example, in one case woman was portrayed as man inside out (Dikötter 1995, 23). Male was *wai* (outside), female was *nei* (inside). Thus it was only *natural* that man was the brain and the public body and woman was the womb and relegated to the private domain (Dikötter 1995, 27–28).[13]

These understandings of biology, bodies, and gender were, for a short time, undermined by the Chinese Communist Party's focus on producing revolutionary subjects. During the revolutionary period (1949–79), the notion of natural gender difference was subordinated to political struggle and the much more pressing concerns of class difference. But since the economic reforms and China's "opening up" (Farrer 2002), scholars are finding a return to biology to frame gender, gender difference, and sexuality. Discourses about science have legitimized the "naturalization of sexual and gender difference on the basis of biological structures and functions," which creates a "rigid code of normative sexual and gender conduct" (Evans 1997, 34). The naturalization of gender influences current-day workplace relations, where women are routinely seen to be better at certain kinds of (emotional) work and are often discriminated against on the basis of perceived innate abilities (see J. Liu 2017).

What is unique about the current era is the way in which discourses about biology and nature are linked to economic reforms. For example, in the post–Mao Tse-tung era, embodied desires are being defined through a market logic (Rofel 1999). Importantly, the market's power is assumed to derive from the fact that it is "natural," which, then, reinforces the power of biology to create or make sense of social divisions. As the cultural anthropologist Tiantian Zheng starkly put it in her ethnography of sex workers in post-socialist China: "For Chinese men, biology is the ultimate explanation and justification for all violence against women" (2009, 19).

BODILY-PERSONS-IN-FLUX

The second kind of body in contemporary China stands in stark contrast to the first: rather than seeing how "naturalized" bodily differences are the grounds for emerging forms of sociality and inequalities, the literature on Chinese medicine (CM) focuses on how bodies in China are unequivocally different from bodies in the West. For example, scholars of CM convincingly demonstrate that there is no conceptual equivalent in Chinese for the English word *body*. They draw attention to the way the Western concept of (physical) body cannot be fully understood without its Cartesian counterpoint of (metaphysical) mind. In China, however, the concepts are merged, as illustrated in *shenti*, the compound term often translated as "the body." *Shen* is most appropriately translated as "body-person," implying both a lived body and a life history (see Elvin 1993; Y. Zhang 2007). The term *ti*, by comparison, usually indicates a closed system or individual unit and refers to the flesh of the body (Brownell 1995, 16). But both *shen* and *ti* have a subjective element: "Neither word has the disembodied Western sort of connotation in which a person is somehow inside the body that is experiencing life—a body that is separate from the experiencing subject" (Brownell 1995, 17; see also Y. Zhang 2007, 36; J. Yang 2017, 123). *Shenti* thus combines the body-person and the flesh-body together and can be used synonymously with *person* in everyday usage (Tung 1994). In the context of

CM, then, these scholars demonstrate that there exists a concept of "body" that is inextricably linked to notions of personhood and selfhood, a radical departure from the post-Cartesian Western understanding of body as separate from person or mind.

The literature also points to a second fundamental aspect about bodies in CM that differs from biomedicine: they are constantly in flux, are inherently unstable, and "refuse fixity and discreteness," what the scholar physician Volker Scheid (2002, 28) calls "becoming" and the anthropologist Judith Farquhar (1994b, 82) terms "bodiliness." This bodiliness is a product of the flow of energy (*qi*) and other substances through overlapping and mutually influential bodily systems. In this model, there is very little interest in anatomy (that is, isolated body parts) and notions of harmonious flows in the body take precedence over a unitary idea of a "healthy" body (Farquhar 1994b, 87–91; Y. Zhang 2007). Also contributing to the instability of bodies is the fluidlike boundaries between bodies and the rhythmic but constant motion of "the cosmos" (seasons and weather, for example).[14] In this view, bodies and nature are not static; all bodies are in constant negotiation with their environment to maintain a harmonious existence, and getting out of rhythm with the cosmos is a temporary and personal condition (again based on bodily flows). Bodily-persons are considered healthy when they are balanced, have unimpeded flows of *qi*, and are in rhythm with the cosmos, a personal condition of subjective experiences.

The kinds of differences demonstrated here are not only "different" from the other bodies described, they are *exactly opposite*. Whereas biology and the market reify the materiality of the body to create rigid hierarchies, bodies in CM defy reification. For example, in the medical context, since the "normal" body is one of constant transformation in which there is continual flow of *qi* without blockage, differences between bodies are always of degree, not kind. So instead of having a normative "healthy" body against which all "sick" bodies are compared, bodily-selves in CM are understood on a spectrum of healthfulness where labels are much less stigmatizing and individuals have agency for cultivating their own personal harmony. Or, whereas in consumerism bodies and sexuality are objectified for the purposes of consumption, ethnographies of CM almost always incorporate a discussion of how the model of bodily-persons in CM undermines objectification and enables a more humane relationship between doctor and patient (and doctor and student) than in biomedicine. In Farquhar's analysis of textbooks, for example, she illustrates that there is not one metanarrative about the body, nor is there a prioritized shared objective stance that doctors use to diagnose patients. Instead, doctors' experiences and positionality play a leading role in their ability to successfully treat patients (Farquhar 1994b, 91). Because doctors' expertise comes less from objective knowledge that can be directly transmitted to the student, and more from experiences, relationships between doctors and students tend to take on a more personal element (E. Hsu 1999). It also opens up the space for allowing patients a more agentive role in diagnosing and helping to cure their illness (see also Kleinman 1981).

At first glance these stark differences might seem to be just a consequence of the social domains in which they are occurring. Thus, because much of the literature on CM focuses on clinics and the clinical encounter, and most work on the politics of bodies explicates emerging inequalities outside the medical context, it could be argued that the "kinds" of bodies being discussed are kept separate in social life. Perhaps naturalized gender differences are erased and unimportant when a woman enters a CM clinic? Or a bodies-in-flux model is irrelevant in the context of consumerism and commodification? However, as much of anthropology has taught us over the past half century, rarely are concepts segregated into separate domains in such a way. Moreover, the question of how these different bodies interact in social life is especially compelling given that in literature about the West scholars have shown that there is a clear conceptual mapping of (or tautological schema defining) the biomedical context, gendered bodies, and "naturalized" hierarchies of social categories. Indeed, as many have shown, in the West understandings of bodies in the medical context have had major implications for other domains of social life. For instance, characteristics of biomedicine—bodies-as-objects, bare life, medical "gaze," categorical divisions—have had ramifications for the prevalence of body-based discrimination that has been central to the West's history. As the historical anthropologist Angela Zito and historian Tani E. Barlow make clear, "The subjection of the body in the European post-Renaissance to discourses of biology provided a naturalized ground for the production of racial, ethnic, and gender inequality" (1994, 4).

With this background, then, reading the literature on CM might suggest that in addition to creating a more humane medical encounter, such an understanding of bodies in China would also create a social context that was more dialogic, more fluid, more dynamic. And, sometimes literature does suggest that bodies-as-mode-of-categorizing (gender, race), and the social inequalities that follow (sexism, racism), are part of a Western tradition that is not necessarily appropriate for understanding cultural contexts outside of the West. But, for the most part, the strand of inquiry that focuses on the implications of CM for inequality is restricted to historical accounts of imperial China (see, for example, the historian Charlotte Furth's [1999] finding that CM's notion of the encompassment of *qi* and blood paralleled the gendered hierarchy of Confucianism); the literature focused on contemporary China is almost always silent on any implications these medical ideas about bodies may have for other domains of social life. This is striking, given that CM currently operates in conjunction with (or at least alongside) not only the imported lens of biology but also a long-standing patriarchal social order in which gender is the basis of much social discrimination.

Bodies-as-naturalized-difference and bodily-persons-in-flux are both described (in separate literatures), then, as being central to social life in post-reform-era China. Whereas the first is implicated in emerging body-based inequalities, and inextricably linked to influences of the West, the second, central to practices of CM, is shown to be radically different from bodies in biomedicine. Moreover, whereas in the Western context scholars have shown how medicalized bodies influence other domains of social life—especially body-based inequalities—literature on the Chinese context provides very little indication of interaction between the bodies described by CM and post-reform market society.

BODIES, "CULTURAL" DIFFERENCE, AND THE WEST

These literatures highlight two problems concerning the politics of knowledge production in anthropology. The first is the way that the political motivations of scholars often overdetermine the extent to which "cultural" difference is brought into the analysis. In a disciplinary tradition dating back to the ethnographies of the cultural anthropologists Ruth Benedict and Margaret Mead, "culture" is often mobilized in anthropology to comment on issues "back home" (see also M. Anderson 2019, 40). For example, in much of the literature about CM, differences—in notions of bodies and in medical practices—are used to critique biomedical practice. Thus, whereas biomedicine is shown to rely on an objectification of bodies, a biomedical "gaze," and the reduction of persons to "bare life," writers on CM stress how it more holistically encourages dialogue and sees differences in terms of degree, not kind.[15] Furthermore, as a "cultural" phenomenon or "local" practice, CM is typically not subjected to the same critical scrutiny as the institutions in the West with which it is contrasted.[16] Critiques have been leveled against CM, but they are typically couched in discussions of the changes that have taken place in the recent past. When examining CM within the contemporary milieu, for example, scholars, for the most part, portray biomedicine and late capitalism (or "neoliberalism" or "socialism from afar") as adulterating CM.

The second issue stems from the way in which "the West" is employed as an important analytic and comparative framework. Whether it is assumed that bodies in China are *like* bodies in the West in their material potential for exploitability in the context of late capitalism, or *have become like* the West through imported notions of nature and biology, or are *drastically different* in the two contexts, the West is always present as a cultural Other to China. Scholars interested in bodies in China are very much aware of the long-standing disciplinary problems such "othering" invites, including the dangerous implications of a West/Rest divide and the inaccuracies of conflating "modernity" with "Westernization." As such, they have attempted to mitigate these problems in a variety of ways, including theorizing universal bodily experiences that unite Chinese and North American readers (see, for example, Farquhar 2002), complicating the relationship between "outside" ethnographer and "inside" informants (see, for example, J. Chu 2010; M. Yang 1994; T. Zheng 2009), and positing that culture and cultural categories be seen as processes and resources used by those in different subject positions (see, for example, Y. Zhang 2007; Z. Ma 2012; Zhan 2009). And yet, problems persist because, in almost all of this work, the West is an abstract cultural concept, against which local embodied experiences are contrasted (see Flood and Starr 2019). Thus, whether the ethnography is focused on similarities or differences, the data is unbalanced: the "bodies" are Chinese and are described through ethnographic anecdotes from daily life. These are then compared with "the West," absent any "Westerners."

SITUATED COMPARISON

In this book, I seek to rectify these problems by employing "situated comparison" (Flood and Starr 2019) as a strategic methodology. Such comparisons are based on locally meaningful categories of difference—in this case Chinese and Western women living in Shanghai—that highlight different subject positions and their orientations to a particular cultural context.[17] Allowing local theories of difference to structure the comparison opens up a space for engaging with locally defined ways of being in the world. Moreover, triangulating local differences in a particular context with academic theories makes it possible to be reflexive about ethnographic knowledge production and the way it is informed by culturally particular assumptions, frameworks, or logics.

For example, setting up an explicit ethnographic comparison between the Chinese and Western women I knew in Shanghai allows me to engage with scholarly and local interest about the differences between China and the West without reifying either side. In particular, I am able to resolve the problem of unbalanced data by employing the same kind of evidentiary sources, such as the ordinary language accounts of living informants, on both sides of the cultural comparison. The Western perspective, then, instead of being something that is inherent in me, the ethnographer, or part of a sui generis rendering of a timeless cultural world, is just as embodied in local people in Shanghai as the Chinese perspective. Or, to put it another way, setting up this comparison grounds the so-called Western perspective in actual people, which can then be used to inform a more thorough and nuanced comparison with the Chinese women I knew in Shanghai.

Moreover, the categories of China and the West are very much a part of the local conceptual world in Shanghai (Flood and Starr 2019). I agree with the anthropologist Michael Herzfeld's suggestion that "listening to what 'informants' have to say about each other can generate important insights into the relevance of specific comparative projects for making sense of their everyday lives" (2001, 267), and my use of "Chinese" and "Western" is further motivated by and meant to draw attention to the importance of these categories for those living in Shanghai. This methodological move also reduces the inherent risk in anthropology of creating and re-creating colonial power structures in the production of anthropological knowledge by questioning the nature of otherness in Shanghai. As the anthropologist Rupert Stasch so eloquently says: "Rather than deny otherness of time, or cultural otherness generally, a more adequate way to dissolve misplaced borders between anthropologists' worlds and the communities they study is to engage intellectually with the ways people are involved with otherness in their own lives, including their experiences of otherness when interacting with consociates in a shared place and time" (2009, 10–11; see also Bashkow 2006).

Rather than reifying the categories, then, linking difference to people on both sides of a cross-cultural comparison draws our attention to the fact that neither group is able to "represent" the large cultural categories to which they belong. There is no generic "West" or "Westerner," just as there is no generic "China" or "Chinese person." The potential for misunderstanding is greatest when anthropologists describe unrecognizable Others and then compare them with abstract notions of "the West," which lack any nuanced inclusion of class, gender, race, or other meaningful differences and give the impression that (1) there is consistency within both places and (2) that the ideas described are common to everyone. In situated comparisons, the task of the ethnographer is to contextualize both groups in ways that allow readers insight into the limitations but usefulness of (cultural) categories.

"Situating" the women I knew in Shanghai and not using my own experiences to represent "the West" opens up the analysis to include space for heterogeneity on both sides of the "cultural" comparison.

In addition to correcting certain epistemological pitfalls in comparisons of China and the West, situated comparison also enables the ethnographer to move beyond employing "cultural" difference as a tool to critique the West. Or, put another way, cultural comparison here does not suggest partiality for "local" practices. This is particularly useful in discussions about beauty, which are almost always critical in nature and, much like the literature on bodies in China, link the emergence of certain kinds of body-based hierarchies to "Western" (that is, market-based economic) influences. Rather than focusing on whether the women "really" have agency or not, or having to balance a feminist-inspired agenda with an anthropological interest in local practices, ethnographically motivated comparison enables me to ask not only why the Chinese women want to pursue beautification and whether they do indeed see the pursuit as liberating but also why the Western women feel that rejecting beauty ideals frees them from gender and racial hierarchies. As difference emerges through the comparison, the ways varying notions of bodies inform how the women understand the relationship between agency, self, and beauty can be examined. The themes, issues, and strategies that were important to the women I knew have broader implications for understanding—and opening ourselves up to—various kinds of feminisms in the contemporary late-capitalist world.[18]

By putting "our" theory into conversation with "their" theory in detailed and recursive fashion and by unburdening the anthropologist as representative of "the West," situated comparison allows us to attend to locally important experiences of difference and undermine the privileged place of "the West." This is not meant to claim that any one comparison can be complete or representative. The comparison described here, like all ethnography, is necessarily incomplete. My goal is not to present a comprehensive portrait of what it is to be Chinese or Western (that, in the words of the anthropologist Clifford Geertz, would only "court parody" [1973a, 42]); it is to highlight the way that certain cultural differences, revealed in the context of cosmopolitan Shanghai, can provide insight into multiple ways of understanding and experiencing life in our ever-more capitalistic, consumer-driven, and globalized world.

SITUATED FEMINISMS

Employing explicit ethnographic comparisons can facilitate scholarly reflexivity and highlight the ways that certain theoretical approaches are products of, or at least aligned with, particular subject positions (such as class, race, gender, culture). An ethnographic approach that I term "situated feminisms" treats the pursuit of body politics as culturally informed and context-dependent *social practices* rather than universally applicable goals for which all should strive. Revealing the cultural specificities that underlie what many take to be universals is what anthropologists have been doing for quite some time, and "situating knowledge" has been central to the feminist project since at least 1988, when the feminist scholar of science and technology studies Donna Haraway proposed the concept. The present study opens up the analysis to questions of how power operates differently on differently configured *material* bodies and selves and from different subject positions.[19] Building on the conversations that scholars are having about materialism and feminism, then, this project interrogates ethnographically—rather than philosophically—entanglements of bodies, nature, and power.[20] Thus, rather than suggest that *in general* the biological body does not matter (see Butler 1990, 1993) or that *in general* nature is the basis for cultural life (see Grosz 2004), this book asks for whom and in what context such assessments might be true or relevant to their pursuit of empowerment.

It has become commonplace in anthropology to investigate, as the anthropologist Julie Chu puts it, "what processes make certain 'domains appear self-evident, and perhaps even "natural," as fields of activity in any society'" (2010, 8; quoting Collier and Yanagisako 1987, 35). When scholars confront such naturalizing cultural discourses, especially when related to the body, they are highly critical and often employ a Foucauldian-inspired genealogical or historical account to "disrupt" them (see, for example, Rofel 2007; Farquhar 2002; Zhan 2009). What is important for this discussion is the way this theoretical move is premised on the *explicit* argument that whatever is "historical" or "cultural" is easier to change than what is "natural." As the anthropologist Mei Zhan states, an attention to process, what she calls "worlding," is the only way to "open ourselves to the possibilities of imagining, understanding, and even making different worlds" (2009, 201).

There is no doubt that the political/theoretical project of denaturalizing bodies has immense power in the Western context, where there is a long history of linking body-based inequalities to biology. Indeed, much of early feminism was focused on undermining the "naturalized" bodily differences that were used as a justification for social discrimination in the West. As summarized by Zito and Barlow: "The poststructuralist commitment to rigorous historicizing has allowed a new archaeology of the body to follow upon the long-standing concerns of feminists to denaturalize the bodies they found themselves discursively and materially trapped within" (1994, 4). However, an unreflexive use of this political strategy has the unintended consequence of hindering our ability to take seriously—or understand the power of—the social world on its own.

In the context of China, given the importation of biological science and the emergence of naturalized body-based differences in the post-reform era, it is perhaps no surprise that scholars find a similar approach useful. In the medical anthropologist Nancy Chen's (2002) discussion of *qi* and masculinity in China, for example, she draws explicitly from theorists in the West to critique emerging narratives. Drawing on the gender theorist Judith Butler's (1993) *Bodies That Matter*, she follows a well-worn path for viewing gender as a "political and social performance" that is "not a singular act but always a reiteration of a norm or set of norms" (Chen 2002, 317, 322). Chen's task is to illustrate to the reader the ways that certain bodily traits (such as *qi*) have become associated with essentialized gender difference in the social and political context of post-Mao China. Chen is forthright about her political agenda: she seeks to undermine the naturalizing effect of bodily based difference *by tracing historical change* and thereby illustrating the socially constructed (that is, not "natural") origins of such difference. Importantly for this discussion, like most scholars who are invested in a similar project of "denaturalizing" (bodily) difference, she leaves unarticulated the essential question: Why does it matter if gender difference is "naturalized"? What is at stake when "the natural body becomes the generative device for gender" (Chen 2002, 317)?

A goal of this book is to ask, what are the implications of importing this political project into the Chinese context? As we will see, the Shanghai Western women's particular version of feminism, which is often mobilized in political interventions about beauty, is similar to recent work on anthropology of the body that typically assumes that power everywhere has a propensity to *naturalize*. To overcome this assumption, scholars have employed a well-worn theoretical approach that seeks to reveal that what is assumed to be "natural" is actually "cultural," in order to "open it up" for change. The Western women shared with these scholars the idea that nature—as static and outside the influence of humans—is inherently more difficult to change than "culture." This was embedded in their ideas about authentic selfhood, which in its ideal and original form existed beyond/outside the influence of culture and society. Moreover, they often employed historical accounts of changing beauty ideals to undermine the pressure they felt to pursue a particular aesthetic in current-day Shanghai. The Chinese women also understood identity as being linked to bodily-selves. However, the bodily differences that were most important to them—for both individual and group identity—were those they cultivated through time. They were thus operating with a cultural understanding of modifiable bodies that allowed them to view their identity as bodily and yet not naturalized or essentialized. In fact, for the Chinese women I knew, "natural" bodily traits were actually *easier to change* than socially or historically produced bodily differences.

What an ethnographic approach to situated feminisms can contribute, then, in this case quite compellingly, is to demonstrate a clear cultural link between ideas and experiences of the materiality of selfhood with some of the taken-for-granted assumptions about power and the body central to the political project of denaturalization. Indeed, it is clear that in this case feelings, desires, and affect were not experienced or understood to be natural or as a part of an authentic self for everyone in the same way. Given that theories of power often take for granted a universal mechanism (either invisible processes of internalization or acultural bodily reactions, such as affect) through which power operates on bodies, how does cultural variability in notions of the materiality of self change how the way power operates on those selves might be theorized? Indeed, it is clear that the full range of consequences of that particular understanding of power and its relationship to a particular kind of embodied self has not yet been explored ethnographically.

FIELDWORK: THE WOMEN, "DATA," AND DAILY LIFE

The Chinese and Western women I came to know while living in Shanghai, to whom I refer by pseudonyms throughout the text, were all outsiders to the context of Shanghai. They had all moved there for professional reasons, for example, to build a career, to try out something new, or to jumpstart upward mobility in a company. In general, the two groups of women did not interact (at least not while participating in the practices in which I was interested), and my comparison is based on women who shared a historical moment in Shanghai in which the geopolitical, economic, and cultural context helped shape their social positions and experiences of social life and daily practices.

The Chinese women came from a variety of provinces across China (most were from Anhui and Jiangsu, provinces neighboring Shanghai, although others hailed from the southwest). They were all Han, the ethnic majority, and college educated. Their engagement with the West was local and both intimate and distant: they all worked in international companies, yet none had been abroad. They all had Western colleagues but, for the most part, did not speak much English and thus were only peripherally engaged with their foreign counterparts at work. A variety of imperfect concepts describe these women and situate them in the current socioeconomic context of Shanghai: middle class, white-collar, professional. Together, these concepts suggest possible ways to understand an emerging global middle class.

The Western women I knew were all white and from the United States, Australia, Great Britain, and parts of continental Europe. They were all college-educated professionals—lawyers, teachers, businesswomen—and had varying degrees of knowledge about and experiences living in China.

Some had just moved to Shanghai at the time of my fieldwork; others had lived there for multiple years but did not speak the language; still others had spent ample time and effort learning standard Chinese (Mandarin) and studying about China. However, as middle-class professional women, they all represented a relatively recent shift in the demographic of foreigners in the city. As described by some long-term foreign residents, the days of "cowboy capitalism" were over: the "original" Westerners who moved to Shanghai in the 1980s, self-described as having been lured by the plethora of "easy" business opportunities, were being displaced by a new, younger, more ambitious variety. As Shanghai grew and developed and became a sought-after place to live, the fancy relocation packages offered as incentives for moving abroad (typically including a big salary increase, an apartment, a driver, cleaning services, and so forth) came to an end. So did the novelty of having a few Western restaurants and bars in the city, as now, at least in certain areas, foreign goods and services are relatively easy to come by. The long-term residents and owners of the original restaurants and bars resented the new kind of ambitious foreigner, and many talked of moving to the Philippines to return to their more "carefree" days of living as expats.

My decision to conduct a comparative ethnography focused on two groups of women, instead of a more traditional field "site," developed over the course of my fieldwork. When I first arrived in Shanghai in September 2011 my intention was to use a beauty salon as my main site, a bounded and delimited space within which I could interact with and learn from those who were familiar with the rules and social expectations of that space. I thus set out to find a "home" salon, against which I could compare other sites. But, rather quickly, I realized that beauty salons were not the most ideal place for me to conduct my research. First, they are noisy. From hair dryers to music to the calling back and forth between stylists, prolonged conversation is difficult. Second, salons are not especially conducive to meeting new people. In fact, unless customers come in as a group, salons in Shanghai are not typically spaces for socializing. And sometimes even when groups would come in together, the group members would end up spending the majority of their time in the salon separated from each other, sitting at their stylists' stations. Thus most customers spent the majority of their time in the salons sitting alone (or with the stylist) and looking down at their phones, texting, reading, or playing games. If there was social interaction, it was typically between the customer and the employees and tended to stay at a rather surface level of intimacy (the casual or sometimes intimate chitchat common between stylists and their customers in salons in the United States was noticeably absent). The one exception was in the "spa" section of the salon, where women (and sometimes men) would get a range of treatments from massages to facials. This area was much quieter, and the interactions tended to be a bit more intimate. But the rooms were mostly private, and thus I did not have access to other clients, making such spaces unsuitable for research. Finally, although my initial intention was to try to work at a salon, I was never able to move beyond the role of being a foreign customer. When I inquired about employment, I was told that all employees of the salon must go through a monthlong training at a center outside of Shanghai; only on completion of the training is anyone able to work in the salon. The training was not open to foreigners.

As I was struggling to find my place in the salons—and wondering how I should go about my research—my partner, Adam, a professional musician, joined me in Shanghai. On his second day in the city he met a local musician, and they immediately began performing together in various bars, restaurants, and concert venues in the area. Quite quickly, due to Adam's introduction into the music scene, our social network grew considerably, both with Chinese and with foreigners living in the city. This had profound repercussions for my project. First, I met my closest Chinese friend, Mei, at one of Adam's shows, when a fan of Adam's music, Charlie, introduced me to her. Charlie was from Ireland but had been a manager at a large international firm in Shanghai before he retired. Mei had been one of his employees, and after he retired they kept in contact. Whenever he came through town, they would get together to catch up. On one such visit through town, Charlie brought Mei to one of Adam's shows and introduced us, and we almost instantly became great friends. Shortly thereafter Mei introduced me to her friends, and because we got along so well and enjoyed each other's company I started hanging out with them on a regular basis.

Having Adam in Shanghai influenced my research in a second way, in that it greatly expanded my network of foreigners living in the city. Adam, on his arrival in Shanghai, spoke no standard Chinese. And since the Chinese women with whom I was developing relationships spoke little English, Adam and I began socializing with an English-speaking crowd.[21] It was the first time that I had foreign friends in Shanghai, and the people we met became very dear to us; they also became important sources of data for my project. I was far from being a "lone" ethnographer in Shanghai, then, and my fieldwork experiences—and the project I developed from them—was very much informed by my own kinship relations.

As I got to know some of the Western women in this group, I realized that, just like my Chinese friends, these women were also constantly discussing their bodies—through topics such as the disturbing yet intriguing white privilege they felt in the city, where to work out and what to eat, and the moral concerns of caring too much about their bodies—and struggling with the role their bodies played in their lives in Shanghai. In essence, both groups of women talked about similar topics. But, as I discovered, the two groups had drastically different ideas and opinions on these matters. Many of the differences that serve as the basis for my analysis emerged in comparative relief; they became obvious only as I moved back and forth between the two groups of women. This fact, coupled with the prevalent use of the categories China and the West in daily life, prompted me to structure my analysis as a comparison of the two groups, in order to examine how cultural difference is expressed within the urban cosmopolitan space of Shanghai.

My social interactions with these two groups were typically relegated to the sphere of "leisure," and thus our relationships were almost always defined through the concept of "friendship" (see Flood and Starr 2019). The vast majority of my ethnographic data stems from times when I would get together with these women for social outings, including going out to eat or for drinks, getting coffee, taking walks around the city, going shopping, attending a yoga class, getting our nails done, or heading to the salon. During the week, when everyone was busy with work, family, and other engagements, it was not uncommon for me to get together with just one or two women for an evening. On the weekends, we usually planned group outings. Occasionally, the group outings would overlap at one of Adam's shows, for example, but for the most part I socialized with each group separately.[22] All of the events portrayed in this book happened as described. But following the long tradition in anthropology of balancing detailed ethnographic accounts with the anonymity of informants, I have edited some of the details about the people to create "composite characters." Of course, my interactions in Shanghai were not limited to these two small groups of women, but the most intimate details—those on which I base my analysis—stem from my time with these women.

Slowly, as I came to know the women, I realized that moving with them through various spaces in their day-to-day lives allowed me the opportunity to examine how they talked about, worked on, and attached moral valence to body modification practices, thus highlighting the myriad ways in which their bodies were central to their daily lives and identities within the city. This project, then, follows a recent trend toward person-centered or individual-centered research, popular in medical, psychological, and moral anthropology (see, for example, Kleinman 1999; Y. Yan 2003). As the anthropologist Douglas Hollan initially described it, "A primary focus of person-centered ethnography is on the individual and on how the individual's psychological and subjective experience both shape, and are shaped by, social and cultural processes" (1997, 219; quoted in Y. Yan 2003, 10). For the anthropologist Yunxiang Yan, this meant a return to a tradition of detailed ethnography, with a new emphasis on "individual experience and agency rather than social structure or cultural norms" (2003, 10). I employ this approach as a way to investigate how certain cultural themes or norms manifest in different activities of daily life. Moreover, bringing a person-centered approach into an explicitly cross-cultural comparative framework makes it possible to study cultural norms without eschewing individual agency.

This approach seeks to understand what Geertz called "an informal logic of everyday life" (1973b, 10). The ethnographic moments highlighted here were by no means special or unique; in fact, most of the topics and themes addressed were so common and shared by the women that they did not necessitate metacommentary. Moreover, importantly, the activities and conversations on which I concentrate were not explicitly a part of official or state policy in China. As Farquhar notes, "The ingredients and rhythms of everyday life change in a somewhat different manner than the highly visible institutions and state political relations that have made the history of events" (2002, 11). This approach provides a lens through which to see how the women engaged various aspects of larger narratives in their discussions of these practices, without reducing them to agentless subjectivities produced through state or elite discourse (C. Hsu 2007).

● The two parts of the book focus on particular beauty ideals popular in Shanghai and the different ways the two groups of women pursued or critiqued them. Part 1 examines the ideal of being thin and daily practices and discussions of dieting, eating, and working out. I show how the two groups of women were operating with different understandings of the temporality and materiality of selfhood, revealing cultural variability in the degree to which embodied experiences come to be understood as an essential part of an immutable and authentic "inner self." Of particular interest is the Chinese women's focus on *tizhi* and how they understood it to be a defining characteristic of themselves that was always being (slowly) modified by the foods they ate, which they categorized on a spectrum from hot to cold. Within the *tizhi* framework, they had a working definition and experience of bodily-selves as something that was constantly changing; they saw losing weight as just one of many ways to improve themselves. The Western women, by contrast, were focused on eating "what they wanted" but recognized that their wants were vulnerable to the influences of advertising and the consumerist context. They often associated an "unmodified body" with an "authentic self," and they thought altering appearances through dieting to fit society's ideals compromised what they held dear: autonomous selfhood.

Part 2 focuses on the prevalence in Shanghai of white skin and big eyes as beauty ideals and examines the differences in how the women understood the relationship between bodies, race, and nation. The Chinese women were adamant that rather than representing a globalized homogenizing preference for Western appearances, ideals of beauty in China were based on *national* preferences. They resented that Westerners thought they wanted to look like them and were resolute in insisting on the differences in beauty ideals between China and the West; they pointed out that if China really wanted to be like the West, then it would share similar beauty ideals, which it does not. The Western women took for granted that the desire for big eyes and white skin was an indication that Chinese women wanted to look "Western." They were deeply troubled by ideals they saw as based on a Caucasian body type (that is, racialized), which they thought inappropriate in the Chinese context. Although they rejected race as a form of social differentiation, their commentary about "original" and unmodified traits points to a culturally particular notion of race that equates it with unique and natural selfhood that endures through time.

Through explicit comparisons, this book is able to intervene in long-standing epistemological dilemmas in anthropology, demonstrating how body politics are culturally produced. The attitudes about pursuing beauty I encountered in Shanghai were informed by culturally variant embodied selfhood, which has implications for understanding various kinds of "individualisms" emerging in China and the West and the role of "denaturalizing" the body in liberation politics. An attention to different experiences of—and identities associated with—the materiality of selfhood enables a more thorough investigation into the variety of ways power operates on and through bodies in the contemporary world.

PART ONE
THINNESS

ONE
SELF

On a cold, rainy, Saturday afternoon, a few of my Chinese friends and I gathered at Mei's apartment on the outskirts of the city. They were supposed to be teaching me how to prepare some of my favorite Chinese dishes, but as the kitchen was small and our conversation distracting, they soon took over the cooking, while I watched. Our discussion, as was so often the case, found its way to dieting and proper eating habits.

"So you're on a diet?" I asked Mei, our host for the day, after she had been discussing her plans to lose weight.

"Of course!" She exclaimed. We all laughed. "Everyone in China is on a diet. Skinny is beautiful right now. And being fat is unhealthy. So we are all on a diet."

All nodded in agreement. Just then Zhu, whom we had not seen in a few months came huffing through the door with a friend from her hometown (someone we did not know). Back from a trip abroad, Zhu had clearly put on a little weight.

"You got fat!" exclaimed Mei as Zhu walked through the door.

Zhu, still flushed from her walk up the four floors to Mei's apartment, replied: "I know! I've been working so hard lately for that promotion that I've gained weight. I have to go on a diet."

Mei nodded. "Yes, you'll never get promoted if you're fat."

"That's not necessarily true," I suggested. But before I could say anything further, Mei, somewhat annoyed, cut me off.

"Oh, you Westerners are so sensitive about your bodies. You treat them as something special, when they are really just like anything else. Of course being skinny helps you at work. Just like knowing English. It's the same!"

Zhu nodded. She then introduced us to her childhood friend, Wenjing. After saying hello to us, Wenjing inquired about the dishes we were cooking. Mei explained that they were some of my favorites.

"So she's used to eating Chinese food?" Wenjing asked, in reference to me.

"Oh yes, she's used to it," Mei responded with pride. "She's been to China many times."

Wenjing smiled with approval in my direction. Our discussion then returned to dieting plans, and I told them about a documentary I had just watched (*Fat, Sick & Nearly Dead*, 2010) about an obese and sick American truck driver who lost a lot of weight by confining his diet to fruit and vegetable juice for sixty days.

Mei looked appalled. "His body must be so cold now. That's a really dangerous way to lose weight." Addressing the room, she went on: "Your diet has to be balanced and include mostly warm foods. The mistake I made when I was younger was to just eat a few things, mostly cold foods, which really messed up my *tizhi*. I'm still recovering. Being skinny is important, but you must also make sure you are healthy. Otherwise, you'll never influence those around you."

SNAPSHOT #2

After enjoying a delicious meal at a new French restaurant (the chef was from Paris) with my American friends Sophie and Emily, we perused the dessert menu.

"Well, I can't decide," Sophie said, still looking down at her choices. "You guys want to split something?"

Emily put down her menu. "No, nothing for me."

"Really?" asked Sophie, sounding disappointed.

"What are you thinking?" I asked. "I might have a bite or two."

"Well, the crème brûlée looks good, or we could do the chocolate sponge cake with raspberry coulis. Or maybe we shouldn't. I don't know . . . ," Sophie trailed off.

"Why not?" asked Emily, in a somewhat confrontational tone. "If you want something, get it."

"I know but . . ."

"Wait, don't tell me you're on a diet?" Emily exclaimed.

"No, I'm not!" Sophie retorted. "But, I don't know, I just feel so fat here. Everyone is always looking at me and making comments about my body. It sucks."

Emily, with a slight edge to her voice, advised, "Don't let that get to you. I mean, if you want dessert, you should have it. If you don't want it, then that's fine too."

"Well, why aren't you interested in having any, then?" Sophie shot back. "And why did you just have a salad for dinner?"

Emily, softening her tone, replied, "A salad sounded good to me. I've been craving one for a while. Also, I'm full. I don't want dessert."

I jumped in. "Mmm, the chocolate cake sounds good to me."

"Yeah, me too," Sophie replied. "I've been craving chocolate all day. Let's get it! You sure you don't want any, Em?"

"I'm sure. I'm stuffed."

The waiter took our order and asked, "How many spoons?"

"Two," Sophie and I said in unison.

"Actually, make it three," Emily cut in. "I think I want some after all."

When the cake arrived we each grabbed a spoon and took a bite. "Oh God, that's good," Emily said with a smile. "I guess I'll have to have a few more bites."

Sophie laughed. "Mmm. That *is* good. We should each have had our own. You know what, fuck society's norms. How skinny or fat we are just shouldn't matter."

● In Shanghai, an overwhelming array of products are available for losing weight. Everything from weight-loss pills, dieting advice, and massages to self-help books, gym memberships, and workout equipment beckons city dwellers with promises of a "better life," unambiguously connecting thinness with "success." Paired with the ubiquitous images of skinny, beautiful men and women plastered on billboards throughout the city, the milieu of Shanghai makes clear the stakes of having the "right" kind of body. All of this is compounded by the very public way in which people point out and discuss bodies that fall short of the standards, oftentimes casually commenting on those who are overweight, well within earshot.[1] This practice is heightened online, where there is an abundance of "thinness tests" circulating on Chinese social media in which women measure their thinness in various ways (for example, the Thigh Gap Challenge, iPhone 6 Challenge, Belly Button Challenge, and A4 Challenge) and comment on each other's posts.

The Chinese and Western women I knew in Shanghai thought about thinness and how to navigate—in their daily practices of eating—the overt pressures they felt to fulfill the ideal. When the concepts important to them in their culinary choices were explicated, quite different notions of "self" emerged. Both groups were focused on self-cultivation and were operating with a sense of self that was individualized, bodily, and linked to health and appearance. However, their understandings and experiences were not the same, nor were the two groups working with similar cultural understandings of individual "psyches." In fact, they had quite different ideas about how their bodies—and embodied experiences—were integral to who they were. The significance of those differences will become clear in an examination of the analytic link scholars often posit between emerging forms of selfhood (and practices of self-cultivation) in China, "the body," and inequalities/subjectivities particular to the current political-economic context.

To suggest that the Chinese and Western women I knew in Shanghai were operating with different ideas about "selves" engages debates about the nature of selfhood in China and the differences between China and the West, especially in their modern forms. Ethnographies of rural China from the 1980s and 1990s overwhelmingly presented Chinese selves as continuing in a "traditional" vein: social in nature, malleable to context, focused on interpersonal relations, and defined by a traditional Confucian ethic of family and descent line.[2] These "relational" and "context-dependent" selves were almost always contrasted with their assumed counterpart in "the West": individual psyches that are thought to exist independently of and prior to any social context or relationship and that are authentic and stable.[3] Harking back to the French anthropologist Marcel Mauss's ([1938] 1985) seminal work on self and personhood (see Carrithers, Collins, and Lukes 1985), then, these comparisons presented "selves" in China as a timeless manifestation of an ancient "Confucian" tradition that was culturally different from the more modern self-as-psyche in the West.[4]

As many scholars have pointed out, there were substantial problems inherent in these "cultural" comparisons, especially in the way they ignored any historical, political, or economic context and were overly structuralist, leaving little to no room for individual agency to shape or engage with cultural norms. Scholars working in the reform and post-reform eras responded by demonstrating (1) how Chinese subjects contribute to and shape ideas about selfhood as they negotiate their daily lives (see, for example, Kipnis 1997) and (2) the way that the political and economic reforms/ruptures of the past century have radically transformed the role of the self in social life. The shift away from the politics of class struggle central to social life in the Maoist period toward consumption-based self-cultivation and self-realization in the post-reform era has led to the emergence of "inner selves" and "psyches," especially for the urban middle class. But rather than assume that these inner selves were exact replicas of selfhood in the West, more recent iterations of China/West comparisons have focused on important historical and political differences between the two contexts, including the way that individuals in China have to navigate the competing forces of an entrepreneurial market and a controlling state, producing a "divided self" (Kleinman et al. 2011, 1–14; see also Kipnis 2012b, 1–4; Zhang and Ong 2008).

While the cultural differences described in this literature have greatly enhanced understandings of contemporary China, most of the work detailing post-reform-era notions of selfhood omits a discussion about bodies.[5] When bodies are brought into the discussion they often serve as a point of similarity, either explicitly or implicitly serving to demonstrate how late capitalism produces a particular kind of body-self relationship that is vulnerable to commodification. For example, a growing literature documents the way that selves in contemporary China have become embodied in desires and feelings, with newfound ideals of self-expression, emotional intimacy, sexual preference, and personal happiness.[6] In fact, the way that desires have become "naturalized" as a part of "inner" selfhood is, according to the anthropologist Lisa Rofel, one of the central differences between Maoist China and reform-era China. According to Rofel's (2007) informants, they are just being "who they are"—gendered, desiring subjects seeking to know and enjoy themselves—without the imposed constraints of the communist state. This parallels quite closely observations in places such as the United States, for example, where "feelings" have become "the most potent and real aspect of the self" (Lindholm 2008, 65). Being "authentic" depends on individuals' displaying, monitoring, and, most importantly, *being* their true feelings. In both contexts, then, linked to the current economic system (described with terms such as *neoliberal* or *late capitalist*) and the rise of consumerism, as individuals attempt to fashion their identities in a flexible labor market and through consumption, seeking out pleasures and enjoyments has taken on almost sacred undertones as individuals strive to "be themselves." In China, this has led to a self-help boom, perpetuated by the party-state, that is geared toward cultivating "happiness" in the face of structural and economic hardships (J. Yang 2017).

The bodily nature of selfhood in post-reform-era China is also described in literature about the pursuit of *suzhi*, especially by the urban middle class. Roughly translated as "quality," *suzhi* is frequently employed by the state and in popular culture to describe emerging hierarchies, often along an urban/rural divide, with those of "high" quality enjoying greater income, power, and status than those of "low" quality. Qualities that define high *suzhi* include educational achievement, fashionable clothing, refined comportment, and tall, toned bodies—all requiring substantial income and tasteful consumption. The ability to improve one's (or one's children's) *suzhi* has thus become central to class mobility and stability. Because cultivating *suzhi* is above all based on the notion that it is not something inherent in bodies—it must be built into them—the emerging framework of *suzhi* has been viewed by anthropologists as troubling, exacerbating inequalities and creating a kind of self-cultivation in which investment in the body, and the body as a site of investment, has become an obsession.

Scholars interested in the bodily nature of *suzhi*, although often positioning their work as theorizing the relationship between bodily-selves and recent economic reforms in China, typically take for granted that the "materiality" of bodies makes them vulnerable to social differentiation. The anthropologist Ann Anagnost (2004), for example, drawing on a tradition in anthropology that views the body as a particularly salient site for producing inequality in a capitalist system (see, for example, Bordo 1993; Butler 1993; Foucault 1973, 1978, 1979), laments the way that neoliberalism in China has (re)produced a context in which actualizing *the body's* latent potential is the means for capital accumulation. She warns of the dangers lurking behind "opening the body to a regime of exploitation perhaps unparalleled in human history" (Anagnost 2004, 201).[7] In her critiques of neoliberalism and *suzhi*, Anagnost uses a concept of "body" that is decontextualized and unproblematized. By doing so, she assumes that differences rooted in bodies are always naturalized (that is, assumed to be inherent and unchangeable).[8]

The cultural comparisons in this book address these conversations in two ways. First, engaging with Rofel, I interrogate the extent to which desires and pleasures were assumed to be an inherent part of selfhood for the women I knew in Shanghai. While Rofel grouped together a wide range of desires, including, at the forefront, sexuality, I focus on the presumed relationship between the self and the pleasures of the palate, another domain of desire that has long been associated with authentic selfhood in the West. Contrary to the "neoliberal" subjects central to Rofel's account, neither group of women I knew in Shanghai assumed a clear or unhindered correlation between what they "wanted" to eat and "who they were." In fact, far from being defined by "natural" desires, the Chinese women I knew conceptualized selfhood as being produced through time; they were much more concerned with the implications of the foods they ate on a regular basis than the foods they "liked." And although the Western women did seem to conflate what they "liked" or "wanted" to eat with authentic selfhood, they were aware that the consumerist context provided a direct threat to their ability to decipher which "wants" were a product of advertising and flavor concoctions and which ones were genuine. Rather than the current economic context producing a particular kind of naturalized inner self-hood-as-desire, then, the discussion demonstrates cultural variability in the degree to which embodied experiences come to be understood as an essential part of an immutable and authentic "inner self."

Second, rather than avoiding describing the nature of "the body" or taking it for granted as a bundle of appetites and the material basis of neoliberal or market-based emerging inequalities, I demonstrate its variability as it informed the kinds of selves experienced by the women I knew in Shanghai. This is revealed through the link between the kinds of embodied sensations that came to represent selfhood and the extent to which political importance is ascribed to bodies in general. The different temporal natures of the embodied sensations that were associated with selfhood for the two groups of women are significant, demonstrating the culturally particular nature of the assumption that when selfhood is embodied as a result of neoliberal / free market / consumerism / economic transformations, and liberated from Maoist politics, it is "naturalized."

In this ethnographic case, then, employing the critical methodology of "situated feminisms" explicates how acultural and Foucauldian-inspired theories about bodily discipline and self-development actually align with a culturally particular model of embodied selfhood. Thus, on the one hand, the Shanghai Western women mobilized a familiar Western critique as they sought to undermine the beauty ideal of thinness they encountered in Shanghai by showing that it was not "natural." On the other hand, the Chinese women pursued certain ideals not because they presumed them to be "natural" but because they saw such ideals as part of a *socially* produced milieu in which they sought advancement.

For many of the Chinese women I knew in Shanghai, introducing me to their acquaintances accomplished dual objectives: it assured that I would do the same for them and it demonstrated their ability to cultivate a broad network, one that included foreigners. Thus throughout my time in the city, I attended quite a few introductory outings where I met friends, colleagues, or family members of my close friends. The gatherings would almost always include an opportunity for us all to eat together, either at home or at a restaurant. On arriving at the chosen location for the evening, we would exchange an improvised assortment of greeting practices—handshakes or hand-holding, pats on the back, half hugs, lots of chatter—indicating both our excitement to be meeting each other and our desire to be culturally sensitive to one another. On sitting down to our table, inevitably my new acquaintances would ask two questions about me (directed sometimes at me, sometimes at my Chinese friend): could I use chopsticks and was I accustomed to eating Chinese food. The answer to the question about chopsticks was easy: yes, I could use them. The other question was a bit more complicated.

One of my earliest memories of learning Chinese—and the painful mistakes that come with it—is of a small banquet hosted by some of my Chinese teachers and friends. At the banquet someone asked me if I was used to eating Chinese food. For a beginning Chinese speaker, the word for being "used to" something, *xiguan*, sounds a lot like the word for "liking" something, *xihuan*, and I thus responded enthusiastically that yes, I liked Chinese food very much. My response, greeted with embarrassed grins and a few chuckles, was clearly not quite right, and my teacher clarified that the person asked me not if I liked Chinese food but if I was accustomed to it. "Oh," I said. "Yes, I suppose I am accustomed to it." At the time this distinction—between liking something and being used to it—did not stand out to me as anything too significant. I did not quite understand the difference, and I assumed it was merely a matter of word choice, not something conceptually important. But as I spent more time in China, I came to understand that being "accustomed" to eating a particular food had a specific meaning and implication for my Chinese friends. During my fieldwork, whenever the question arose about whether I was used to eating Chinese food, Mei, my best friend, would answer with pride that, yes, I had been to China many times and was thus used to it. Sometimes she would offer up the fact without any prompting from others, especially in moments when she was boasting about me to those who did not know me.

Most people explained the difference between liking a food and being used to it in similar terms. Being used to a food has to do with how long one has been eating it, which influences how much of it one can eat and the way one feels after eating it. As one of my friends explained: "If you are used to eating something, you feel full after the meal and are able to go back to work immediately and concentrate on what you are doing. The food sustains you until the next meal." The amount one can eat before feeling "full," as I learned firsthand, is oftentimes the main indicator of whether one is used to eating something. On occasions when I did not eat as much as my friends thought I should, for example, they would often disapprovingly say to each other, "Oh, she's not used to this," and then ask me if we should order something else. Their disappointment palpable, no amount of expressing that I just was not hungry could change their minds.

They described liking a food, by contrast, as something one could tell in one bite; it was based almost solely on the flavor of the food. And, according to the women I knew, it did not say much about who one was as a person. It was not that liking foods was not important. In fact, it played a large role in being a good host. My friend's mother, who often cooked for the group, took an active interest in finding out our favorite dishes and would try to make them for us every time we visited their home. But when I asked people what was more important for getting to know someone, liking a food or being used to it, everyone agreed that being used to a food was much more significant, because it said something about a person's history. When discussing the topic, my friend offered the following example: Her outgoing and friendly cousin had moved to England a few years back, and now, whenever she returns to China to visit her family, she just sits on the couch and does not talk to anyone. "We all think she's become used to their food, which is cold, and it's changed her personality." She went on to say, as for liking something, "You can tell in one bite what someone likes, and so it's just not that interesting."

FOOD AND SOCIALITY IN CHINA

Food and eating—banqueting, table manners, food preparation, food taboos—are central to cultivating Chinese social life and affirming family dynamics (see, for example, Chang 1977; E. Anderson 1988; M. Yang 1994). Following a long tradition in anthropology, researchers have focused on how sociality is created through food, explicating the ways that practices and discourses about food create meaningful and moral contexts within which social, political, and group identities can be established and maintained (see, for example, X. Liu 2002; Oxfeld 2017). However, they have often left unexamined how people assess the food they eat, and how they decide what to eat, in relation to their bodily-selves.

In my experience in (urban) China, there is a highly developed and complicated discourse about eating that theorizes a relationship between the food one eats and one's character, personality, and appearance. In certain ways, I think, this is connected to the seemingly common knowledge throughout China that describes the personalities of certain regions as emerging from that region's food preferences. Perhaps one of the most common distinctions made in this way is between northern and southern China: in the north, people eat (or traditionally have eaten) flour-based staples like noodles and dumplings; in the south, people eat rice. On this basis, a variety of comparisons are made between the people of the north and south and what they are "like." For example, a relatively common distinction is to say that northern people are like flour/noodles: straightforward, bold, and careless about details; southern people are more like rice: gentle, delicate, and focused on details. These comparisons sometimes extend beyond the ingredients, to the way people eat those ingredients. Thus northerners are rough and straightforward because they eat quickly and swallow big bites of noodles and buns; southerners are more refined because they focus on the smaller details and the tastes of their food and savor their dishes.

While these kinds of regional stereotypes are rarely taught as part of an official curriculum on China, discourse about these differences and their relationship to food is pervasive enough that most people in China know them (an abundance of social media posts are about these), and there are surprisingly consistent versions of how certain foods produce certain kinds of personalities.[1] For example, regardless of whether I was in Beijing, Qingdao, Shanghai, Guizhou, or Chengdu, everyone described Sichuan people as being straightforward, bold, short-tempered, and stubborn and linked these traits to their spicy cuisine. In short, they always said, the people are "spicy" because the food is spicy. But the connection is sometimes more complicated. In Sichuan, for example, where the weather is typically damp, spicy food (the chilies to be precise) is understood to help dispel the bodily discomfort associated with humidity. So there is an entanglement between a region's weather, the kind of food that is eaten there, and the personalities of the people. Of course, depending on which region someone is from, the presumed traits might be presented in a more positive or negative light, but a relationship between food and regional personalities is rarely questioned.

The Chinese women I knew in Shanghai extended these ideas to "self," exemplified in their discussions about being used to a food, and the concept of *tizhi*. Indeed, rather than focusing on how their personality was linked to the region from which they came, they theorized the relationship between their bodily type, the foods they were eating, and their personalities. This is not to suggest that they prioritized cultivating bodily-selves over their social relationships; the two aspects of eating were inherently entangled for them and took an equal amount of their focus. For example, the women sometimes asserted their individual needs when choosing to eat only some among several foods offered. The sociality of the situation was not compromised by such individual selections—oftentimes it was actually bolstered by the sharing of personal information about health. Or, when I did not eat as much as my friends thought I would, it demonstrated that I was not "used to" the food and *also* indicated a lack of sincerity or enthusiasm for our social relationship.

The way that food is theorized in relation to self is alluded to in ethnographies of contemporary China, often in reference to interpersonal relations. For instance, the anthropologist Xin Liu (2002) recounts a banqueting scene where men discuss the food they are about to eat. I quote at length to illustrate the detailed attention these men pay to the food and its effect on their embodied selves:

> Although laws prohibited the consumption of many animals, they continued down the throats of businessmen and their guests. One young man who was always asked to accompany officials on their visits said, "You see, people like rare animals because they are good for health. They eat rare animals not because they simply taste good, you know, but because they are nutritious."
>
> "Really? But a lot of things are nutritious, such as carrots," I said.
>
> "Well, that is different. How long can you live? How long does a turtle live? See the difference? A turtle lives for a thousand years, but you cannot live more than a hundred. You see the difference? Then you understand why he likes turtles. You eat more turtles, you will be likely to live longer. This is what I mean when I say they are good for your health. This is what everyone believes and why everyone enjoys turtles."
>
> "If so, one should not eat chrysalides. They live only for a few hours, if I am right."
>
> "You are wrong. They eat chrysalides not for that purpose. Young women in particular like them because they are supposed to be good for one's skin. You know, you don't want to have skin like a turtle's, do you? Then you have to eat something like chrysalides for a change. Eating them helps keep your skin young precisely because they live only for a few hours. After you have enough turtles, you

must have something else for different parts of your body." He was completely serious, and he continued, "Each animal, especially rare animals, has its own potential to increase your health. Snake, for example, is good for your kidney, and the kidney of the snake is good for your eyes. The only danger is that if you eat too much turtle, although you may live longer than others, you might also become more like a turtle in character or appearance. Don't you think that those officials look a bit like rare animals? I guess that part of the reason is that they have eaten too many such animals." (X. Liu 2002, 58)

Although Liu positions his work as explicating selfhood in contemporary China, he leaves unexamined the way that food is linked to the men's health, appearance, and character; instead, he moves on to examine how power operates within these banqueting contexts. He argues that rare animals symbolize power and that because only certain people have the means to eat such animals, these men are literally "eating power." I agree that this is indeed the case (not everyone is able to eat turtle), but the focus on the social implications of these situations does not address the way that the men understand themselves—and their bodies—as being formed through the foods they eat.

Much like the men whom Liu knew, my Chinese friends in Shanghai were preoccupied with the impact that certain foods would have on their bodies and bodily-selves. The concept of *tizhi* was central to how they conceptualized food and bodies, which informed how they made choices about what to eat each day. Dovetailing with the temporal understanding of self implied in being "used to" a food, *tizhi* points to an understanding of bodily-selves that are continuously being modified—or made—through food. The women's willingness to pursue being thin, either by dieting or through other weight-loss programs, depended on dieting's compatibility with the temporal aspect of self embedded in their daily eating practices.

TIZHI: UN-ESSENTIALIZED BODILY-SELVES

My language tutor, Li Zhang, first introduced me to the concept of *tizhi*. A twenty-eight-year-old from a small village in the nearby province of Anhui, Li worked at one of the many language centers in Shanghai, where native Chinese speakers teach foreigners standard Chinese. They offer small courses and, for a slightly higher fee, one-on-one tutoring. In search of some assistance in explicating the texts I was using about bodies, I sought her help—she came highly recommended. Li focused mostly on tutoring and tried to tailor her lessons to the interests of her students. When I explained that I was researching practices of bodily self-improvement in daily life, she became quite enthusiastic about working with me. As she put it, she had always been interested in Chinese medicine (CM) and had lately encountered some health troubles. She was adamant that she was not qualified to teach me CM, but since she was interested in the topic, she thought it would be fun to survey some of the information available online and in books and work through the material with me.

Li described herself as conservative, as she preferred a "simple life" to the busy, chaotic life of the city. She had worked hard in school to learn English and cultivate the proper standard Chinese pronunciation and was now making a relatively good living in Shanghai. But she was worried that the stress of city life was making her sick and often contemplated returning to the village where she grew up. She was profoundly confused and disgusted by how some of her friends spent their money, sometimes blowing hundreds of dollars at a time just to purchase a fashionable purse. And she was relentlessly curious about the differences between China and the West; we often spent our time not only reading about what was happening in China but also comparing whatever we had just read to life in the United States.

Li and I worked together throughout my eighteen months of fieldwork and, over time, developed a close relationship. Some days we focused on written material, and other days we spent our time chatting about her health and her recent trips to the doctor's office. We stopped meeting at her downtown office, a fairly bland space with florescent lighting and gray carpet and walls, and instead would meet at coffee shops and restaurants.

Her favorite place to meet was McDonald's, where she would order french fries and hot tea. About halfway through my time in Shanghai, we realized that we lived only four blocks from each other (an incredible coincidence in a city spanning almost twenty-five hundred square miles), so we would sometimes meet in the neighborhood or at her house, where she lived with her husband and mother. Although I never met her husband, I did get to know Li's mother, who was also interested in CM and was absorbed with the task of figuring out how to eat healthfully. She had moved to the city to help support Li, her only child, in the hopes of one day taking care of a grandchild. Li and her husband were trying to conceive but were not having success, and Li's health had been deteriorating. During the time we worked together, Li and her mother became more and more focused on Li's health and well-being. Sometimes, after a session, Li would invite me to accompany her to see her doctor.

One of the very first things Li brought in for us to read together was a description of the different kinds of *tizhi*, a concept, she said, that was essential to her own understanding of her body. She was not an expert in CM, she reminded me at just about every meeting, and could only tell me what was important and interesting from her perspective. So in one of our first meetings, we read fairly brief descriptions of the nine types of *tizhi*: balanced, weak yin, weak yang, weak *qi*, wet phlegm, stasis blood, wet hot, gloomy *qi*, and special endowment. Li explained to me how a person's *tizhi* was important for deciding what to eat, since food—which she organized according to properties, from hot to cold—affected each type of *tizhi* differently.[2] Not everyone could eat the same thing and be healthy.

Tizhi is typically translated as "bodily composition," and contemporary discussions about *tizhi* have their roots in canonical teachings and texts in the CM tradition. However, although referenced in *The Inner Canon of the Yellow Emperor* (Huangdi neijing; ca. 2000 BCE), theories about *tizhi* types and their relationship to illnesses were not developed in China until the late 1970s, when Wang Qi and Sheng Zengxiu proposed *tizhi* studies as a new direction of research in traditional Chinese medicine (TCM). In 1982, they published their official text *Theories of Bodily Composition in Chinese Medicine* (Zhongyi tizhi xueshuo), which, among other things, outlined the nine types of *tizhi*. Since the 1980s, *tizhi* studies has become increasingly popular; in 2011, it was officially recognized when the National Administration of Traditional Chinese Medicine listed it as one of the schools of contemporary TCM.

About three months after first reading about the nine types of bodies, and after meeting and getting to know many other women in Shanghai, I was beginning to see that *tizhi* was an important concept shaping how many women thought about themselves and how they decided what to eat each day. So, on an afternoon trip to a bookstore with two close friends, Dandan and Mei, I decided to shop around for popular books about *tizhi*.

Book City, one of Shanghai's largest bookstores, is in an immense six-story building, where each floor is home to thousands of books and an entire half of the first floor is dedicated to food, eating, and *tizhi*. As we walked in, *tizhi* was the first section we encountered, and it was brimming with all kinds of people, including men and women, old and young. The number of people taking an active interest in their health was not too surprising, given the recent rise of medical costs and the elimination of most state help for medical care (see, for example, Chen 2008, 127; Zhang and Ong 2008, 11; Blumenthal and Hsiao 2005; French 2006). As many take on managing their own health, and with the amount of interest shown at the bookstore, it seems clear that food and *tizhi* are central to how people are seeking to cultivate their health.

Books about *tizhi* abounded. They ranged in topic from self-cultivation and self-improvement to beauty methods and work habits. Because *tizhi* is modified through food, all of these books contained information about proper eating habits. In general, most books agreed on the nine kinds of *tizhi*. But certain books catered to particular demographics. For instance, one book on self-cultivation claimed that for modern people living in an urban environment, there are three main kinds of *tizhi*: weak yin, internally hot, and wet spleen.[3] There were books offering solutions to white-collar workers struggling with "internal heat" as well as books geared to either gender.

Besides being essential to one's health, *tizhi* was offered as an explanatory framework for why a person might be encountering social problems in the world. The following blurb was published on the back of an introductory book about *tizhi* (translation from Chinese):

Why am I always drifting away from the group and feeling isolated?

Why doesn't he (she) understand me?

Why are his (her) suggestions so unsuitable for me?

I'm out of strength, but he (she) continues to argue with me.

I'm working so hard, so why is my performance at work mediocre?

Lately my boss's attitude toward me has changed. What did I do wrong?

There is no need to doubt yourself. You acknowledge your faults and understand the deficiencies of others.

Every person's *tizhi* is different, and it is differences in *tizhi* that lead to all kinds of personalities, which ultimately determines how you deal with situations.

Your habits do not determine your fate; your personality does not determine your fate; it is your *tizhi* that determines your fate! (Wang 2012)[4]

After browsing the selection for some time, I bought a few books, and we settled into a nearby coffee shop for an afternoon of reading and chatting. As we were surveying our newly purchased books, Mei picked up one of mine: *Nine Types of Tizhi: A Nutrition Plan* (Jiuzhong tizhi: Yingyang fangan). She started flipping through it, nodding in agreement with what she read. The book, written by Ji Jun, was a dense 315 pages and included an introduction written by the "*yangsheng* [nourishing life] expert" Wang Fengqi. The cover was full of "official" endorsements of the author's qualifications, including the fact that Beijing People's Radio Station named Ji an "ambassador of public welfare for self-cultivation and health." It had a picture of the author, clad in a Western suit, smiling with his arms crossed in a pose suggesting self-confidence. Mei said, "You found a good one," and then turned to Dandan and asked what kind of *tizhi* she had.

Dandan, after thinking for a moment, admitted that she was unsure. She thought she might be lacking yang, because she was always cold and tired, but she did not know for certain. Mei thought it was possible Dandan had a weak *qi tizhi* and decided it would be a fun task to figure it out. We spent the afternoon reading through the book together, learning about *tizhi*, and deciding which *tizhi* best described Dandan's current situation.[5]

The book began by describing what *tizhi* is:

> When we speak of *tizhi*, we are pointing to what makes up an individual, including innate disposition and cultural (non-innate) lifestyle. Whereas one's innate disposition is the foundation for the form of *tizhi*, lifestyle factors influence and change it. One's innate disposition includes things that are relatively stable, such as growth and development; the process of getting older; biological structure; function and activities; metabolism; and psychology. The environment, your habits, food, sicknesses, and medicine are all considered nurture factors. Of all of these, food is perhaps the most important factor in determining and changing your *tizhi*. (Ji 2012, 5)[6]

Tizhi is thus a combination of both nature and nurture. And although the foundation of one's *tizhi* is inherited, one's lifestyle and habits alter and change it. The author pointed out, contrary to popular beliefs, that bodies are much less stable than most people think:

> We have all heard the saying "Your body (hair and skin) comes from your parents." But actually research has shown that although the foundation of your *tizhi* is inherited, what you eat, the environment in which you live, your feelings and sentiments, the medicines you take, and any sicknesses you've had can all change and influence your *tizhi*. (7)[7]

Because one's *tizhi* is a combination of both inherited and lived factors, and the goal is not to return to one's "original" *tizhi* but instead to work toward a balanced and healthy body, there is not too much interest in trying to parse out what is inherited versus what is attributable to lifestyle. One is not more difficult to fix or change than the other. What is important is that food, combined with exercise and healthy habits, is the means through which one can become healthy again. Furthermore, gender and age also play a role in determining one's *tizhi*, and because *tizhi* is apt to change, it is necessary to constantly pay attention to one's body to know what kinds of foods are most suitable for oneself.

Following a definition of *tizhi*, the first section of the book consisted of nine quizzes, each corresponding to a particular *tizhi*, which are meant to help readers determine what kind of body type they have at any given time. Mei, Dandan, and I casually worked our way through each one, discussing the questions as we answered them. Each quiz consisted of either seven or eight questions, which we answered by circling a number, one through five (1 = never; 2 = rarely; 3 = sometimes; 4 = frequently; 5 = always).[8] For example, the quiz questions for the weak yang *tizhi* were as follows:

1. Are your hands and feet often cold?
2. Does the inside of your stomach, back, or waist dread the cold?
3. Do you have to wear more clothes than other people to stay warm?
4. Are you less able than others to endure the cold (winter chill or summer air-conditioning)?
5. Do you suffer from colds more than most people?
6. When you eat or drink cold things, do you feel uncomfortable?
7. After eating or drinking cold things, do you often have diarrhea? (Ji 2012, 16)[9]

The questions for the wet phlegm *tizhi* were

1. Does your chest/heart/mind feel melancholy? Does your stomach feel bloated?
2. Does your body feel uneasy?
3. Is your stomach plump and soft?
4. Is your forehead oily?
5. Are your eyelids more swollen than other people's?
6. Does the inside of your mouth feel sticky?
7. Do you have a lot of phlegm, especially in your throat, which gives you the feeling of being stuffy?
8. Is the coating on your tongue thick and heavy? (20)[10]

And the quiz for the weak *qi tizhi* contained the following questions:

1. Do you tire easily?
2. Are you often out of breath (your breaths are short, do you have a hard time catching your breath)?
3. Are you easily flustered or nervous?
4. Do you feel dizzy when you stand up?
5. Do you suffer from the cold more than most people?
6. Do you like quiet spaces? Do you often not feel like talking?
7. When you speak does your voice lack energy?
8. When you exercise, do you perspire a lot? (23)[11]

These questions covered a range of issues: bodily sensations (for example, being cold); likes and dislikes (for example, quiet spaces); and personality traits (for example, being easily flustered). After answering all the questions for each quiz, we calculated our scores, based on a simple algorithm, to determine which *tizhi* type we were closest to. Dandan, it seemed, had a weak *qi tizhi*; Mei (still) had a weak yang *tizhi*, which she already knew; and I had a relatively balanced *tizhi*.

We continued on, reading the descriptions of each *tizhi* type, pausing to discuss the ones that were most relevant. For example, about Mei's weak yang type, we read:

> 3. Weak yang: There is a principle in Chinese medicine of "yin and yang balance." If your body does not have enough yang, your *tizhi* will eventually become one of weak yang, which has the characteristic of being too cold. We often hear the saying "All things depend on the sun,"[12] which of course includes people as well. If your body doesn't have enough yang, you are always cold, especially your hands and feet, you always want to sleep, and if you drink or eat something cold, you will immediately have a stomachache. People with weak yang *tizhi* are typically women. Even in the summer they wear heavy clothing and don't like to turn on the air-conditioning or even electric fans. They don't like to work out, and because of this, they often give the impression that they are lazy and depressed. If these people don't take care of themselves, their *tizhi* will become even more unbalanced. (Ji 2012, 29–30)[13]

After reading the description, Mei recounted how when she first came to Shanghai, five years ago, she became exceedingly ill. She was sick for quite some time and was so weak that her boyfriend had to carry her up and down the stairs to their apartment to go see the doctor. Ever since then, her body had become an extreme version of weak yang. She had spent the past three years working to rebalance her body, but it was still too cold. She told Dandan that maintaining a healthy and balanced *tizhi* is very important—once it gets unbalanced it takes a lot of work to make it better. Dandan agreed that one had to be careful and promised to start taking better care of herself. She had just moved to Shanghai two years earlier, after graduating from college, and was working as a headhunter for an international company. She explained that it was the busy season, so she was working a lot of overtime and did not have time to cook for herself. Mei nodded in sympathy as we continued down the list to weak *qi tizhi*.

4. Weak *qi*: If your body doesn't have enough *qi*, your breath will diminish, and the function of your organs will decrease. Those afflicted with a weak *qi tizhi* are always tired. When they climb stairs, by the time they reach the top, they are out of breath and exhausted. They have little stamina, so if they have to work late, a good night's rest is not enough for them to recover their energy, and the next day they cannot keep up with their colleagues. These people sweat a lot; sometimes eating just a little bit is enough to cause them to be soaked with perspiration. They have very little endurance and are always catching colds. (30)[14]

The descriptions did not fit perfectly, which was normal, because *tizhi* is constantly changing.[15] For instance, although Dandan does did not perspire nearly as much as the description of a weak *qi* indicated, the other characteristics were accurate, and her score showed that she was leaning toward that body type. We thus all agreed that she was most likely lacking *qi*. We spent the next hour or two examining the chapters dedicated to our types of *tizhi*. The weak *qi tizhi* chapter, for example, began with a description of why *qi* is important and outlined the five different types of *qi* flowing through the body. As the author described the body in such a way, he was careful to point out that this model is particular to CM. He then gave reasons for why one might be lacking *qi*, including the following: the *tizhi* of one's parents was weak when one was conceived; one has damaged one's spleen and stomach (through heavy dieting); one works too hard and does not get enough rest; or one has been sick. All of these reasons could lead to one's *qi* being harmed or diminished. The rest of the chapter was a detailed description and analysis of the kinds of food a person with that particular *tizhi* should eat, which vary depending on the season.

On reaching the part of the chapter detailing which foods to eat, Mei asked Dandan about her daily diet. "Do you ever eat hot or cold foods?" she asked, referring to a categorization system common in China where food is organized on a spectrum of hot to cold, referring to properties internal to the food, not its temperature (although temperature is also important).[16] The question about hot and cold foods was important because, as the book had just explained, for people with a weak *qi tizhi*, taking care of the spleen and stomach is essential for their recovery; it is therefore imperative that they avoid eating foods that are on the extreme ends of the hot–cold spectrum. Dandan replied that she tried not to, but she loved eating watermelon (a notoriously cold food), especially in the summer. Mei admonished, "You'll never get better if you eat watermelon! You need to focus on eating balanced (neither hot nor cold) or slightly warm foods."

"OK," Dandan responded. "My mom is moving here soon to be with me, and she will have time to cook and pay attention to such things. Let's see what foods he [the author] recommends."

Mei replied, "Your mom is coming? Great. That will be helpful for maintaining a healthy diet."

Dandan nodded and explained that her sister lived in the city as well (they were from a small town in Jiangsu, a nearby province) and that their mother was coming to town to live with them and help support them as they pursued their careers. Returning to the page, Dandan read out a list of recommended foods, including lotus seeds, Chinese yams, red dates, rice, honey, red tea, chicken, and certain kinds of fish. Mei nodded in agreement and then, pointing to another section of the page, told Dandan she also needed to be eating sweet potatoes, Chinese pearl barley, gorgon fruit, and peanuts, as these help the stomach recover.

The afternoon continued in this way, with each of us garnering information about what we should be eating on a daily basis, as well as how our eating habits should vary according to the season. Overall the book outlined a complex understanding of the integration of one's innate disposition, lifestyle choices, daily habits, medical history, and feelings and sentiments. And although every person is born with a particular type of *tizhi*, the environment in which they grew up alters and modifies their body type over time. Everything from living in urban to rural settings to stress from work, job type, hours of sleep, and exercise has an impact on one's bodily-self. And because the body type one was born with is not at all important when trying to attain a healthy body, there is no desire to return to or to authenticate an original or authentic self. Everyone can attain a balanced *tizhi* if they follow the appropriate ways of eating, taking into account their present *tizhi*, seasonality, the needs of different organs, and the properties inherent in different kinds of foods. And eating is the most important factor for regaining a balanced *tizhi*. For Dandan and Mei, the book reinforced and filled in important details about principles that they saw as important for healthy eating, self-improvement, and understanding their bodies and personalities. Mei's knowledge of the topic far exceeded Dandan's. The concept of *tizhi* was certainly not new to Dandan; she just did not know the details of each particular type of *tizhi* or what foods would be best for her to eat given her current state. They both agreed that the only way to achieve a healthy life was by cultivating a balanced *tizhi*.

TIZHI IN DAILY LIFE

Throughout my fieldwork, as I cultivated relationships with a growing number of women, I was frequently eating or drinking with them and thus witnessed firsthand the importance of *tizhi* for their daily food choices. For example, Mei would often invite me over for dinner during the week. She and her husband owned two apartments in the suburbs surrounding Shanghai: her parents lived in one, and she and her husband lived in the other. Mei was originally from a small town in Anhui and had moved to Shanghai to pursue a professional career. She was college educated and was doing well in her job at an international firm. Because she was their only child, her parents followed her to the city a couple of years after she settled in Shanghai (much like the parents of Dandan and my tutor Li). The apartment of her parents was much closer to her work, so Mei often stayed with them during the week. And because her mother cooked every night, Mei was able to eat home-cooked meals Monday through Friday. So whenever Mei invited me over for a meal, we usually ate with her parents. I would often arrive early, before Mei got home from work, to help her mother cook. As we cooked together, her mother would explain to me why she was cooking particular foods. Her reasons were typically about seasonality and the amount of hot/cold foods appropriate for her family's health. Meat, such as beef and lamb, was almost always served in moderation, since it is a hot food and Mei's father had problems with his internal heat. Mei, by contrast, was lacking heat (she was weak yang *tizhi*), but according to her mother, eating foods that were too hot was not healthy for her either. Balancing one's *tizhi* took time, and overcompensating for the lack of one element by eating too much of it could be dangerous for one's health. Thus Mei's mother tried to serve dishes that were appropriate for the season and were in the warm part of the hot–cold spectrum. She also included dishes that were meant to boost women's beauty (beneficial for skin and hair), such as wolfberries and white radish.

In addition to explaining the value of foods for altering one's health and appearance, Mei and her mother stressed their importance for modifying one's character, especially in regard to anger (stemming from internal heat) and lack of energy (stemming from a lack of *qi*). These bodily states were perceived to be responsible for certain behaviors: having too much internal heat could cause a person to have a quick temper, be impatient, and want to accomplish things too quickly; not having enough *qi* could cause a person to avoid exercise, dislike noisy spaces, refrain from talking too much, and fail to enjoy the company of friends and family. For example, Mei's father's "food therapy" was meant to reduce his high internal heat as well as his propensity for bouts of anger. Dandan's weak *qi* made her shy and quiet.

It was generally assumed that when her *qi* flow returned to normal, she would be more talkative. Instead of associating such likes and dislikes with someone's innate personality, then, such character traits were understood to be shaped and molded through a person's body and dietary choices.[17]

Thinking that Mei's mother's knowledge about *tizhi* was something she was "handing" down to Mei, I asked her about it one afternoon while we were cooking together: "Did you learn how to cook and about the importance of *tizhi* from your mom?" She chuckled in a way that made me realize the naivety of such a question. "No, when I was growing up we had almost nothing to eat, so we were just grateful to have a meal. No one had the time or interest to talk about food—we were all busy doing other things." As a woman in her late fifties, Mei's mother would have been born during the early years of Mao's rule, and she would have lived through the starvation that came after the Great Leap Forward and the social turmoil of the Cultural Revolution. "No," she repeated again, absent any smile, "I've learned all of this from books and TV shows that I've read or watched in the past few years." She went and found a few of her books about *tizhi* and proper eating habits, which she said I could borrow. In content, they were quite similar to Ji Jun's book: descriptions of the various kinds of *tizhi* and the health problems associated with them, followed by in-depth advice about what to eat, during each season, for cultivating a more balanced bodily disposition. She explained that since health care is so expensive now, it is necessary to cultivate healthy habits, especially in relation to eating.

Like Mei, most of my Chinese friends preferred to eat at home during the week. Over the weekends, however, we almost always met up for a meal out, which they saw as a less healthy alternative to home cooking. Because Shanghai has a seemingly never-ending supply of restaurants, deciding where to eat was always a challenging, but pleasant, task. To find a restaurant we would use Dianping.com, a popular site, which, in 2014, listed over seventy-one thousand places, organized by style, region, neighborhood, and price.[18] In addition to restaurants serving cuisine from all over China, the site lists restaurants specializing in foreign cuisine, especially Japanese, Korean, Southeast Asian, Western, Mexican, and Indian. Although it had a wide assortment of options, it did not include the innumerable small noodle stalls, dumpling stores, or individuals serving various breakfast foods for a few hours each morning. Nor did it include many of the restaurants not located in the city center or in food courts, which are a popular one-stop way to access a variety of foods in shopping malls or subway stations. Nevertheless, my friends and I would often look up restaurants on the site to find a good place to eat. It is similar to the US website Yelp, in that each restaurant is reviewed by its customers.

Recent scholarship on food and eating out in contemporary Chinese society has focused on how locals experience foreign restaurants, where the food is seen as secondary to the atmosphere. For instance, at McDonald's in Beijing, most adult customers reported not liking the taste of the food and feeling unsatisfied after eating there.[19] But they continued to go to the restaurant, drawn there by its ambience and the feeling of equality among its diners and by their children's less discriminating tastes (Y. Yan 1997). This notion is echoed in other work about eating and cosmopolitanism in Shanghai, which foregrounds the importance of atmosphere over food in foreign restaurants: "Their interior design signifies cleanliness, impersonality, and a world that can be carried anywhere. They foster the idea that you are what you eat. But the food is actually not the attraction" (Rofel 2007, 120).

Atmosphere was certainly a factor influencing where my friends chose to dine out. But wherever we ate, there was always much commentary on the food that was on the table. For instance, one of our favorite Sunday brunch spots in Shanghai was an Italian/French restaurant that was impeccably decorated with marble floors and elaborate chandeliers, and, with plenty of space, even when it was crowded it felt open and airy. For brunch, the restaurant offered four or five set meals, each including five or six small portions of various breakfast foods plus drinks. When ordering, my friends always made changes to the set meals depending on what they could and could not eat. Sometimes that meant substituting more fruit, eggs, or potatoes for the meat option; at other times it involved making sure that none of the drinks were served too cold. My friends typically took the time to explain to the waiter or waitress why they were making such changes (with the hope of ensuring that the server would pay attention and make the necessary changes). Mentioning that they needed to pay attention to their *tizhi* and not eat foods that were too hot or cold typically brought a nod of approval (or at least understanding) from the waitstaff.

This practice was repeated at every meal we shared. My friends regularly pointed out which food items were good for what parts of the body and what food items they were avoiding because they were either too hot or too cold. What we ordered was typically (although certainly not always) about what was good for us given a particular season. Healthy choices were often individualized, according to a person's type of *tizhi*, but there was a general rule of health that all of my friends followed: foods at the extreme ends of the spectrum were considered more dangerous for creating an unbalanced *tizhi*, and thus one should eat mostly foods in the middle of the spectrum.

FOOD, BODILY-SELVES, AND PURSUING BEAUTY

As with any ethnographic situation, daily practices were informed by many interrelated themes, premises, and factors. It is noteworthy, for example, that many of the parents of the professional Chinese women I knew had moved to Shanghai to support a daughter, often their only child, due to the one-child policy under which these women were born. Thus, their social mobility included a physical movement away from the smaller villages and towns where they were raised (that is, "home") but not away from "family." Due to the stress and time constraints of the women's budding careers, in many of the households their mothers did the cooking and paid attention to cultivating bodily health. But just as Mei's mother explained to me, it was not that the mothers were "teaching" their daughters about "traditional" techniques for cultivating health; in many cases, they were learning together through recent books and popular TV shows that focused on the relationship between CM and food. Clearly informed by the contemporary moment— monitoring their own health, moving to urban centers to pursue career opportunities, and focusing on self-improvement for social mobility—the women's daily practices cannot be divorced from the political-economic context in which they occurred.

Of key importance are the implications—in the current milieu—of the women's understandings of the relationship between food and bodily-selves for their openness toward pursuing beauty ideals. At first glance, the Chinese women were clearly attentive to an *individualized* sense of self that was intimately connected to the foods they ate. Far from the "social" selves of "traditional" China, then, these women had a highly theorized and personal concept of self that they actively sought to cultivate through material means. In important ways, this seems to validate the argument that the current neoliberal context is producing "selves" in China that are becoming more "like" their Western counterparts—individual and focused on self-improvement.

However, a closer look at the concepts of *tizhi* and being "used to" a food makes clear that rather than understanding their individualized selves as "inner" in nature, able to be authentically represented by their unchanging wants and desires (see, for example, Rofel 2007), the Chinese women saw bodily-selves as created by daily practices. They actively talked about what they liked to eat, but the significance of those conversations for "selfhood" was limited; of far greater importance was being "used to" a food, something that emerged through time and had an impact on one's personality/character. Moreover, as their discussions about *tizhi* make clear, they were not at all concerned about deciphering their "original" type—the focus was to figure out one's current bodily state to be able to cultivate a balanced body by eating the appropriately hot/warm/cold foods in the current season. Their "individualized" selves, then, were personal iterations of already established categories of bodily types, which included attributes such as appearance, character, personality, and health, all of which were modified by daily life.

These ideas about self engendered an open and accepting attitude for dieting and pursuing thinness. For example, *tizhi* provided a conceptual framework within which the properties of food linked together notions of "self" with health *and* appearance. At just about every meal we shared, in addition to a discussion about the hot/warm/cold nature of each food, and what everyone should be eating for their own bodily health, there was much discussion about what foods were good for bolstering one's appearance, including how to improve one's complexion, bring luster to one's hair, look younger, lose weight, and so on. Thus, as the women chose food in the name of cultivating a balanced *tizhi* they also sought items that were good for beauty, including those helpful for losing weight. Dieting as a concept, then, fit seamlessly into their already highly theorized daily practices of modifying various aspects of self through eating. Put another way, dieting—eating or not eating certain foods in the pursuit of bodily aesthetics—was exactly what the women were already doing: thinking about the properties of food, and what they should eat, in relation to their bodily appearances.

In addition, within the *tizhi* conceptual framework, ever-changing bodily-selves, including appearance, were meant to be improved on for the purposes of social mobility. There was no "original" or "unmodified" version to which the women attached special significance. Thus pursuing beauty ideals did not compromise one's selfhood and was not distinguished from other domains of self-improvement. In "Snapshot #1" in chapter 1, for example, when Mei commented that pursuing thinness was much like learning English, she was being explicit about how, to be successful in the current moment, learning "skills" and pursuing beauty were conceptually equivalent: they were both ways to improve the self and had equal significance and potential for creating better career opportunities. As such, among friends there was copious attention paid to one another's bodily appearance, in a manner similar to how the women showed concern for their friends' health, which they also linked to success. For example, in chapter 1's opening vignette, Mei's exclamation that Zhu had gained weight demonstrated that she cared about Zhu, her health, and her successes in the world, which were inevitably entangled with her appearance. As my relationships developed with these women, they became more explicit in commenting on my body as well. Often, when first seeing them, I was greeted with observations about my recent weight loss or gain, any blemishes on my face, or changes in my skin color from exposure to the sun. This was typically followed up with advice about what I needed to eat to correct the unwanted changes.

Our in-depth discussions about cultivating bodily *tizhi* revealed the extent to which they connected properties of food to a historically produced bodily-selfhood that needed constant attention to ensure a balanced and healthy person. The way the women emphasized the relationship between eating and cultivating bodily health aligns with literature on CM and the pragmatic or functional element of attending to bodily changes for maintaining healthfulness. These women's daily practices were thus shaped by a medical tradition preoccupied with change and bodily permeability.[20] However, for them, food choice had implications not only for health but also for personality, character, and appearance, all of which they associated with an ever-changing sense of "self."

Taken together, then, their understandings of selves as inherently individualized, integrated with bodies that were continuously being modified, and linked to health and appearance engendered an approach to food that made them especially open to dieting and modifying their bodies in the pursuit of being thin. In short, the materiality of selfhood for them informed their body politics, especially in regards to eating. The Western women I knew in Shanghai, in contrast, were overtly anxious about the political implications of modifying their bodies through dieting and pursuing thinness. They had an obsession-like focus on their cravings, likes, and dislikes when deciding what to eat each day, which they linked to an unchanging aspect of self that they actively sought to apprehend.

THREE
CRAVINGS

Being "true" to oneself was a mantra of everyday life that the Western women I knew in Shanghai took very seriously. In the context of food, this meant eating what they "wanted," regardless of any societal pressure they might feel to do otherwise. However, they acknowledged that their wants were vulnerable to outside influence, and therefore much of their discussions and attempts to decide what to eat each day was focused on interpreting their desires. Reflecting an American notion of "authentic" selfhood (Lindholm 2008), one of the most difficult aspects of figuring out what one "wanted" to eat was deciphering whether that want originated in oneself or was coming from an outside source. That personal culinary preferences came to represent, both to the women themselves and to their friends, an important part of their identity in the city added to the complicated nature of deciphering the nature of their wants. In fact, for those new to the city, "settling into" their new home required figuring out the culinary scene in the cosmopolitan megacity, which offered an overwhelming number of "new" foods to try.

Home to tens of thousands of restaurants, Shanghai is a foodie's dream destination. The city offers an incredible variety of culinary options, and with the appropriate language skills, "taste," and sense of adventure, residents can enjoy flavors from all over the world. However, for foreigners who do speak standard Chinese (Mandarin) or who are not willing to pick a menu item from an assortment of pictures, the choices become much more limited. These include plenty of fast-food options (with menu items often listed in English), but most foreigners I knew found the food less than ideal and the long lines deterring, especially for eating out on a daily basis. Much more appealing were the "foreign" restaurants, many of them clustered in select parts of town, including Xujiahui in the city center and Hongqiao, a western suburb that was home to one of the most popular international schools in Shanghai.[1] Although all catered to an English-speaking demographic, these restaurants offered different kinds of culinary experiences. Some tried to imitate restaurants in "the West" and create an atmosphere that feels like "home." Others crafted an "international" vibe (or "fusion," as it is often called in fancier restaurants), allowing diners to imagine themselves as part of a global cosmopolitanism that extends beyond the borders of any one place. Still others rooted dining experiences in the "local" context of Shanghai or China, more broadly conceived.

Three of my closest Western acquaintances, Kate, Sophie, and Emily, were engaged in different expat food "scenes" and made very different choices about what to eat each day.[2] Whether they ate "locally" or ordered delivery from McDonald's, their food choices—not at all surprisingly—were guided by their likes and dislikes. Tellingly, though, as they navigated their culinary options in Shanghai, they all relied on a similar register to legitimize their personal eating preferences: the notion of a CRAVING. Cravings, as they told me, are bodily sensations that are "true indicators of what one wants." The ways in which the women mobilized the concept—always as a means to link their culinary choices to selfhood—reveal that they rooted "self" in an *unmodified* "body." As such, and in great contrast to the experiences of the Chinese women, dieting—or modifying the body through specific eating practices—was especially troubling for them, as it threatened what they held most dear: authentic selfhood.

FOREIGNER STREET

"Let's get Indian food," Sophie said as I greeted her at the entrance to Foreigner Street (Laowai Jie), our chosen destination for dinner that evening. "I've been craving it all day. And this place [*pointing to a spot a few doors down*] has a great buffet." I happily agreed, both with her choice of Indian food and with the restaurant—I had eaten there before and the food was delicious. As we walked to the restaurant, we watched a French family with two young kids make their way down the pedestrian walkway—a rather narrow path (given how crowded the street typically was) set between the restaurants and their outdoor seating areas. The kids, one just learning to walk, were comfortably meandering down the path as it made its way past the thirty or so restaurants (most of them Western) and bars that line the 480-meter-long street. Quite a few diners smiled and waved as the littlest one toddled by, and some Chinese tourists snapped a picture of the family. The kids were clearly enjoying the attention. Sophie thought aloud, "I wonder what it's like to grow up here? It must be fun to be around so much diversity."

At the restaurant, we sat outside on the patio. Before we could even get up from our table to get our first round of food from the buffet, we were approached by an elderly woman, dressed in rags and hunched over, begging for money. She brought one hand up to her mouth while pretending to hold food in the other. As Sophie reached for her purse, our waiter approached and shooed the beggar away. She reluctantly left, and we watched as she made her way down to the next restaurant.

The Indian restaurant was tucked between one of the few Chinese restaurants on the street (Amy's Restaurant) and an Iranian place, so there was plenty of commodified cultural diversity on display for us to watch as we ate our selections of Indian food. In fact, just as we sat down to our first round of food, an Iranian belly dancer came out onto the street to perform her nightly ritual of two or three dances, accompanied by loud Persian music and the unrelenting clapping of a man who appeared to be her boss. As usual, some pedestrians stopped to watch; diners turned their heads, at least for the first few measures. Sophie and I pondered the relationship between the dancer and her boss. "I wonder if she wants to be dancing or if she has to," Sophie muttered as she used her garlic naan to scoop up the last of her chicken masala. "I mean, is that exploitative? It's a cool dance, but . . . does she have to wear such skimpy clothes?" "Yeah, I don't know," I managed, as I pondered her reaction to the man and woman. Watching the scene unfold, him clapping, her dancing, the music blasting, my friend's skeptical but interested interpretation, Chinese tourists taking pictures, blond kids running past, it was hard to reconcile the commodification of cultural difference with the genuine socializing occurring. People seemed to be enjoying themselves in part, if not completely, due to the "diversity" of the scene.

When the dancing finished, our conversation turned to Sophie's recent breakup with her boyfriend back home, something he initiated. She was sad but also understood why it might be a good time to part. "I don't know. It's been more than six months since we've seen each other, and I feel like I've really changed since being here. Like today. It's the first day I've ever *craved* Indian food. Back home we never ate Indian food. And now I'm craving it. I'm finally becoming me. I know it doesn't sound like a big deal, but I think it is. Anyway, it's probably for the best. I just wish there were more options for me here."

Sophie came to Shanghai to teach English at one of the many schools employing foreigners as teachers. With the rather forgiving criteria of being a native speaker of English and having a college degree (and, oftentimes, being white), these jobs drew young college graduates who wanted an adventure abroad. On a one-year contract, she was given a small apartment on campus and a meal card, which she used for breakfast and lunch in the school's cafeteria. The school was on the city's northwest side, quite a distance from the city center and Hongqiao, the suburb where we met for dinner. Sophie liked living in an all-Chinese part of the city; it made her feel like she was really living in China. But in the evenings, she was drawn to places such as Foreigner Street for their "diversity" and "international vibe." The main reason Sophie wanted to come to China was to have a chance to explore the world a bit before she settled down in the States. Being in China not only afforded her an opportunity to know more about the country but also introduced her to a cosmopolitanism that she longed for back home.

After picking up a couple of cookies at a French bakery, we decided to call it a night and began walking toward the subway station. Foreigner Street dead-ends at bustling Hongmei Road, right across the street from Pearl Market, one of the largest markets for fake goods (and real pearls) in Shanghai. The market, a five-story building crammed full of stalls selling anything from fake North Face jackets and Louis Vuitton bags to Chinese paintings and all kinds of stone jewelry, is almost exclusively visited by foreigners. Bargaining is the name of the game, and it is not uncommon to hear a heated back-and-forth between customer and vendor. The block immediately outside the market is also full of peddlers offering their goods, most notably Tibetan women selling turquoise and silver jewelry laid out on yellow felt blankets lining the sidewalks. As we walked past one such blanket, a pair of earrings caught Sophie's eye, so we stopped to look. The Tibetan woman approached us and asked if we were interested. Sophie said, "No, just looking," and we moved on.

As we waited for the subway to take us home, a young woman approached Sophie and handed her a pamphlet. We watched her walk away and hand another pamphlet to an overweight woman a few feet down the platform and then to an overweight expat a few more feet away. Sophie looked down at the pamphlet and read aloud, "Join our gym. Lose weight fast." She looked up, annoyed. In the direction of the young woman, now quite a ways away, she said, "I'm not fat. I'm *not* fat. *I'm not fat.*" Then turning back toward me, she complained: "That's so annoying. I'm not fat. I work out at a gym almost every day. I'm not going on a diet. I just want to eat what I want to eat. Ugh. I hate it how everyone is always assessing my body here. It shouldn't be that important!"

THE AVOCADO LADY

In the Shanghai expat community, the Avocado Lady is legendary. She is the owner of a "hidden gem," one of the most popular places where in-the-know foreigners shop for groceries in the city center. On first glance her unmarked fruit stand looks like any other on the tree-lined Changle Road: a small concrete structure, opened to the street by two large raised garage doors, with produce and other foodstuffs overflowing out onto the side-walk. But peeking in, one will see that the store is packed with foreigners (and maybe a few curious locals), all either milling around searching the cramped shelves for their desired product (how they all fit into the stall is a mystery) or waiting patiently to make their purchases, often using their newly learned Chinese when their turn comes.

The story of the Avocado Lady, Jiang Qin, is as compelling to her customers as her location and assortment of produce: a local heroine who overcame destitute poverty through recognizing a need in the market (foreign food goods) and then working extremely long shifts (nineteen hours a day, seven days a week). She is nice, humble, and eager to please her foreign clientele, something relatively rare in the service industry in Shanghai; most foreigners will bemoan that the city lacks the "service" they know and expect back home. Qin is originally from Nantong, a small rural town north of Shanghai. The story goes that after high school she moved to Shanghai to earn money for her family. In 1990, she was selling eggs and a few vegetables. A French chef, who lived nearby and was struggling to find the items needed for his cooking, suggested that if she started selling imported goods, foreigners would flock to her store. She took him up on the idea. One of the first foods she tried selling was avocados (hence her nickname). With the best prices in town (no one knows how she does it), she instantly gained a steady flow of customers.

Based on her success, she started importing foods from all over the world, be it cheese from Europe, olive oil from Greece, or fruit from South America. Her store is stocked full of goodies expats long for, including fresh mints, tropical fruits, Kaffir lime leaves, artichokes, beetroot, shiso leaves, dill, kale, basil, bean sprouts, tomatoes, olives, coconut oil, imported wines, whiskey, Limoncello, coconut water, lamb, prosciutto, salamis, tuna, Aussie beef mince, Amelia's sausages, salmon, steak, yogurt, mozzarella, ricotta, mascarpone, mustards, tahini, pomegranate molasses, flour, yeast, chickpeas, lentils—the list goes on and on.

She runs the store with her husband, her husband's business partner, and her daughter. She is notorious for working long hours, beginning her days at 4:00 a.m. and not closing until well after dinnertime. Expats speak appreciatively of her desire to understand their wants and her ability to fulfill them. One chef in the area told me that if he ever needs something, he always asks her first, to see if she can find it. Much to his delight, she almost always locates the item and is able to sell it at a price much cheaper than he thought possible.

Most expats shopping at the Avocado Lady's store are concerned with finding the best and most "authentic" foods possible (olive oil from Greece, cheese from France), while still paying attention to the local scene and the environment (her best-selling produce is from Yunnan, in China's southwest, known for its scenic landscapes and "exotic" minority groups). Moreover, they are able to have a "local encounter" with Qin; she has an extensive English vocabulary of food products, but she operates mostly in standard Chinese and is exceptionally patient with foreigners practicing their Chinese while doing their shopping. The foreigners who shop at her store are typically those who plan to be in Shanghai for more than a year; they have outfitted their kitchens with ovens and have learned or are learning Chinese. They frequent Chinese restaurants and know all the varieties of "Chinese" food offered throughout the city.

My good friend Emily was very much a part of this scene. Emily was working on a doctorate in history and had been researching and writing in Shanghai for more than three years. She lived with her partner, Rob, in the former French Concession, a beautiful neighborhood in the city center and home to many foreign restaurants. They both spoke standard Chinese and were self-described foodies. One day Emily invited me over to her apartment for an afternoon of writing (we often worked together); we then planned for our partners to meet up with us for dinner. At around three o'clock we started discussing dinner plans. Emily gave me an assortment of local options: the small (four tables and a kitchen) but great Buddhist vegetarian restaurant right down the street, the Hunan place that has an amazing spicy fish dish, or a new French bistro that opened just down the road ("the chefs come directly from Paris"). She also offered that we could cook a meal in. After a brief discussion we decided to cook—she and her partner had stocked their kitchen with the appliances and tools necessary for cooking Western food, and we decided it would be fun to cook a meal together.

They lived just up the street from the Avocado Lady, so we hopped on bikes and headed down to pick out our dinner menu—Emily preferred to go to the store without a list and just buy whatever looked good that day or appealed to her. Emily and her partner ate mostly vegetables, legumes, and fish; they typically did not eat a lot of meat. When we got to the store, she first grabbed a bunch of fresh spinach. Then she started picking out steaks for us. "It's so strange. I'm really drawn to the meat case. Yeah, I'm craving meat. Meat and spinach. I must need iron. Do steaks sound good for dinner?" I agreed that they did, and so we bought the fixings for steak, roasted potatoes, and an arugula salad with goat cheese.

Our route home from the Avocado Lady took us by Baker & Spice, a local coffee shop and bakery, and we decided to stop in for a cappuccino. To order, one waits in a line that files past a beautiful display case of delicious in-house baked goods and pastries. As we were waiting, Emily, eyeing the case, asked, "Do you want to share a chocolate croissant? Theirs are to die for. I've been craving a little something sweet all day."

"Sure," I said. "I'm always up for something sweet."

"Or maybe we shouldn't. I mean, I'm not on a diet, but I probably don't need the calories. I feel like all I do is sit all day writing, and I can tell I'm gaining weight. I mean, I don't care, but . . . ," she trailed off, glancing down at the croissants in the case.

"Let's get the croissant," I said. "We had a productive day today and deserve a little treat."

Nodding in agreement, Emily ordered the croissant with her coffee.

When we got home we started prepping for dinner, and, before long, Rob and Adam joined us to help complete the cooking tasks. When we had all finished eating (a rather delicious meal), Rob stood up to go to the kitchen. Rather innocently and without thinking, he said, "Em is on a diet, so she probably won't want dessert. Anyone else? Coffee?"

Emily, looking appalled, shot back, "I am *not* on a diet. I've just been eating healthy lately. I just want to eat healthy. My body's been craving veggies. It's not a diet!"

Rob, not yet good at picking up on his wife's cues, looked at her questioningly and asked, "I thought you were trying to lose weight?"

Emily, getting more annoyed and embarrassed by the minute, responded emphatically, "No. I am *not* on a diet."

"OK, so do you want dessert?" he asked in a soft tone.

"No, I had a chocolate croissant with my coffee this afternoon, so I'm good."

GRAND GATEWAY

Kate, an American from the Midwest, was in Shanghai to further her career. She worked at a US-based company that was expanding into the Chinese market, and her boss offered her a position in the firm's new office to help with its transition. The transfer was for three years, although it could be extended for as long as she liked, and included a raise, housing, and a round-trip ticket to Shanghai, perks that were hard for Kate to pass up. She was newly single and looking for something to snap her out of the rut she was quickly settling into, so she accepted the position, excited for "something new." This would be her first long-term experience of living abroad, and she was not sure what to expect. But since a good friend of a good friend lived there, she would at least know someone when she first arrived. She accepted the offer and within a month found herself outside the arrivals gate at Pudong airport, standing in the hot humid air, waiting in a long line for a cab with one of her colleagues, who was to escort her to her new apartment in the city center.

Before arriving in Shanghai, Kate thought of herself as adventurous—she was always up for new experiences back home, or, as she put it, she "loved to be out exploring the town." She thought she would love the hustle and bustle of Shanghai, and, as she tells the story, for the first week the city amazed her. There was so much to see, so many new foods to try and new places to explore. But, rather quickly, she grew tired of the disorienting feeling that shadowed her much of the day: she could not communicate with anyone on the street, so simple things like asking for directions or a quick conversation while waiting for the bus were impossible or incredibly awkward. And the city was crowded, very crowded. And people did not know how to walk on their side of the sidewalk. And they were always spitting out their phlegm, which produced a cacophony of sounds she preferred not to hear. And—her biggest pet peeve of all—no one stood in line (except at the airport), and instead people would push and elbow their way to the front of the mass of those waiting. The pushing and shoving was exhausting to her—and endlessly annoying.

Furthermore, Kate found her apartment less than desirable. She lived in the city center, in an apartment complex whose exterior looked nicer than her apartment's interior. Her kitchen was inadequate compared to what she had back home. With just one electric burner, a wok, and a few utensils—and lacking an oven—it was hard for Kate to imagine cooking any suitable meals there. This meant that she went out for just about every meal. Again, what started out as a fun proposition—exploring the city's culinary offerings—quickly turned into a tiring chore. For all that Shanghai had to offer, Kate's culinary world was rather restricted by her limited Chinese and her hesitation to eat local food.

When she first arrived, she was eager to try the new foods Shanghai offered. In the mornings, she eagerly followed her co-workers (the ones "trying to be local") out into the morning heat to taste some local breakfast cuisine. They introduced her to a variety of options, which included pastries (*bing*), fried dough crullers (*youtiao*), and her favorite, egg crepes (*jian bing*). But by the second week, the excitement wore off, and she was beginning to feel homesick and longed for familiar foods. So she stopped eating like a local and instead chose to frequent restaurants that served foods resembling what she ate back home, such as sandwiches and salads (foods that were not at all part of the local cuisine).

This pattern was easy for her at lunch and dinner, since her office was in Xujiahui, a bustling shopping district (about four metro stops south of her apartment complex), known for its sparkling marbled and chandelier-adorned shopping malls. Conveniently, her office was a block away from one of the biggest intersections in the city, a five-corner crossing of three major roads with two mega-malls on either side. The Grand Gateway 66, one of the two malls, was a beautifully kept, massive, six-story structure, with a good selection of Western restaurants and an outdoor "food strip" with excellent patios—a place to see and be seen in the "expat" community.

Just about every day, Kate would head down to the mall to sit out on a patio and eat at one of her favorite restaurants, Element Fresh or Bistro by Wagas. Both were local chains exceedingly popular with foreigners, since they were known to serve fresh Western-style cuisine. This was a major selling point for Kate, who was a bit skeptical of the food quality in Shanghai, given all the recent food scares.[3] Most days she chose Element

Fresh, which was started in Shanghai in 2002 (and has now expanded to other major cities in China) and serves organic foods, mostly sandwiches, salads, and an assortment of hot meals, including "Asian Creations" (dishes such as Vietnamese noodles or sesame-ginger tofu). But when it was too busy or when she felt like something a bit different, she would go to Bistro by Wagas, which serves a good mix of "everyday food," including coffees, smoothies, sandwiches, wraps, salads, pastas, and, like Element Fresh, a few hot "Asian" dishes. Both restaurants were always packed during the lunch hour, and Kate enjoyed the "international scene" of the patio. The patios and interiors of the restaurants resembled what one might find back home (or even better versions of what one could find back home), and the numerous European languages spoken by customers were intermixed with the Chinese of the waitstaff. All in all, the place had an international vibe that was consistent with Kate's vision of diversity: a North American / European upper-middle-class lifestyle sprinkled with some predictable local flavor.[4]

More often than not, when Kate was explaining to me why she ate what she did, she invoked the notion of a craving as the legitimizing source. In fact, she seemed to understand and rely on her cravings as the guiding light for determining what she should eat and how that defined her within the context of Shanghai. Thus when she spoke of eating at Element Fresh, although motivated by the restaurant's use of organic foods, it was her *craving* for one of its sandwiches that continually brought her back. Her body wanted it. And she was happy to oblige. This idea came out best one day when we were discussing breakfast options in the city. We were hanging out with our friends John and Amber, and John suddenly blurted out, "So, I ordered breakfast delivery from McDonald's *again* this morning."

Kate laughed and rather sheepishly, but with a hint of pride, said, "I'm glad to know someone else is doing it too! I've been ordering McDonald's for breakfast every morning for the past *two* months." She began to imitate—in a mock accent—the voice that greets you when you call the delivery number: "How many people are you ordering for today?" They both laughed.

"One," John said.

Kate, playing along, placed her order: "I want one sausage-and-egg Mc-

Muffin and a hash brown. With ketchup. Ketch-up. *Ketchup.* Tomato sauce. *Fanqiejiang.* For fuck's sake. Ketchup!"

Frustration mixed with amusement clearly visible, Kate told us about her morning struggle to get the person on the other end of the line to understand that she wanted ketchup with her order. "I don't know why they can't understand me. I say ketchup a million times and then try the Chinese word my tutor taught me. But I know I don't say it right, and they of course can't understand me, so then I go back to saying ketchup. Sometimes it comes with my order, sometimes it doesn't." She continued, "Honestly, I can't believe I'm eating McDonald's. I *never* eat McDonald's back home. But here it just . . . ,"

John jumped in, "reminds you of home."

"Exactly," Kate slowly nodded in agreement. "I'm not sure why. But I can't help it. It's what I crave in the morning. It's who I am, I guess."

Throughout the time we knew each other, Kate's attitude toward her food choices changed dramatically. After her first month in the city, she complained to me that figuring out what to eat each day was the hardest part of her life in Shanghai. She was not sure how to explore the food options around her, since everything was in Chinese, and she was afraid of getting sick. It made her feel isolated and like a failed adventurer. But a few months later, after she discovered restaurants like Element Fresh and Wagas, she was settling into her culinary choices and was much more comfortable with the fact that she "wanted what she wanted." This attitude culminated toward the end of her first year when an American Chinese restaurant, Fortune Cookie, opened in Shanghai, serving all the Chinese foods that Americans love (but which do not exist in China), including fortune cookies and crab rangoon and "some of the best sweet and sour chicken in all of China." Fully aware of the irony, but not caring, Kate could not contain her excitement: "Finally! I've been craving Chinese food all year!"

CRAVINGS AND THE MATERIAL BODY

The ethnographic scenes described offer insight into the complex array of historical/cultural/political/economic vectors shaping the culinary experiences available to Westerners in Shanghai, including the local politics of eating out, foodie cosmopolitanism, exoticizing the Other through food, and cultural commodification. These dynamisms no doubt overdetermined the particular culinary scenes to which the Western women were drawn. Kate, for example, with her quite limited and highly ethnocentric notion of the "global," actively sought out spaces that allowed her to experience an "international" vibe disconnected from Shanghai, a place she found to be less than ideal for daily living. She was thus drawn to places that served food similar to what she ate back home, albeit with some "new" options available for the days she was feeling "adventurous." Emily, by contrast, understood "authentic" experiences (and culinary options) to be fully rooted in the "local" and took active measures (including learning Chinese) to integrate herself into daily life (outside of foreign circles) in the city.

Clearly engaged in quite different culinary scenes, the Western women nonetheless shared a cultural framework in which deciphering and pursuing what they "liked" and "wanted" to eat was a central concern. They understood culinary preferences as an essential aspect of selfhood that they actively sought to apprehend, and their cravings were the embodied sensations to which they ascribed such selfhood. For Kate, the notion of a craving was used to make sense of—and legitimize—why, somewhat to her embarrassment, she ordered McDonald's for breakfast on a daily basis. She was not especially proud of eating at McDonald's, but she explicitly linked her cravings for it to selfhood ("it's who I am") and had a resigned sense that it was something she could not change about herself. Sophie, in a similar manner, understood her craving for Indian food as a sign that she was finally able to "be herself." She was saddened by the consequences of who she was—she was no longer intimately connected with her past boyfriend—but was proud that her travels and adventures had unveiled aspects about herself that were hidden before. In this way, these women can be understood as a product of a long cultural history in the West where the pleasures of the palate exemplify individuality.

However, the desire to eat what one wanted had added significance for these women in Shanghai, a context in which they felt especially vulnerable to "society's" influence. They heard frequent comments about their appearance and were often singled out for certain weight-loss or beauty products. What happened to Sophie at the subway station—when she was handed the advertisement for the new gym—was by no means an isolated incident. All of the Western women I knew experienced similar encounters. As such, they often complained to me that they felt as if their bodies were on display in Shanghai and resented the overt pressure they felt to be thin. They were anxious about how the milieu of Shanghai was making them internalize certain standards of thinness, and as they actively sought to push back against such pressure, being "true" to themselves—that is, eating what they "wanted"—became key to personal empowerment. While they were adamant that "bodies shouldn't matter," they also wrestled with the fact that they cared about their bodily appearance and confessed that all the attention on their bodies made them insecure about their weight.

There is a fairly extensive literature discussing Western women's preoccupation with (and contradictory attitude toward) body size and eating (Bordo 1993; Millman 1980; Counihan 1999, 76–92; see also Kulick and Menely 2005). In this literature, the tension for women and their eating habits is typically attributed to an unresolvable Cartesian divide between body and self, in which an uncontrollable body is conceptualized (and experienced) as an enemy to self-control. For example, the feminist scholar Susan Bordo describes anorexics' attitude toward hunger:

> These women experience hunger as an alien invader, marching to the tune of its own seemingly arbitrary whims, disconnected from any normal self-regulating mechanisms. . . . It is experienced as coming from an area *outside* the self. . . .
>
> In this battle, thinness represents a triumph of the will over the body, and the thin body (that is to say, the nonbody) is associated with "absolute purity, hyperintellectuality and transcendence of the flesh." (1993, 146, 147–48; italics in the original)

Bordo places this body/self divide in a long tradition in the West, historically rooted in Augustine's struggle of the "two wills" (one of the flesh and one of the spirit) and Plato's vision of complete liberation as being an abandonment of body (147). Similarly, "food rules" among college students in the United States have been described as being about self-control, "the ability to deny appetite, suffer hunger, and deny themselves foods they like but believe fattening" (Counihan 1999, 114). In both cases, "body" is seen as something to be controlled by "self," indicating a division between the two concepts, at least in regard to eating.

In the register of cravings employed by the Western women I knew in Shanghai, bodies were the authenticating location of selfhood, not an enemy to it. Indeed, rather than a self/body divide, the cultural logic of a craving in Shanghai framed an adversarial relationship between authentic selfhood, as located *in* the body, and societal norms and influences, including body ideals. Thus rather than something that the self needed to control—like hunger—cravings could be trusted because they "came from" the body. In certain ways, this version of self-as-body epitomized in cravings is quite similar to recent work on modern American ideas about authentic selfhood and consumerism. Specifically, the way the women overtly linked their culinary desires to their identity clearly situates them within a paradigm of embodied selfhood that blurs the Cartesian divide. Domains that used to be relegated to "the body," such as pleasures and desires, are now a central way to know and be true to the self.

On further examination, though, the craving is noteworthy in how it was the means through which the women directly engaged (or confronted) their suspicion that their desires and pleasures were being manipulated within consumerist contexts.[5] Indeed, the reason the women had to work to decipher whether their culinary wants and desires were "really" a part of selfhood was that they were no longer able to trust their embodied sensations from eating as a means for representing those selves. This was because, in addition to recognizing the impact of the advertising that bombarded them as they moved throughout the city, they were keenly aware that certain foods were designed in a particular way to make them want and like them. The women recognized that companies actively sought to concoct flavors and tweak ingredients to increase sales and were, in effect, able to produce desire and enjoyment. For the women I knew in Shanghai, this meant that the pleasures of the palate could no longer be trusted as the site of genuine selfhood.

If the embodied sensations of pleasures and desires associated with eating were no longer trustworthy, what, then, were the women referring to when they invoked the "wants" of "the body"? What, exactly, was it about "the body" that made it genuine and trustworthy? In addition to indicating an unchangeable aspect of self, the embodied sensation of a craving could also communicate a nutritional need. Emily employed the concept in this way when she found herself craving meat and spinach. She interpreted the sensation as her body telling her that she needed iron, or that her body "wanted" to eat these. The other women did this frequently as well, most often when they were craving something healthy, such as a salad—it was a sign that their bodies needed/wanted the nutrients. Significantly, then, when the women were eating foods that could most easily be associated with "dieting," invoking the nutritional requirements of the body was the most convincing way to justify and legitimize their choices as a part of selfhood.

When put in the context of the well-documented anxieties of middle-class white Westerners about fashioning their identities through (excessive) consumption, this looks like an iteration of invoking the "biological" to legitimize certain behaviors as more moral than others. The "foodies" whom the food studies scholar Isabelle de Solier (2013a, 2013b) describes, for example, invoke the needs of the body as a way to justify the overt pleasure they derive from eating; they see food consumption as "a natural activity based on biological needs," which they understand as morally superior to the problematic accumulative nature of other consumerist activities (de Solier 2013a, 16). Interestingly, de Solier, building on the anthropologist Richard Wilk's (2004) work on the morality of consumption, sees this move as "diminishing the role of the self" (de Solier 2013a, 16), because "in eating . . . our own agency is called into question by the natural compulsion of need, which leads us to constantly search for the dividing line between necessity and luxury, the needs-driven, and the wants-driven" (Wilk 2004, 23; also cited in de Solier 2013a, 16). However, for the women I knew in

Shanghai, rather than justifying their choices as necessary—in contrast to luxurious or conspicuous consumption—they invoked bodily needs (framed in terms of nutrition) as representative of genuine selfhood.[6] Thus rather than seeking a dividing line between wants and needs, they happily blurred the distinction as they moved between invoking a craving as an embodied desire of genuine selfhood, a "want" of the body, and a nutritional "need."

Presuming that the body "knows" what it needs and wants and can communicate this aligns nicely with scholarly descriptions of the recent wellness movement, in which the body is considered "wise" and "listening" to it is an important part of being "well" (see, for example, Cederström and Spicer 2015). This is all part of what the French politician Hervé Juvin calls a new regime of bodily truth in the West, where "to the upright citizen of today, man or woman, the real is that which speaks to the body as sensation, as experience, as enjoyment, or as representation" (2010, 41). What these accounts miss, however, is the way that certain sensations are privileged over others in the search for what is "real." What made "the body" the site of authentic selfhood for the women I knew in Shanghai was not some innate wisdom or the nature of its materiality. The truthfulness of the body was, instead, rooted in its ability to oppose the influences of society. Indeed, in great contrast to the vulnerability of self-as-likes, the women assumed that certain material necessities of the body were impervious to outside influence and provided a trustworthy channel of communication for one's "true" wants and desires to emerge. This desire to differentiate what is changeable from what is not is a culturally particular preoccupation, central to critiques about the body's role in social life.

CRAVINGS, BODILY-SELVES, AND DIETING

The conceptual significance of cravings for the Western women sets up a productive comparison with the Chinese women from chapter 2 that can further understandings of the various articulations possible of "selfhood" within late-capitalist contexts. First, because the two groups of women were clearly operating with different notions of "self" in relation to bodies and food, it is not surprising that they had such radically different attitudes about dieting. The Chinese women understood selves to be ever changing, produced through their daily practices, and influenced greatly by the foods they ate. Dieting was thus a mere extension of what they were already doing with food: modifying and improving various aspects of the self, which gave rise to their open attitude toward pursuing thinness.

For the Western women, however, culinary choices were supposed to represent "authentic selfhood," which was rooted in an unmodified body. Within their cultural logic, eating "properly" had more to do with eating what one "wanted" than eating based on societal concepts of health or nutrition. This is not to say that they ate junk food all the time or that health was not important to them. But when they did eat "healthfully" they justified it on the basis of cravings, which were either a signal that the body "needed" something or a trustworthy channel of communication for wants of the self. For them, eating salads because one was craving them was categorically different from being on a diet: the former was linked to individual/ bodily wants, needs, and desires and the latter to society's imposition of unreasonable and oppressive body ideals. Dieting, then, as both a concept and a practice was threatening to the personal empowerment they sought in their ability to choose what to eat.

Not surprisingly, then, there were striking differences in how the women supported each other in their pursuit of self-cultivation. Unlike the Chinese women, who were happy to comment on each other's weight gains and aspects of bodily appearance that needed tending, the Western women illustrated their concern for one another by policing the degree to which one's wants were influenced by society. This typically included helping their friends decide if what they were eating, especially when healthy, was what they *really* wanted or, when deciding to eat desserts or other unhealthy foods, making sure they were not abstaining because they wanted to be skinny. In short, they saw to it that their friends were being as true to themselves as possible (see also Flood and Starr 2019).

Second, there were differences in how the two groups understood the relationship between self, health, and appearance. Within the *tizhi* framework, the Chinese women had a working sense of self that included both health and appearance, each meant to be improved on for the purposes of social mobility. Again, and in great contrast, the Western women typically differentiated appearance from the kinds of self-cultivation they associated with being healthy. In fact, "taking care of oneself," which they explicitly linked to good health, oftentimes meant being careful to *not* think about one's appearance. For example, most of the Western women practiced yoga on a regular basis before arriving in Shanghai. They were quite happy with the level of instruction they could find in the city, which they found to be quite impressive, but they all complained extensively about the mirrors that were in all of the studios. They went to great lengths to try to find places without mirrors—actively discussing their options with friends and acquaintances and sometimes traveling a good distance to get to them— without much success. This was greatly disappointing for them, as they unanimously agreed that yoga was meant to be done without having to look at one's body. Many of them described how seeing their bodies—really, seeing the flaws of their bodies—got in the way of being able to focus on anything else as they moved through their routines.

On first glance, this seems to suggest that at the same time the women assumed a material basis to selfhood (the craving) they also rejected it (their appearance). But actually, there is continuity in the link they made between an *unmodified body* and authentic selfhood. In fact, the biggest problem of seeing their bodies while doing yoga was how it made them want to change/improve them. The point of yoga, as they understood it, was to become aware and content with the self. Wanting to improve their bodily appearance, then, ran counter to that goal. Again, it was not that they did not care about their appearance. They did—and were quite explicit about it. But they assumed that as they cultivated a healthy self, their appearance would exude such "health" and their *own kind* of beauty would emerge.

One night at a dinner party hosted by Emily and Rob, Emily introduced me to another one of her close friends, Hannah. We were casually chatting about our experiences living in Shanghai while also perusing Emily's book collection in her spare bedroom. As Emily led the way back to the dining room, Hannah commented: "Emily, you're really owning your body right now. I can tell by the way you carry yourself. You've got confidence and it shows."

Emily, turning around, smiled. "Thanks! Yeah, I guess I haven't seen you in a while. I've been trying hard to take care of myself. I've been doing a lot of yoga and I feel good. Yeah, I'm at a good place right now."

Hannah nodded in encouragement, clearly impressed. "I need to get back into yoga."

Thus, whereas dieting in the pursuit of thinness was seen to compromise selfhood (by betraying one's true wants) and something quite troubling for these women, looking good because they were "taking care of themselves" was something to be proud of. It was a topic that could be broached in casual ways with acquaintances of varying levels of intimacy. Running quite counter to the wellness phenomenon, in which cultivating selfhood for white middle-class women has become synonymous with being obsessed with improving "the body," these women were operating in a conceptual framework that was focused, first and foremost, on deciphering which aspects of "bodies" were trustworthy for representing authentic selfhood.

● The ethnographic material presented suggests that the Chinese and Western women I knew in Shanghai were operating with different understandings of selfhood that shaped their choices about what to eat and their attitudes about modifying their bodies through dieting and losing weight. Although all of the women were operating with a sense of self that was individualized, bodily, and linked to notions of health and appearance, they had strikingly different ideas about the nature of the materiality of the self. These differences shaped not only the kinds of political importance they attached to certain parts of their bodies but also the way they experienced and interpreted embodied sensations as a part of selfhood.

This ethnographic context enables a better understanding by expanding on approaches for theorizing how "power" operates on bodies in the contemporary milieu. Why do some women *want* to pursue certain beauty ideals that, at least in some sense, perpetuate their marginalized status as women? Although scholars have taken different approaches to this political conundrum, all of their theorizing, informed by Foucault and Gramsci, has assumed that power operates through an invisible and acultural mechanism that makes certain desires appear as "natural" in embodied selfhood. Thus, they argue, as women seek to improve the "self" it is evident which ones have "internalized" the norms to a greater or lesser extent by their willingness to pursue them. Moreover, in "resistance" theorizing, women who sought the ideals in search of their own individualized empowerment were not considered to be "resisting" because they were not contesting the ideology that served to marginalize women on the basis of their bodies/appearances (see, for example, Weitz 2001).

The ethnographic comparisons highlight the limitations of these approaches. To presume, as these models do, that women who pursue beauty ideals that conform to social standards have "internalized" problematic norms more than others leads to the less-than-appealing conclusion that the Western women in this case are less victims of false consciousness than the Chinese women. Moreover, continuing with this line of reasoning, the "cultural" differences I have described become the means to make sense of this disparity: the way the Chinese women understand their bodily-selves makes them more susceptible to internalizing the beauty standards in the current milieu, whereas the Western women are able to "see" how problematic they are and thus reject them. These conclusions do not satisfactorily unpack the complexity of the ethnographic context I have described.

What the ethnographic comparisons really highlight is the way that these approaches—and the politics informing them—rely on culturally particular ideas about bodies, selves, and empowerment while presuming a universal applicability. In particular, the approaches take for granted that self-as-desires would be "naturalized" by all selves in the same way. Or, put another way, they assume that all people (in an assumed neoliberal or capitalist context) understand "self" to be "natural" (that is, outside the influence of "society"). Thus as such selves have embodied desires, those desires are taken to be a product of nature, which is what gives them their power.

These ethnographic examples make clear that embodied experiences were not naturalized as part of inner selfhood to the same degree for these two groups of women. Neither group assumed that their pleasures were "natural" or that they were able to authentically represent selfhood in a consumerist context. But the Western women did seem to rely on an essentialized (unchanging and deriving its virtue from being authentic) reading of selfhood through their embodied cravings. For them, bodies were the site of the "really real" because they were viewed as outside the influence of humans and society. Even if something changed—for instance, Sophie's newfound like of Indian food—it was assumed to be indicative not of historically and socially produced selfhood but of the ability to find out who one "really is" apart from the hindrance of social influences. And while other cravings come and go—Emily's iron craving or Kate's comfort foods, for example—and are thus "historical," these are typically understood to be reflecting changes that are "biological" and body-based, not socially determined. In short, the Western women I knew had an enduring-through-time experience of selfhood, which they authenticated in bodily experiences they deemed outside of society's influence.

However, the temporality of the Chinese women's sense of self inverted this assumption. Indeed, the embodied sensations they associated with selfhood were assumed to be created through continued and habitual eating of a certain food. And, furthermore, although this was seen as an important indicator of who one is, it was never assumed to be essential or unchanging. This is not to suggest that selfhood was less "inner" in nature; it was just less essentialized by being located in an ever-changing bodily-self. Thus balancing of one's *tizhi* had nothing to do with figuring out or returning to an original or authentic state of bodily-self, but instead hinged on being able to read the body's signals (reflecting its current state and context) correctly and then to eat accordingly. For the Chinese women, the bodily experience of "feeling full" was not solely based on one's stomach sending "natural" signals when it had had enough; instead, it had to do with the relationship one had with the food one was eating (*and* those with whom one was sharing the meal). In fact, feeling full before one had eaten a sufficient amount was often *the* indicator that one's stomach was not used to a food. Thus, on the one hand, subjective sensations such as feeling satiated and being able to work immediately following a meal were indicators that one was used to a food. On the other hand, the bodily sensation of being full could not be trusted on its own, as it must correspond with the amount of food one has eaten. For the Chinese women, then, bodily experiences of feeling full and being satiated were "historically" contingent (on a lifetime of experience): they were based on what one had been eating throughout one's life. And, accordingly, this said something about a person.[7]

This sense of temporality extended to embodied selfhood in general, as illustrated at a dinner party I attended at Mei's parents' home when her former boss, Charlie, came to town. After Charlie retired and moved back to Ireland, he frequently returned to Shanghai and would always call on Mei to catch up and offer his help and advice for developing her career. On one such visit, Mei invited Charlie, me, and a few of her Chinese friends to her parents' house for dinner. Sitting around a crowded dining table filled with an impressive array of delicious dishes, Charlie and I chatted about his recent travels and I translated the Chinese conversations happening around us.

As we began to eat, Mei's friends were discussing their recent attempts to lose weight. One of them had lost considerable weight, and all the women congratulated her on her success. She was clearly proud of her accomplishment and began giving advice about what to eat to be successful (and not ruin one's *tizhi*). As she started to give such advice, Charlie, who was itching to be a part of the conversation, chimed in: "What's all this talk about losing weight? You are all successful women. I think you are beautiful just the way you are." When he finished, there was anticipated silence around the table for the translation. I hesitated, not knowing the best way to phrase his sentiments. Mei took over: "He said 'we are already very beautiful [*women yijing hen mei*].'" What is noteworthy is that Mei in her translation included a temporal element absent in my reading of Charlie's statement. Instead of having some authentic or atemporal state of "just as you are," she placed their bodily-selves in the current moment. Her friends, wanting to be polite, all nodded in agreement. There was then a lull in the conversation, before another friend asked: "So how did you lose the weight? I want to find a new job and I'm too fat right now. I must lose a bit of weight."

In striking contrast with the Western women, then, what mattered most to the Chinese women was what was produced in the social world and through time. They were not interested in uncovering "true" aspects of an unmodified self, nor did they assume that certain embodied sensations were more or less trustworthy for communicating the wants/needs of an "authentic" self. Moreover, as they sought ways to improve the self, they understood "natural" bodily traits as actually being *easier to change* than socially or historically produced expectations about bodily differences.

How, then, do these differences in understanding and experiencing the materiality of selfhood help expand understandings of the way that power might be operating on and through bodies in the contemporary milieu? In this ethnographic context there is a clear link between a "naturalized" sense of self for the Shanghai Western women and a propensity to understand empowerment through recognizing that societal pressures are "cultural" and not "natural," very much in line with the "denaturalizing" approach scholars take as they seek to undermine the power of body-based categories for producing and maintaining inequality. Indeed, it was the same idea about nature—that it was harder to change than culture—that provided the framework for the Westerners to legitimize wants of the self and delegitimize the ideals that threatened their ability to "be themselves." In short, empowerment for these women meant recognizing and rejecting the influences of others so they could "be" their natural selves, which is what made "denaturalizing" social norms seem like an effective approach.

However, the Chinese women did not view "self" or the beauty standards they pursued as natural. Thus, if "self" is understood as something cultivated through time (rather than "natural"), then how might the process of internalization in relation to those selves be rethought? Moreover, what can be said about women who are actively pursuing ideals that they do not think are "natural" at all? Put another way, what is empowering about making "visible" what is already apparent? Indeed, the Shanghai Chinese women were familiar with and rejected the self-empowerment narratives the Western women employed, typically on the basis (1) that they presumed the body was inherently more political than other aspects of self and (2) that being able to "be oneself" was an indication of being empowered. Embodied selfhood for the Chinese women was just as cultivated as other aspects of self, and thus they found this particular way of pursuing empowerment to be an imposition of Western values on to the Chinese context. Far from understanding "resistance" as emphasizing the way that societal norms are artificial impositions that do not reflect "natural propensities" and that undermined individuals' ability to "be themselves," then, the Chinese women were operating with a sense of empowerment that sought out ways to influence others *based on* society's norms.

The implications of these differences were especially critical for how the women understood themselves as racial or as national subjects, as part 2 examines.

PART TWO
BIG EYES AND WHITE SKIN

SNAPSHOT #1

Emily greeted me at a coffee shop one Saturday morning with a mischievous grin. "I have a mission for us today," she said. "I'm out of my face lotion from home and I want to find something comparable. Let's see if we can find something without any whitening agent in it." I smiled at the task, knowing she meant it to be both a challenging agenda item to complete and a challenge to the beauty ideal that made it so. We had talked about skin whitening on numerous occasions: on a sunny day when she lamented the way that most women were carrying umbrellas to shield themselves from the sun; while riding bikes in the summer heat and noticing that the female bikers around us were wearing long sleeves and gloves; after numerous conversations with her Chinese co-workers about the importance of staying out of the sun and taking good care of her skin. I knew she was uncomfortable with the amount of energy, effort, and money that many people in China seemed to spend working to make their skin whiter.

As we sipped our cappuccinos, I asked her about our strategy for the day. Should we go to a mall that carried name-brand Western goods? Should we see if we could find something in the district where our coffee shop was located, an area often referred to as the French Concession, which had a relatively dense amount of places catering to Westerners? After a brief discussion we decided to stay in the area and do a "walking tour" of our options, including the small boutiques that lined many of the nearby roads as well as the larger chains and department stores within a reasonable walking radius from where we were.

We left the coffee shop and headed in the general direction of Watsons, a well-known health-care and beauty supplier in Asia. Similar to Walgreens or CVS in the United States, the store carries an impressive assortment of products, and we thought its selection might be broad enough to include a lotion or two without a whitening agent. It was quite a few blocks away, so as we meandered our way there we had plenty of opportunities to shop in the multitudes of small stores we passed. We were not sure what we would find, but, at that moment, Emily seemed to have high hopes that there would be something she could buy and use to her satisfaction.

In each of the stores, we had a remarkably similar experience. Emily would approach the sales clerk and, practicing her newly learned standard Chinese, would say something along the lines of "I'd like to buy some face lotion, but I don't want white skin." The women—it was always women working behind the counter—would look at her and, with a nonchalant attitude typical of the service industry in Shanghai, respond with a shake of their heads, "None here." Sometimes we would peruse the selection offered in the store before asking; sometimes we would go straight to the counter, as we did when we got to Watsons. The woman, on seeing us approaching, gave us a half smile. Emily asked her by now well-rehearsed question. The woman cocked her head to the side, thinking, "Uh, we have some sunscreen that is popular with foreigners."

"No, I don't want sunscreen. Thanks. Lotion for, uh, after a shower or something."

"Without a whitening agent?" she asked with a shake of her head. "No, we don't have any of that." Emily thanked her, shrugged in my direction, and we left yet another store empty-handed.

The day continued like that, and, getting weary of our shopping adventure, we decided to try one more place, a larger department store with a floor full of stations selling makeup, face products, and other beauty supplies. Approaching one booth, Emily repeated her description of what she was looking for to the women working there. The women looked at each other and then shook her heads. "We don't have any," one replied. Then, looking at me, she said, "But we have a lotion that will help you get rid of those red spots on your face." "No, thanks," I responded. Emily, curious at the exchange, asked what the woman had said. When I translated for her, Emily said, scrunching up her face, "How rude." We walked out and contemplated what to do next.

Emily's mood had clearly soured, and as we started toward the subway station to head home, she blurted out:

"Ugh. Whitening products are so annoying. I just want a lotion that moisturizes my skin. Why do they all have to have stuff to whiten it? I mean, that stuff doesn't actually change your skin color. You can't *really* change your skin color anyway."

"What do you mean?"

"Well, skin color is skin color. It is something you're born with. Changing it with products is artificial. As soon as you stop using them, it goes back to its natural color. These products are just a ploy to get people to keep buying them. Anyway, why do they want to be white? I wish they could just be happy with who they are."

SNAPSHOT #2

Less than a week later, I was, quite serendipitously, back at the same department store, this time with my good friend Mei. We were on our way to brunch at Mei's favorite restaurant in the French Concession, and she wanted to stop by a store to get some more of her favorite face lotion, which was running low. She parked her car in the nearby lot, and we walked in, heading straight to the booth that carried her brand. As she told the woman behind the counter what she wanted, Mei described to me with pride the power of the whitening agent in it. The woman, listening to Mei's description, smiled and nodded: "It's a little more expensive but worth it." After finalizing Mei's purchase, the sales clerk looked at me and asked what I wanted. When I shook my head, she asked, "Don't you want something for the redness on your cheeks? I've got something that will work well to make your color more even and whiter." When I declined her offer Mei sent me a sidelong glance and said disapprovingly, "She doesn't pay nearly enough attention to her skin as she should." They both sighed.

Interested in Emily's and Mei's contrasting attitudes, I relayed to Mei as we walked back to the car the critiques that Emily had made about women in China wanting to whiten their skin, including that it seemed they wanted to look Western. Mei, familiar with such critiques, was annoyed at the suggestion. She rolled her eyes, pulled out her phone, and remarked, "If China really wanted to be like the West, then we would share similar beauty ideals." She handed me a photo of Lucy Liu displayed on her phone (fig. 1). "But we don't. You Westerners love big mouths and tan skin. Like Julia Roberts. Even in Asian women. See, in every picture of Lucy Liu, her big mouth, darker skin, and 'Asian'-shaped eyes are highlighted."

Mei took back her phone and, pulling up another image, handed it back to me. "In China, we prefer big eyes, white skin, and a small mouth. Look at Fan Bingbing. She's the epitome of beauty in China right now" (fig. 2). Putting her phone away, she added, "Anyway, why do Westerners always think it's about them? We don't want to look like you, we have our own standards of beauty here!"

● The beauty ideals of having big eyes and white skin, much like being skinny, were prolific in Shanghai and elicited much commentary from the two groups of women I knew. Their attitudes toward these ideals were, on the one hand, consistent with those for being thin: the Chinese women were happy to pursue them; the Western women found them deeply troubling. However, unlike their discussions about dieting, which focused almost solely on the significance of eating for cultivating or knowing one's "self," the women typically discussed big eyes and white skin in terms of either their racial or national implications. Their drastically dissimilar ideas about the nature of such body-based differences were reflected in how they discussed differences between China and the West and in the kinds of categories they invoked in discussions about beauty ideals. What was at stake when the Western women critiqued the Chinese women for not understanding the "politics of their bodies" and when the Chinese women disapproved of how the Western women took their bodies "too seriously"? These differences enable insight not only into culturally different body politics but also into

FIGURE 1. The American actress Lucy Liu at Comic-Con 2012, in a photo similar to the one that Mei showed me. Distributed under a CC BY 2.0 license.

FIGURE 2. The Chinese actress Fan Bingbing at the Cannes Film Festival in 2018, in a photo similar to the one that Mei showed me. Distributed under a CC BY-SA 4.0 license.

some of the ways that the individualisms central to social life in China and the United States are culturally distinct as well.

As cosmetic procedures and products have increased in number, and as certain beauty trends have become more "global" in scope, scholars have become interested in not only why women want to modify their bodies (in general) but also what the racial implications are of wanting to modify certain traits in certain ways. Of concern are the political consequences of modifying the body in permanent ways through procedures such as nose jobs, eyelid surgery, chin reconstruction, face-lifts, liposuction, breast augmentation, and so forth that make certain body ideals "the norm." In the global context, besides critiquing cosmetic surgery for its gendered implications, then, they see the normalization of a certain kind of ideal face and body as a racialized practice, in which the white Caucasian body is the ideal (see, for example, Balsamo 1992; Hunter 2005). As described by the feminist scholar Kathryn Pauly Morgan, "What is being created in all of these instances is not simply beautiful bodies and faces but white, Western, Anglo-Saxon bodies in a racist, anti-Semitic context" (1991, 36).

According to many of these scholars, women who modify their bodies in the pursuit of such racialized traits are victims of oppressive, idealized standards of beauty that stem from a global racial hierarchy. However, as many of them point out, one of the persisting "paradoxes" of the racialization of the ideal face is how non-white people routinely deny that they want to look white, even as they continue to ask for what appear to be explicitly white features, such as white skin, double eyelids, and higher noses.[1] Paired with the seeming valorization of "multiculturalism" and the inclusion of non-white people in advertising, it appears as if beauty is not a racialized discourse, when in fact it is (Hunter 2005, 57–67).

Attempting to make sense of the discord between what they see as obviously racialized beauty trends and their informants' denial of it as such, and very much mirroring theories of beauty, power, and agency, most scholars attribute the discrepancy to what they call an "internalization" of a global hierarchy. Regardless of how women "feel" or "think" about what they are doing, their choice to pursue certain traits indicates an *unconscious desire* to look like the dominant racial group. As women pursue seemingly white traits, then, scholars deem that women have come to accept—without knowing it—a racial ordering of the world. More troubling still, because they cannot see it for what it is, their actions serve to reproduce the hierarchy that works against them as non-white women. As the sociologist Margaret Hunter concludes, "In the long run, the practice of Anglicizing features through cosmetic surgery just perpetuates the inequality the individual is trying to escape" (2005, 67). Thus in important ways, for these scholars, racial oppression operates much like gendered oppression in terms of beauty ideals: the "internalization" of social norms, based on hierarchies of bodies, produces the desire to look a particular way.

The beauty ideals that were prevalent during my time in Shanghai—big eyes and white skin—have been central to these discussions, although typically in locales outside the context of China. The anthropologist Eugenia Kaw (1993) contends in her account of Asian Americans wanting to have eyelid reconstruction surgery, for example, that their desire to change their eye shape is a product of how, in the United States, Asian facial features have historically contributed to negative Asian stereotyping. This is particularly the case with respect to the shape and size of eyes: smaller eyes with a single eyelid are often correlated with sleepy and less intelligent people (81). However, in an all too familiar pattern, Kaw's subjects largely dismissed the notion that they were trying to look Caucasian; they emphasized instead the socioeconomic advantages of having a certain eye style. Moreover, they often viewed changing their eyes as an individual experience of liberation (87). Kaw, like the other scholars described, was deeply troubled that the women could hold such views in the face of obviously racialized ideals.

The comparisons in the following chapters question the "obviousness" of this claim by asking, rather than taking for granted, what it *means* for a particular physical trait to have racial implications or to be "racialized." I do not question, in any way, the seriousness of the rampant racial discrimination operating in societies around the world. However, building on the work of scholars who draw attention to the "Orientalist gaze" inherent in seeing the ideals as "Western" and those working to further our understandings of race and beauty, I contend that the majority of the critiques of racialized beauty ideals not only rely on a presumption about what race *is* but also take for granted what kinds of actions would serve to undermine a racialized world.[2] Put another way, there is often slippage between how scholars employ the concept of "race" as an analytic and the culturally particular meanings of race that might exist in different contexts. And while some scholars who are interested in such "racialized" beauty ideals are attempting to (re)theorize what race is and how it is related to such ideals, few examine the link between culturally particular experiences of embodied selfhood, race, and how certain norms are "internalized." Indeed, the reason the logic applied to gender oppression is also applied to racial oppression (that is, that both operate through a mechanism of "internalization"), especially in relation to beauty ideals, is due to the presumption that since race and gender are both body-based categories, the mechanisms through which power creates hierarchies—internalization—is also the same. This will become relevant in a comparison of the two groups of women in Shanghai.

For example, in a study of skin-whitening ads in the Indonesian *Cosmopolitan*, in which one of the models is "Caucasian" and the other "Japanese," L. Ayu Saraswati (2010) argues for a move away from theoretical orientations that assume whiteness is only a trait of Caucasian bodies, inherently linked to the Euro-American racialized hegemonic model. For her, because the kind of whiteness in these ads clearly is not limited to a particular race, efforts to challenge the hegemony of whiteness must incorporate a theory that is not limited to a racial/ethnic distinction. She proposes "cosmopolitan whiteness" as a means to achieve such ends, arguing that the ads are not actually marketing a kind of racialized hierarchy but instead work to produce a desire "to embody the 'affective' and virtual quality of cosmopolitanism: transnational mobility" (17). In certain ways, such "cosmopolitan whiteness" resonates with how in Shanghai lighter, untanned skin is a marker of higher-class white-collar indoor labor that is contrasted with lower-class manual labor outdoors in the sun. This explicit class-based notion of whiteness, connected to untanned skin, has been prevalent in a variety of cultural/historical contexts, which existed independently of one another and predated the transnational racialized hierarchy that typically links whiteness with Caucasian bodies.

However, while I am sympathetic to Saraswati's arguments about the need to disentangle whiteness from Caucasianness, her work leaves unexplored the possibility of culturally distinct bodies. Throughout her work "the body" as an acultural "physical substance" is taken for granted. As she rethinks whiteness as a quality of transnational cosmopolitanism, she seems to move *away* from the body and its materiality. She contends that whiteness in the ads, as well as the cosmopolitan ideal, is not about biology but is "a virtual quality, neither real nor unreal" (18). Although she does not completely unpack the difference between the "real" and the "unreal," she hints at it when she says, "This notion of virtuality is important in understanding cosmopolitan whiteness because virtuality highlights the lack of 'traditional physical substance'" (17; quoting Laurel 1993, 8). Or, as she continues, "I argue that cosmopolitan whiteness is a signifier without a racialized, signified body" (17–18). In this way, by delinking whiteness from bodies, she is able to show that the desire for white skin in Indonesia is not actually about race. However, as she extends her analysis not just to the ideals but to the way ideals can be embodied, she goes so far as to suggest that because whiteness is a virtual trait, "the body can only be virtually white" (31).

Throughout Saraswati's work, the questions of *whose body* or *what kind of body* are never posed. Nor does she leave any space for any kind of differing perspective or "reading" of the ads. In her account of the desire for cosmopolitanness, for example, she argues that such "feelings" emerge from "affect," or "bodily sensations" that produce and are produced by a feedback loop of positive impressions: "That is, as the audience feels good looking at beautiful pictures, they will have an orientation toward these beautiful women as being good" (28). She continues, "Simultaneously, she [the model] becomes the point of positive affective identification: she looks good; she makes the reader feel good; the reader will feel good if she has her good looks and good skin, achievable by consuming the advertised cream" (29). Here, then, decontextualized "bodily affect" is linked to a decontextualized "audience" that is "reading" the ads and "feeling" a certain way. One only knows that these feelings—unmediated, primal, bodily reactions—exist because of their effect: the desire for white skin.

Finally, and perhaps most relevant for this discussion about bodies, power, and beauty, Saraswati employs the same theoretical apparatus, affect, to examine how race and gender are "constructed." She writes, "My argument that whiteness is cosmopolitan and transnationalized (transcending race and nation) leads us to this article's larger theoretical claim: gender, race, and skin color are 'affectively' constructed" (27). Seemingly uninterested in what gender, race, and skin color are in a given context, and how that might inform the way ads are read, she focuses her attention on how race and gender are produced through the acultural "body." Thus, even though whiteness in this case is not about "the real body," the way that race is constructed is similar to gender and the desire for white skin: through the primal, unmediated feelings that are then interpreted through culturally particular emotions. In sum, then, to make her case about the global and transnational influence of racial hierarchies of whiteness, Saraswati must presuppose that power works everywhere the same through the acultural mechanism of affect. Indeed, a decontextualized "body" is at the heart of how she theorizes not just the desire for cosmopolitanism but also how race and gender hierarchies *come to be*.

My ethnographic and "situated feminist" approach in the following chapters offers a way to incorporate a variety of points of view—and culturally particular experiences of bodies—into the same analytic framework about race and racialized beauty ideals. Indeed, one of the benefits of conducting ethnography is that one does not have to assume that ads will have evoked the exact same "feelings" from women in different times and places or that power "operates" through "affect" the same way everywhere. Understanding race and what appears as racialized ideals necessitates an attention to culturally distinct ideas about the materiality of self and identity. In this case, far from being "virtual," the women I knew in Shanghai understood the traits of whiteness and big eyes to be "real" attributes (that is, part of the materiality of bodies), but that did not mean they understood them or experienced them as part of their identity in similar ways. In fact, the differing ways that power operates in and through disparate materialities of selfhood arises from cultural variation in the domain of "real" bodies.

In particular, setting up an explicit comparison shows that the two groups of women in Shanghai had strikingly different assumptions about body-based differences—and the categorization of those differences—that overdetermined the extent to which they saw modifying certain features as problematic or not. The Western women understood race as a "natural" and unchangeable aspect of their bodies that they linked to self. Not surprisingly, then, they saw wanting to change those traits as a denial of one's "true" self; they often remarked that they wished Chinese women could just be happy with "who they are." Moreover, the Western women assumed conceptual similarities in the relationship between race/self and gender/self that informed their political inclination to denaturalize racial categories as a means to undermine their power. However, the Chinese women saw race in quite different terms: they thought it was the physical characteristics of the body that *could change*. Most were quite certain that changing one's race was not only possible but more easily done than changing one's ethnicity. For them, both race and ethnicity were *body-based* categories, but that did not mean differences were assumed to be "natural" or essentialized. In fact, the bodily differences attributed to nationality by the Chinese women were almost always historical, mirroring their understandings of bodily-selves as produced through time. It was these historically produced bodily differences—rather than surface ones such as skin color or eye shape—that were considered more central to one's identity and more difficult to change.

The political significance ascribed to certain bodily features is the outcome of different understandings of the physical nature of race, which also shaped the extent to which the women recognized certain body-based identities as socially significant—or problematic. This has implications far beyond critiquing the pursuit of beauty and leads to questioning received notions of the concept of "race" in China. Scholars disagree about the extent to which racial differences have been important in Chinese forms of othering. At the root of these disagreements is the extent to which "race," as a concept, is necessarily linked to an essentialist notion of biology and genetics, as it has been in the West. The way "race" is operating in contemporary China is especially intriguing given the Chinese Communist Party's seemingly contradictory narratives that, on the one hand, "racism" is a problem of the West and, on the other hand, "Chinese" people are all linked genetically, as can be traced through the archaeological record.

The radically dissimilar ideological frameworks of anti-racism for the Western women and nationalism for the Chinese women were direct outcomes of their dissimilar ideas about the nature of the materiality of selfhood and body-based differences. The following chapters bring together insights about race and ethnicity in China with conversations about whiteness, both as a racial identity for the women I knew in Shanghai and the way it informs certain kinds of anthropology, to demonstrate that the propensity to denaturalize racial categories as a means to undermine their power is informed by a culturally particular assumption about the materiality of self.

FIVE
"CHINESE"
IDEALS

The Chinese women I knew in Shanghai assumed bodies to be a central aspect of selfhood. Certain body-based distinctions were also fundamental to how they understood their "identities," most thoroughly elaborated in the distinctions they made between Asian/yellow and Western/white bodies and between being Chinese and Western. However, the categories and explanations they invoked when discussing the pursuit of beauty revealed that not all bodily traits were equally significant for them, nor did they assume that all traits were produced or created through similar means. Importantly, running parallel to how they conceptualized and experienced bodily-selves, the bodily traits they found most significant for their identities were those produced through daily practices.

Rather than contrasting "physical" differences to "cultural" ones, as much work on race tends to do, this discussion begins by explicating the kinds of body-based features that were most important to the women. Their ideas about body-based identities were underpinned by nationalism and are thus relevant to debates about the nature of "Chineseness" in contemporary China as well as the way that racial categories are employed in daily life. All of this offers more to ponder than if the women had or had not internalized a global racial hierarchy as they pursued big eyes and white skin. To set the scene for analysis, I begin with an ethnographic account of an afternoon I spent with my friends discussing beauty.

Walking into the white marbled lobby of a recently remodeled (but clearly underused) hotel in the Xujiahui district, I saw Mei chatting with her friends at the top of a grand staircase. Dressed to the nines, in a black fancy dress and a pair of stilettos, she was standing at the end of a red carpet that guided guests from the door, across the lobby, and up the stairs. Backlit by a magnificent crystal chandelier, she looked as if she were about to enter an awards ceremony, with all the extravagance of the Grammys. Taking in the scene, I was glad I had opted for my "nice" sandals, although my jeans and tank top were clear indicators that I had greatly underestimated the occasion. Mei had invited me to a "beauty workshop" organized by one of her friends who owned a salon in town. It was a luncheon, meant to bring together women who were interested in learning more about the essentials of beauty; the event was to culminate in a lecture by an "expert" on beautification. Mei thought it would be fun for me to meet some of her colleagues—and she wanted to support her friend's salon—so she bought a bunch of tickets and invited us all to join her.

Almost as soon as I saw her, Mei saw me, waved enthusiastically in my direction, and headed down the staircase to greet me. She was with our friend Dandan and two colleagues whom I did not know (they were much less dressed up than Mei but definitely not as casual as I was, in what I can only call my "anthropologist" uniform). After brief introductions, and some friendly conversation, we headed up the staircase to the ballroom, where the event was to take place. The room had been elaborately decorated, with a stage at one end and ten to twelve large round tables, set for lunch, with name tags in front of the chairs, indicating our assigned seats. Mei had purchased enough tickets for an entire table, and we found our spots and settled in for the afternoon. There were plenty of new faces around the table, so we all introduced ourselves, and as we ate from the plentitude of dishes served, Mei facilitated a conversation about our interests, where we came from, and our typical beauty routines.

Most of the women at our table reported intensive skin-care regimens, and we talked at length about the importance of staying out of the sun and using soaps and lotions that contained safe kinds of whiteners. Some of the cheaper products, they warned each other, used dangerous ingredients that could actually do damage. It was better to spend a bit more and buy trusted brands. During the conversation, one of Mei's colleagues explained to me why she thought having white skin was so important: first, it has long been a beauty ideal in China, and, second, it represents class status. Those of lower economic status have to farm or work outside and therefore have darker skin. As the woman was talking, Mei, nodding fervent support, leaned over and put her arm next to mine: "My skin is lighter than yours! You see, the white skin we want is a trait of Asians. You white people have a different color. Also, you have so much hair on your arm!"

As lunch was winding down, Mei's friend and salon owner gave a speech thanking us for coming and then introduced the "expert" on beautification, who had published numerous articles on the subject in various popular magazines. He took the stage donning a white medical coat and, to much applause, thanked everyone for coming. As a show of respect, the room grew quiet; we were all attentive. He started with a brief discussion about the golden ratio and how it applied to the face: there should be symmetry, and the size and spacing of features should be governed by a constant ratio, 1:1.618 (known in mathematics as the golden ratio). This was not the first time I had heard about the importance of symmetry or the golden ratio for beauty. It seemed to be a common theme in fashion magazines in Shanghai and was a regular part of discussions about the aesthetics of the ideal face.[1]

As he was describing the way the ratio pertained to faces, he asked us to consult the handouts at our tables, which included an image of the "perfect" face. He explained that almost no one was born with a perfect face and that different races have different problems. Asian eyes tend to be too small, but, he said, some have beautifully large eyes too; black people can have large noses; white people have large mouths. The problems with asymmetries are different too. He assured us, though, "With technology and scientific advances we can use the laws of nature to improve on the bodies given to us by our parents." Finally, he explained that although the ratio of beauty is the same for everyone, each race has its own ideal version and each place has its own beauty preferences. The women at my table all nodded in unison. He then asked us to take a few minutes to use the handout to assess the faces at our tables: "What's out of ratio? What's too large or too small? Are there any asymmetries?"

Dutifully, we went around and described the imperfections we saw. Mei volunteered to go first, holding the image of the perfect face next to hers.

We noted that her eyes were too close together and her face was not symmetrical. She nodded and told us about the makeup tricks she used to make her eyes look further apart. The next woman had eyes that were too small and a chin that was too large. Someone noted that having eyes too small was the easiest problem for Asians to fix; it was just a simple double eyelid surgery, common in China. Speaking from experience, another chimed in: "A few snips and a couple days of puffy eyes and it's done!" The next woman had a nose that was too large; then another had a mouth that was too far below the nose. We made our way around the table—I was the last one to go. Although my face was pretty symmetrical, my ears were too low, my eyebrows were too thick and too long, and my mouth was too big.

Just as we were finishing up, the speaker called our attention back to the stage. He wanted to move on to the next phase of his talk, the importance of being beautiful. "For whom are you trying to be beautiful?" he asked. "Don't be shy—call out an answer!" Amid hushed giggles, women began yelling out responses: Our boyfriends! Our husbands! Our friends! Our parents! Our colleagues! Our bosses! With each answer, he shook his head and looked disappointed. Finally, one woman called out, in a voice filled with mockery, "Ourselves?" The room erupted in laughter. The speaker, somewhat taken aback, nodded in agreement: "Yes! It is for yourselves!" A collective groan went up from the women. Mei looked at me, shook her head, and, with a roll of her eyes, started talking with her colleagues about an issue they had encountered at work the previous week. Almost in unison, women at the other tables began talking to each other as well.[2]

It was clear he had lost the room. In fact, the chatter was so loud it was difficult to hear him anymore. And as much as he tried to engage the women—and admonished them for talking—he never regained their attention. However, when he finally ended his lecture (I am pretty sure he cut it short) there was great applause and lots of smiles, and someone went onstage to give him flowers of appreciation. Then the luncheon was declared over; on our way out, we were given goodie bags filled with face masks and samples of lotions and soaps.

After saying good-bye to friends and colleagues, Mei offered to give me a ride home so we could debrief about the outing. On the way to the car, I asked if she thought the speaker was upset that everyone stopped listening to him. "Oh, no, probably not," she said. "We gave him face at the end by clapping and giving him flowers, so it's all good. My friend will be happy with that. Anyway, we all know that being beautiful is for other people. It's meant to have an effect on others. I mean, sure, it boosts your confidence, but that just helps you influence others too." We hopped in her car and paid the garage attendant, and she continued: "The idea that beauty is for the self, well, that's just too Westernized. We Chinese people know that's not the case. We do it for others. He's clearly been influenced too much by the West, so we lost interest in what he was saying."

● The luncheon I attended that day was a special event, catered to a particular demographic of middle-class women who had the time, money, and desire to spend an afternoon talking about beauty. However, the commentary I heard at the event, especially with regard to big eyes and white skin, was repeated to me again and again throughout my time in Shanghai. In fact, the consistency with which I received the same answers and heard the same comments about these ideals was remarkable, particularly given that the topics are, for the most part, outside of state discourse. Thus although the women did not talk about these ideals nearly as much as they did about thinness and dieting, the content and consistency of their answers—contextualized within their broader conversations about the nature of China/West comparisons—merits consideration.

Two overlapping foci occupy the attention of scholars of race in China. The first is the extent to which there is a "racial" element to Chinese identity and to the ethnic categories (*minzu*) employed by the state within the nation. This literature is focused on the presumed nature of such categories (that is, if there is a "bodily" or "essentialist" element to them) and the feelings and experiences associated with national belonging (and, of course, the exclusions on which such belonging is founded). The second is the way that racial categories (*zhongzu*)—the ones that would be familiar to a Western audience, such as those based on "skin color" or other physical features—have become incorporated into Chinese forms of othering. Inquiries into racial categories tend to ask, in one form or another, the extent to which *historically* China had something conceptually akin to "race" prior to contact with the West and the ways in which *contemporarily* racism and racial hierarchies are operating at the levels of state discourse and in daily life. Connecting these two queries are debates about the appropriateness of "race" as an analytic for explicating social life in China (and the inequalities central to it) and the extent to which there are (or conceptually could be) local "Chinese" ways of understanding "racial" differences.

Inquiries into racial forms of othering in China typically begin in "traditional" times (221 BCE–1912 CE), when attitudes toward the "Other" were somewhat ambivalent. The intellectual foundation of Confucian scholars was based on the Five Classics (Book of Odes, Book of Documents, Book of Changes, Book of Rites, and the Spring and Autumn Annals), which posited that the world was one great community (*datong*) consisting of the culturally superior and civilized Chinese at the center and the "Others" at the periphery (Dikötter 1992, 2). On the one hand, although the distinction between civilized human (Chinese) and barbarian animal existed, identity was not considered static, and barbarians could become civilized (and, by extension, human) through acculturation. Many concepts, such as *laihua* (come and be transformed), *Hanhua* (transform into Chinese), and *jiaohua* (transformation through teaching), reflect the belief that barbarians could be transformed and culturally absorbed (Dikötter 1992, 2). The superiority of the Chinese was intertwined with their concept of virtue and their assumption that people are drawn to morality and strive to become virtuous. Since those outside of humanity were lacking virtue, the barbarians, it was assumed, would naturally be drawn to and submit to those with superior morals, that is, the Chinese. These ideas applied as well to positions of leadership; as long as it accepted and upheld Confucian political principles, even a foreign dynasty—such as the Qing—could occupy the symbolic center of Chinese society (Ebrey 1996, 20).

On the other hand, there were political theories that sought to harden the "natural" boundaries between Chinese and the "Other," maintaining that there *was* a fundamental difference between them. Because barbarians were not part of the civilized world, they were often seen as belonging with the animals. Indeed, most of the ideographs used to designate these people included an animal radical (Dikötter 1992, 4). These theories claimed that the Chinese and the barbarians belonged to different natural categories, which could not, and should not, intermingle (Dikötter 1992, 18–19). The historian Frank Dikötter argues that the Chinese appealed to these categorical differences for legitimacy when their sense of cultural superiority was threatened; thus these attitudes were heightened in times of conflict, rebellion, and invasion. Accordingly, physical characteristics—especially skin color—were symbolically incorporated into the concentric spatial hierarchy ordering the world, with "white" Chinese royalty at the center and "black" uncivilized laborers and barbarian others at the edges (Fennell 2013, 247). Consequently, scholars such as Dikötter contend that there was *racial* ordering in the Chinese "symbolic universe" from a very early time. For him, the fact that "attitudes about skin colour and physical characteristics are of great antiquity in China" demonstrates that "some form of racial categorisation, however unsystematic, existed well before the arrival of Europeans in the nineteenth century" (Dikötter 2015, 1–2). As such, he rejects the idea that "race" should be seen as a solely Western notion. In fact, he contends that the narrow sense of race as a Western phenomenon, in which white people oppress people of color, has distorted the comprehension of race problems in non-European societies.

However, even though skin color was an element of categorical divides, it did not have the essentialist connotation that it did in the West. Rather, as described by the political scientist Vera L. Fennell, "Ideas about skin color and the recognition of skin color differences were not absolute; attaining civilization defined skin color" (2013, 247). Much like the other characteristics of group differentiation in traditional Chinese hierarchies, then, physical traits were assumed to change as one became more "civilized." Thus for other scholars, Dikötter's contention that premodern China had "racial" forms of othering was an ethnocentric and problematic projection of a Western concept onto the Chinese context. Some call attention to the need to examine local categories on their own terms and to recognize the influence in recent centuries of racial orderings of the world disseminated by the West (Stafford 1993; Dirlik 1993; Lan 2016, 300). Moreover, the historian Patricia Ebrey's (1996) work on patrilineal surnames from the Tang (618–906) through the Yuan (1215–1368) periods demonstrates how Chinese notions of relatedness were starkly different from Western notions of biology and race. She argues that what made someone Chinese during those periods was twofold: acting Chinese and Chinese ancestry. Because lineal ancestors shared family names (but marriage partners did not), patrilineally transmitted surnames (in the written form) became a key to group membership, with certain names becoming a marker of "Han" (ethnic) identity. Importantly, Ebrey (1996) points out that this notion of ethnicity defined by patrilineal descent was quite different from the Western idea of "genetic inheritance"; in the Chinese case there could be little connection between physical traits and patrilineage membership, since such traits were "inherited from many forebears randomly" (including females and female-linked kin), while membership in a patriline came only from father-son links (32).[3] Thus, in an important contrast to Dikötter, Ebrey argues that, "kin-based metaphors of ethnic solidarity like China's do not lend themselves easily to racial categorizing" (32).[4]

Fundamental to these debates are (sometimes tacit) different working definitions of what race "is" and differing levels of confidence in the ability to divorce the term from its Western cultural baggage. For example, in the Western context, race-as-biology comprises dual characteristics: differentiation based on physical features and a notion of genetic inheritance that views those features as a static aspect of bodies/identity. Dikötter tried to pull the two elements apart to allow for "race" to be any categorization based on physical features, regardless of whether they could change or not. But he did not theorize why he chose that particular definition of race and what he sought to achieve by disentangling the essentialist nature of the concept central to its meaning in the Western context. He thus did not always successfully or consistently disentangle the two factors, appearance of physical traits and their transmutability across time. As he explains in the preface to his account, to make his argument that the Chinese had racialized group differences before interacting with the West he translated six different terms—zu (group), zhong (type, kind), zulei (kind, category), minzu (people), zhongzu (race, ethnic group), and renzhong (person type)—all into "race" based on how they "appear to stress the biological rather than the sociocultural aspects of different peoples" (Dikötter 1992, ix). At the same time, he suggests that "physical composition and cultural disposition were 'confused' in Chinese antiquity" (3), and the titles of his chapters, in the form of "Race as . . ." (for example, "Race as Culture," "Race as Lineage," and "Race as Nation"), indicate his comfortability employing "race" as a means of understanding a variety of *kinds* of differences. In short, it is unclear exactly what Dikötter means by "race." Given this lack of theoretical clarity, and the dual meanings associated with race in the Western context, it is not surprising that his critics typically highlight the fluid and relatively porous nature of categories as a way to argue against the notion that China had a "racial" ordering of the world before contact with the West (not to mention that having to translate six terms into "race" indicates that perhaps the Chinese had many ways of classifying people, not just racial versus cultural).

The question arises, then, is it possible to interrogate local meanings of "race" in China without smuggling in Western assumptions about the nature of biological difference?[5] If so, how does one maintain clarity about when race is being employed as an analytical tool (that is, when it relies on its Western meaning) and when it is being analyzed as a local concept? And, finally, what is at stake in the scholarly project of demonstrating cultural variability in the conception of "race"? Answering these questions in contemporary China (rather than historically) is in some ways simplified and in some ways complicated by the fact that racial categories—the ones based on the West's reified ideas about skin color—are now in circulation.[6] Ethnographically, then, it is possible to interrogate what such "racial" categories meant to contemporary women in Shanghai as they employed them in daily life. However, assuming that categories of skin color are indeed "racial"—and other body-based differences are not (or maybe are?)—seems to reproduce the same problematic assumptions about what race "is" that are inherent in Dikötter's work and that hinder the possibility of a full account of culturally variant understandings of the concept.

Once again, to solve these epistemological problems, "situated comparison" is useful as a critical methodology. A benefit of setting up this ethnographic comparison between the two groups of women in Shanghai is the ability to triangulate their ideas about body-based differences with academic theories of race, highlighting both the discrepancies and the overlaps in the conceptual frameworks at work in each. Moreover, and perhaps more importantly, rather than trying to decipher whether certain kinds of body-based distinctions are indeed "racialized" or not, I compare how different ways of understanding the *nature* of physical differences shaped how the women experienced identity and selfhood, and vice versa.

(ASIAN) BIG EYES AND WHITE SKIN

When discussing big eyes (*da yanjing*) and white skin (*bai pifu*), the Chinese women I knew in Shanghai inevitably invoked the category of "Asians" (Yazhouren) or, sometimes, "yellow people" (*huangren*). This was more often than not contrasted with "white people" (*bairen*), although some-times "Westerners" (Xifangren) would be used instead. For example, when remarking that someone had "small" eyes, they were typically referring to the "Asian" trait of having no fold in the upper eyelid, or having "single" eyelids (*dan yanpi*), rather than "double" eyelids (*shuang yanpi*). According to these women, single eyelids made eyes look small, droopy, and sleepy and just were not as aesthetically appealing as larger eyes. This sentiment was echoed throughout the city. It was common to see—on billboards and in most fashion magazines—advertisements and pictures showing the dramatic change possible by undergoing "double" eyelid surgery.

Having single eyelids was a flaw they understood as being particular to Asians, although not all Asians, which was an important caveat for them. In fact, they all described the pursuit of bigger eyes as wanting to be the most beautiful Asian they could (it was not just white people, they pointed out, who had double eyelids). Moreover, the kinds of surgeries available—creating a crease on the upper lid (Asian blepharoplasty), lowering the lower lid, lengthening the eye (medially and laterally), and creating a lower eyelid "love band"—were often described as "Asian" surgeries that sought to maintain traits particular to Asian eyes while also improving one's look.[7] Changing one's eyelids in these ways, then, in no way meant one was seeking to look anything other than "Asian." And, the women often commented, the reason there are such high numbers of cosmetic surgeries in Korea (a popular topic of discussion) is because of the fact that Korea has more Asians with single eyelids than China does. Reasons given for why big eyes were considered beautiful in China ranged from seeing them as a traditional standard of beauty to linking them to the aesthetic of women depicted in Japanese anime and thinking that not all Asians have big eyes and thus they have become a marker of distinction. These details were always contrasted to beauty standards and procedures in the West that were assumed to exist for historically and culturally different reasons.

In similar fashion, discussions about white skin typically included a comparison between "Asian" whiteness, which was desirable, and the hues of "Western" or "white people," which were considered (more often than not) less beautiful. For example, when highlighting the differences between Asian and white bodies, my Chinese friends would often comment about the "ash" or "deathly gray" hues of Western skin, which they found to be unhealthy looking. Moreover, the women I knew would frequently point out (very much in line with scholarly work on the topic; see, for example, Fennell 2013, 247) that having light skin was an important marker of beauty in China well before there was any significant contact with the West, as indicated in the ancient proverb *Yi bai zhe baichou* (White skin can hide a hundred flaws).[8] In addition, they always linked the historical significance of white skin in China to class status, rather than racial difference. As Mei's colleague described at the luncheon, because farmers and menial laborers worked outside, they typically had tanned or darker skin; the more elite were able to stay indoors and shelter their skin from the sun. This distinction continues today, a clear unabashed merging of class status with the beauty of white skin.

There were other physical traits the women associated with differences between ethno-racial categories, including some that they found to be aesthetically pleasing and others that they deemed unappealing. For example, "high" (prominent) noses (*gao bizi*) and body hair (*ti mao*) were both traits the women often pointed out on white people they saw in person or in advertisements, on TV, or in movies. While high noses were generally regarded as a positive feature of white faces, the abundance of hair on white bodies was typically scorned as an inferior trait. The women often highlighted it, just as Mei did at the luncheon, when discussing differences between Asian and white bodies. In fact, it was often one of the reasons cited in support of why Asians were more beautiful than Westerners. Interestingly, although dark skin was a trait the Chinese women avoided themselves, they often commented that black people tend to have smooth skin and less body hair than white people, traits that they found to be beautiful. However, because big noses and hairiness were not as important to beauty as big eyes and white skin, commentary about them was less frequent. Moreover, while there were procedures available, such as nose jobs for those seeking a "higher" nose and waxing for those seeking to rid themselves of body hair, they were not nearly as common or as important to the women I knew as double eyelid surgery and whitening products.

Although both big eyes and white skin were described by the women as being "Asian," they were modified in different ways. Pursuing bigger eyes was (typically) a onetime procedure (however, follow-up procedures were not uncommon) that was quick and relatively inexpensive and had an almost immediate impact on one's looks. For these reasons, according to the women I knew, it was popular among a wide demographic, including young and old, men and women.[9] It was even quite common to hear younger women discuss the procedure with their parents, often receiving advice about the benefits of undergoing the surgery. Skin color, however, was modified slowly, through time. It took a combined effort to avoid getting darker—by sheltering away from the sun (with parasols, broad brimmed hats, long sleeves)—and using products to enhance or boost whiteness. As a material entity, then, skin, like other bodily-selves (*tizhi*) was constantly being modified by one's environment, and it took continual effort to shape it into the best form. Additionally, not all "skin" was alike: the Chinese women frequently commented that they had to strenuously avoid the sun because their skin tanned more readily and got darker than white people's skin. Thus, although the ideals held differing levels of significance for class status, both were linked to "Asian" bodies. Moreover, for neither trait was there an "original" form or color to which they attached significance for selfhood or identity.

The way the women employed the concepts of "yellow," "white," and "black" suggests a conceptual linkage to racial categories that were imported from the West during the late nineteenth century. Most scholars, including both those claiming that Confucian values predisposed Chinese thinkers to perceive a racial order of the world (for example, Dikötter) and those claiming that Western racial theories contributed to a major departure in Chinese thinking about difference (for example, Ebrey), agree that the nationalist movements of the republican era (1912–49) proved a pivotal moment in the history of race in China. The encroachment of the Western imperial powers and the decline of the Qing dynasty destabilized the Confucian worldview of Chinese elites, who cast about for ways to understand China's new situation. Nationalist thinkers at the time, including Yan Fu and Liang Qichao, heavily influenced by their time abroad, began to categorize the world on the basis of racialized color groups (white, yellow, brown, and black and sometimes red). However, as the color schema entered Chinese discourse, and as Chinese elites grappled with China's place in the world, they mobilized these imported categories in new ways to craft a nationalist narrative of identity about the "yellow race."[10] Far from just reproducing Western racial orderings, which positioned white above everyone else, they saw white and yellow at the top of the racial order, locked in a battle for supremacy (see Dikötter 1992, 83–87). As the cultural anthropologist Shanshan Lan describes, "Although the idea of the yellow race was initiated from the West, the Chinese reformers had significantly transformed its meaning such that it became an ideological weapon with which to contest white domination" (2016, 303).

However, this hierarchy of racial ordering was short-lived. When the Chinese Communist Party (CCP) took power in 1949, the official discourse about race—like most things—changed dramatically. First, rather than assuming an affinity between whiteness and yellowness at the top, "Mao aggressively pursued an anti-imperialist and anti-racist political agenda by supporting African Americans' struggles for civil rights in the United States and by building coalitions with developing countries in Southeast Asia and Africa" (Lan 2016, 304). Indeed, part of the CCP's international political strategy of undermining imperialism included building solidarity between China's masses and black Africans and the black diaspora in the United States, most notably by linking racial discrimination to the colonialism of the white West (Fennell 2013, 257, 262; Lan 2016, 304). The subtext, then, was that "race" was a problem of the West that had been improperly incorporated in Chinese ideas about identity and the world order. Fast forwarding to today, although it is no longer couched in terms of class warfare, the CCP continues this vein of official discourse, especially with regard to building Sino-African cultural and economic "friendships" (see Fennell 2013; Lan 2016).

What all of this means for daily life in China today, and for differently positioned people within the contemporary Chinese nation-state, remains unclear. For example, despite state discourse uniting China and Africa and claims that race is a Western problem, there are numerous accounts (both scholarly and in popular media) of racial discrimination by Chinese against black immigrants, whether from Africa, the United States, or Europe (see, for example, Sautman 1994; Dikötter 1994; Cheng 2011; Lan 2016; Mathews, Lin, and Yang 2017). However, not all scholars agree that "race" is at the root of these problems. As Lan notes, "Others read it as symptomatic of broader issues such as nationalism, increasing social inequality, and [Chinese] students' quest for democracy" (2016, 304).[11] Scholars such as Lan (2016) and Gordon Mathews, Linessa Dan Lin, and Yang Yang (2017) have thus begun the important work of examining experiences of black immigrants in China as well as explicating popular perceptions of Africa and African immigrants and the various meanings attributed to blackness in contemporary China. However, there has been little work deciphering the meanings attributed to other color-based categories in the contemporary era, particularly in the efforts to understand how "race" is operating in conjunction with Chinese identity and nationalism. In fact, most scholarship in this vein takes for granted what race is.

For example, in one of the few accounts examining ideas about the body-based nature of differences between China and the West, the cultural anthropologist Louisa Schein (1994, 148) understood cosmetic surgery as a practice that enabled women to move beyond the impermeability of naturalized (that is, bodily) gender and racial categories (Mercer 1990; Balsamo

1992). She proposed that the popularity of cosmetic surgeries in which argu-ably "Western" bodily traits were pursued by Chinese women was producing "hybrid" bodies, evidence that the "racial" boundaries between China and the West were breaking down in contemporary Chinese cosmopolitanism. As she described, "For those with enough money, the Western look could be had in the most intimate way—not simply by dangling a beeper from one's belt or by donning fishnet stockings and spiked heels, but by cosmetic surgery, to amend the Asian body, deracializing it in some small measure to shorten the distance between 'us' and 'them'" (Schein 1994, 148).

Given the almost twenty-year gap and the quite far-reaching changes that have taken place in China between Schein's writing and my fieldwork, I can-not speak to the relevance of my arguments for her informants. However, clearly her assumptions about race and racial boundaries were not entirely applicable to the women I knew. Most obvious was the way Schein assumed that white skin and other traits pursued through cosmetic surgeries were "Western" in nature. My friends were quite clear that they wanted to look "Asian" and thought that certain traits of Asians were more beautiful than those of white people.

More important, however, was Schein's idea that modifying certain kinds of physical traits reduced the racial divide between Chinese and Western by "deracializing" bodies. Schein's dissatisfaction with the notion that her in-formants were merely reproducing or internalizing Western ideals matches that of my Chinese informants. However, for Schein, opting to pursue cer-tain so-called Western traits through cosmetic surgery was a means through which the women could disrupt "the East-West binarism through which so much of identity politics and critique have been negotiated" (1994, 149). Hybrid bodies, then, by unsettling the essentialist nature of racial difference, enabled what Schein called an "imagined cosmopolitanism," lessening the political significance attributed to differences between China and the West.

While sympathetic to Schein's arguments, I think the notion of "deracial-izing" bodies is an importation of the dual Western meanings about race that include both physical characteristics and a particular way of defining the nature of racial categories (such that creating "hybrids" would challenge categorical divides). In certain ways, the Chinese women I knew invoked the categories of Asian/yellow and white/Western suggesting a familiar rendering of "racial" difference that aligns with the race-as-phenotype that Schein was describing. They clearly linked certain color-coded categories with geographical location, as indicated by the frequency with which they substituted "Asian" with "yellow" and "white" with "Western."[12] Moreover, they associated certain physical traits (such as hairiness, big mouths, high noses, African black skin) with racial categories, and in their pursuit of big eyes and white skin (desirable traits potentially associated with Western bodies), they were adamant that they wanted to have the "Asian" version of those traits.

However, this did not mean that "race" was associated with the unchangeable features of the body. In fact, the women I knew thought that "race" could change. During my time in Shanghai, for example, there were various reports of people in China getting facial reconstruction surgeries to look like particular people, sometimes famous figures from the West. In one such case, as documented in 2011, the author Zhang Yiyi was reportedly planning to spend upwards of $200,000 to undergo surgeries that would make him look like William Shakespeare (see, for example, McCrum 2015). For the most part, the women I knew thought it was a rather silly and over-the-top idea. However, when we were discussing his plans, the women often indicated that they thought it was possible—through such cosmetic surgeries—for Zhang to "change his race" and become "white." Thus, even though they denied that the kinds of traits they sought were "Western" or "white" in nature, they were open to the idea of people being able to change their race through (albeit quite drastic) cosmetic surgery.

Finally, although the women discussed big eyes and white skin in terms of Asian/yellow and white/Western bodies, they did not hierarchically order the world according to those categories. There were certainly physical traits they deemed superior to others (Asian whiteness was much preferred over Western whiteness and the hair on white bodies was a less-than-desirable feature), and they were annoyed that people in the West would assume that they wanted to be like them. However, they never invoked any *color-coded* hierarchy of ability or "modernity" to go along with those traits. In fact, aligning with state discourse, they typically referred to racial discrimination as a problem confined to the United States and not something found in China. However, this did not mean that they thought race "didn't exist" or that they pursued a "color-blind" stance. Quite the opposite. Race for them—at least in how they discussed Asian/yellow and white/Western—was a concept that referred to appearance *only*. And, like most physical traits, it was assumed to be modifiable. In this way, altering one's body through procedures like cosmetic surgery or using whitening products was not significantly different (or more problematic) from the bodily changes that came from eating and other mundane activities. For the women, their bodily-selves were by nature subject to constant change and body modification practices did not threaten an idealized or essentialized version of self, body, or identity. But there was no sense that a person could be "without race," and even though changing race was considered to be theoretically possible, there was no reason to think that the most common cosmetic surgeries would lead to a "deracializing" of the body.[13]

In some ways these ideas aligned with how the Western women I knew understood race, especially in regard to rejecting a color-based hierarchy of the world. However, as I show in the following chapter, the Western women I knew had starkly different ideas about the nature of "racial" features of bodies and what modifying them indicated about a person/self.

"RACIALIZED" NATIONALISM (OR "BEING CHINESE")

Conversations about big eyes and white skin almost always included comparisons between China and the West. Indeed, the nationalist subtext to the way the women situated the pursuit of beauty was perhaps most explicit in their arguments that they did not want to look Western and that the ideals represented "Chinese" preferences. Moreover, although they invoked the category of "Asian" in their discussions of big eyes and white skin, in their daily lives they did not attach much significance to it as a part of their identity, especially in comparison to the substantial element of "being Chinese." The way the Chinese women I knew framed differences between China and the West suggests interesting discrepancies between how they understood their identity as "Chinese" and the highly political official discourse about

China as a nation that is concerned with geopolitics, separatism, and creating a sense of shared national belonging. Most significant was the way they attributed fundamental and bodily differences between Chinese and Westerners as coming from food and eating, including differences in health (and what bodies can handle), differences in capabilities (being strong or flexible), and differences of what might be called cultural personalities (being aggressive or passive).

Part of the scholarly interest concerning race in China includes an examination of the nature of "Chineseness" in the contemporary nation-state. Is how people understand themselves as Chinese based primarily on "bodily" experience or a "genetic" inheritance? How "racialized" is the concept of *minzu*, a term used to categorize the "ethnic" groups within China, but also employed as a moniker for all those of Chinese "descent" (*Zhonghua minzu*)? What makes these questions particularly compelling is that while the CCP has deemed "race" a Western problem and racial discrimination a product of Western colonialism, it has also pushed "since the 1980s [a discourse] that epitomizes 'Chineseness' with explicit racial taxonomies in a mystified association with the Chinese land" (Cheng 2017, 577–78). Most of this discourse is centered around identifying common ancestors from long ago, such as Peking Man, as a means to link together all "Chinese" *minzu* within the contemporary nation-state.

The overt efforts of the CCP to create a shared lineage stem from the (quite common) tension inherent to modern nation-states seeking to unite "diverse" peoples within their borders. The concept of *minzu* has been central to this tension in China since 1949 and the founding of the People's Republic of China (PRC). The newly established nation was to be a "fraternal cooperative family" of *minzu*, typically translated as "cultural-ethnic groups," each with official representation in the government (Fei [1947] 1992). To deal with the problem of incorporating ethnic diversity within an ideal unity, China adopted a Soviet model of multinational state building (Dreyer 1976, 2006; M. Zhou 2008) and embarked on the task of identifying all of China's minority nationalities (*minzu shibie*). Thus, Chinese ethnographers were sent out to survey the population and categorize its constituent groups according to Soviet leader Joseph Stalin's four criteria for a nation: common language, common territory, common economic life, and a common psychological makeup (McKhann 1995, 47). As part of this project, the "Han" were to be understood officially as just one of the fifty-six *minzu*, which was a significant departure from their pre-PRC status as "Chinese," a "residual category, comprised of all those who were not barbarians" (Ebrey 1996, 26). While hundreds of groups applied for nationality status, only fifty-six were officially recognized by the state (leaving many smaller groups aggregated into units they considered not their own), with the Han constituting a large majority, about 92 percent of the population. Politically, the problem of incorporating diversity was solved by "positing ethnic minorities alongside a majority and giving everyone a *minzu* . . . [making] this aspect of identity equally shared" (Blum 2001, 59).

However, the pretense of unification based on an equality among ethnic groups was contradicted by state policies toward minority groups that fluctuated between tolerating ethnic distinctiveness and assigning the groups to a place in a social evolutionary hierarchy. Thus at the same time that the PRC, in an effort to protect the minorities' ability to maintain their own way of life, established autonomous regions and counties for the minority groups (Rossabi 2004, 7), Chinese ethnologists used a Marxist version of the nineteenth-century American anthropologist Lewis Henry Morgan's theory of social evolution to label minority groups backward and primitive and place them on the lower rungs of a hierarchy headed by the more modern and civilized Han (McKhann 1995, 41–42). From the initial creation of *minzu*, there was thus a tension between viewing the minorities as an integral and unproblematic aspect of the nation and viewing them as less modern than the Han.

Everyone having a *minzu*, then, was not quite the same as creating a shared sense of Chinese national belonging, especially for groups who sought independence.[14] Thus an important addendum to creating an image of "colorful" minorities happy to be part of the nation (see, for example, Gladney 1994, 95) has been the CCP's efforts to use archaeological evidence in support of a shared line of descent for all citizens of the PRC, what it calls Chinese ethnicity, or *Zhonghua minzu*. In some sense, this idea echoes the racialization of Chinese identity in the nationalist movements of the early twentieth century that asserted that all the peoples within Chinese borders were descendants of the (mythic) Yellow Emperor (a similar racialization of national identity was occurring in much of the Western world around the same time) (see Dikötter 1992, 2015; Sautman 1994; Cheng 2017).[15] However, the CCP is currently mobilizing science-based ideas about biological genetic inheritance that are typically linked to "race" in the West, which is why scholars are concerned with a racialization of Chinese identity.[16] Moreover, in addition to its politically motivated uses, the discourse about "racial nationalism . . . has become more accessible in society and therefore more popular owing to the invention of new rhetoric and dissemination devices" (Cheng 2017, 596). This popularization, according to the historian Yinghong Cheng (2017, 596), includes linking, in "patriotic songs," a common line of "Chinese" ancestry to certain physical traits, such as black eyes, black hair, yellow skin, and blood. In short, "cultural continuity has been transformed into racial genealogy" (596).

Interestingly, although there is clearly official and popular discourse circulating about the biological/genetic nature of Chinese identity, the women I knew never invoked such ideas as part of their nationalistic discourse about beauty, big eyes, or white skin. This is not to say that they were not interested or invested in theories about differences between China and the West. It was a common topic of discussion and, more often than not, included a bodily element, especially when they wanted to emphasize dissimilarity. However, rather than "genetic" differences, the body-based differences that were most important to them were those that arose from food and eating. For example, a commonly stated difference between Chinese and Westerners was the ability of Westerners to eat or drink "cold" foods without any repercussions for their health. This was particularly the case with eating watermelon in the summer and drinking ice water with meals. Oftentimes, in moments when they were describing *just how different* being Chinese was from being Western, my closest friends would tell me about the "crazy" ability of Western women to drink cold water immediately after giving birth and find it refreshing. As Mei put it, "Honestly, I would die if I did that. Just die." Our friends all agreed that it was a particularity of Westerners to be able to handle such a cooling effect when *qi* was already depleted.[17] On a return visit to Shanghai in 2016, five years after conducting my initial fieldwork, I brought with me my two-year-old daughter, Ellie. As Mei showered her with attention and affection, she asked, "So, did you drink cold water after you had her?" I acknowledged that I was pretty sure I had (although I was so exhausted after labor, I could not quite remember). She gave me a knowing look and said, "See, Chinese and Westerners really *are* that different. No way could I survive doing that."

Another close friend, Xueping, narrated a related difference to me one day after I attended her yoga class. Xueping taught yoga at a community center three times a week for housewives who wanted "to get out of the house and lose some weight," and she invited me to join the classes. After a day of strenuous stretching, we were walking out of class and she said, "Today must have been really hard for you." I nodded (my struggles were obvious given my performance in the class). She continued: "Today's class demonstrated one of the main differences between being Chinese and being Western. All the women in the class are new to yoga, but the Chinese women were able to do today's class much better than you did. That's because Chinese are flexible and Westerners are strong. Remember last week when you performed better than the others? That's because it was a strength-based class." I asked her why she thought that was the case. "It's because of what we eat. Rice and noodles make us flexible. Meat makes you strong and hard. The biggest difference between Chinese and Westerners is that our stomachs are different [Women zui da de qubie shi women de wei butong]."

Since the publication in 1978 of Edward Said's *Orientalism*, scholars have shown how ways of "othering" often say more about "us" than "them." More recently, they have begun to apply this reasoning outside the West by looking at the processes of "othering" by non-Western groups (see, for example, Stasch 2009; Bashkow 2006). Scholars of China have focused on how both Western foreigners and Chinese minorities are important Others for the modernizing Han majority (see, for example, Harrell 1995a; Schein 2000). For instance, sexual images of Western and minority female bodies provide Chinese with symbols of the modern and the exotic (Chow 1991; Farquhar 2002; Gladney 1994, 1996; Johansson 1998; Schein 1994, 2000). Typically, in these accounts, the West represents a modern Other that China seeks either to emulate or to dominate.

What does it say about the nature of "Chineseness" for these women that differences between Chinese and Westerners were rooted in bodily dispositions attributed to food choice? First, it connects "selfhood" with "Chineseness" in ways that are radically different from how the Western women I knew were thinking about self and identity. Indeed, selfhood for the Chinese women was intimately tied to *tizhi*, bodily disposition, which was constantly being modified by the foods one ate, in addition to other daily practices. Chinese identity, then, in a similar vein, was understood to be produced through particular eating habits over an extended period of time. Thus the nature of Chinese identity for the women I knew developed alongside and through means similar to those that produced selfhood.

The Chinese women I knew in Shanghai were quite open to various ways of modifying their bodies in the pursuit of beauty. There was, however, one procedure that most of them were opposed to: stapling the stomach in order to lose weight. Almost unanimously, they considered this procedure as "going too far." The Western women, interestingly, were the least troubled by this procedure and often discussed it in terms of "taking control" of one's life. This difference, I contend, has to do with the fact that both individual and group identity for the Chinese women was created through the stomach. Nationalism, then, was in line with, rather than opposed to, the emergence of a culturally situated form of individualism in China. And this was strikingly different from the way the Western women rejected both race and nationalism as aspects of their identity that held any significance for—and sometimes hindered—their ability to "be themselves."

Second, rather than seeking to emulate or dominate the West, or ordering the world based on a linear progression of modernity with the West "ahead" of China, these women were invested in describing differences that had the dual ability (1) to make sense of why the world was ordered as it was (while acknowledging China's rapid twentieth-century rise and catching up) and (2) to argue that there should be space for more than one way of being in the world. Thus, for example, many of the women I knew attributed the expansionist nature of the West to a history of extensive (red) meat eating, which they thought created aggressive behavior. Meat, in addition to making bodies strong and hard (as Xueping noted), also produced aggression and a desire to use that strength for dominance. That is why, the women argued, the West sought out other lands and colonized other peoples. However, they did not invoke this difference to suggest that Chinese people should start to eat more meat in order to be more powerful. In fact, they typically followed it up by bragging about everything China had achieved in its long history without relying on meat or aggression, and sometimes they would attribute aggressive behavior by men in China to the recent influx of red meat in the Chinese diet.[18]

As the women theorized the way that Chinese/Western attributes were produced through time and daily practices, they were also invested in creating, producing, and determining "Chinese" versions of things in the contemporary moment. Indeed, the emphasis they placed on the ideals of big eyes and white skin being "Chinese" was in no way an isolated example. In fact, from art and movies to academic theories and political systems, the women actively discussed—and disagreed about—what the "Chinese" contributions to such fields should be. In sharp contrast to the Western women, they did not think that Chinese people could just "be themselves" and call what they produced "Chinese." For them, in their quest to not "be" like the West, then, they had to produce difference in a thoughtful way. Thus, at the same time that they understood differences between China and the West as bodily in nature, they rejected, for both selfhood and nationality, a notion of identity that just "is." Running counter to the CCP's discourse about genetic unity, then, being Chinese for these women was less about a timeless essence and more about historical processes that were produced through the social world. However, this did not mean that such differences were necessarily "easy" to change. In fact, in contrast to the way the women thought it possible to change one's "race" through cosmetic procedures, they did not discuss the possibility of changing one's identity as Chinese.

Finally, rather than viewing "China" as a unified whole of various *minzu*, it was very clear, at least in the context of beauty and China/West comparisons, that these women equated being "Chinese" with being "Han." Although their identity as "Han" was almost never discussed, the kinds of eating practices they associated with "being Chinese" were very much those typically associated with the Han. In this way, then, in the context of beauty, Han-ness had the same unmarked nature that whiteness has in the United States (see Blum 2001). However, as the following chapter demonstrates, in great contrast to the Chinese women who were actively cultivating their Chinese identity through Han practices, the Western women rejected whiteness as a part of their identity, leaving them at quite a loss for dealing with the overt privileges they garnered by being white in Shanghai.

SIX

"RACIALIZED" IDEALS

The Western women I knew in Shanghai were consistent in their comments about big eyes and white skin: they saw Chinese women's desire for such features as a clear indication of their wanting to look "Western," and they understood such desires as a rejection by the Chinese women of "who they were." When discussing the popularity in China of double eyelid surgery, for example, the Western women frequently commented: "It is so sad that they go to such lengths to look Western. I think Asian eyes are beautiful. Why can't they just be happy with who they are?" Moreover, that Western companies were advertising and selling many of the whitening products available in China was proof to the Western women that the Chinese women were being influenced by a globalized and consumerist-driven power structure that shaped their desires to look Western. Indeed, the conspicuous presence around town of foreign companies' advertising of whitening products, often by including the word WHITE in English, seemed to make such a message clear to both English- and Chinese-speaking audiences.

The Western women I knew, then, were deeply troubled by the ideals of big eyes and white skin, for two reasons. The first, running very much parallel to their understandings of selfhood-as-cravings, was their association of certain physical traits—skin color, shape of eyes, and face structure, for example—with *individual* identity/selfhood. They conceptualized these traits as having an "original" and "unmodified" form that made selves "unique." Like cravings, the traits they most associated with selfhood were the ones they thought were most permanent and most difficult to change. As such, in their critiques of the beauty ideals in Shanghai, they often discussed what "could" and "could not" change about bodies. For Emily, one's "natural" skin color was what one had when one "did nothing" to it. Doing "nothing," for her, meant not using any *whitening* products and "not caring" about how tan one got. She was adamant that using certain whitening products and tanning might alter one's color temporarily, but when one stopped those practices, one's "natural" or "default" color would return. This is why, she argued, one cannot "really" change the color of one's skin. Again, much like cravings in chapter 3, "unmodifiable" bodily traits were, for Emily as well as the other Western women I knew, fundamental to authentic selfhood. Not surprisingly, then, they saw wanting to change those traits as a denial of one's "natural" self, a morally troubling bowing to social pressures.[1]

In great contrast to how these women conceptualized skin color was the way they discussed and actively sought to negotiate wrinkles, aging, and skin "care." For example, most of the Western women I knew moisturized their skin on a daily basis, using products such as face lotions and creams, to keep their skin "healthy" and to delay the effects of aging (hence Emily's desire to find a face moisturizer in Shanghai sans a whitening agent). They understood these products to be "enhancing" or "protecting" their own skin, which they saw as fundamentally different from "changing" its color. When asked about the difference between moisturizing and whitening, the Western women I knew almost uniformly gave some version of this response: "Moisturizing and taking care of what I have isn't changing anything about myself." There was a sense, then, that aging, as a historical process, undermined one's "original" skin (although they did not really discuss it in those terms), and hence, in important ways, slowing the effects of aging was a way to *preserve* selfhood.[2]

The second reason the women were especially troubled by the ideals of big eyes and white skin was that they thought these traits represented a preference for a "Caucasian" body type, indicating a racialized partiality inappropriate for the context of China. Aligning quite closely with academic critiques of racialized beauty ideals, the Western women typically assumed a version of false-consciousness that made Chinese women think that their "Asian" bodies were not as beautiful as "Caucasian" bodies. Thus, not only were the Chinese women rejecting "themselves," but by pursuing these ideals they were also inadvertently supporting/reproducing a highly problematic racialized hierarchy that was a product of Western cultural imperialism. Even more troubling, by desiring big eyes and white skin the Chinese women were buying into the idea that "race mattered," something the Western women vehemently opposed.

Examination of the Western women's ideas about beauty, bodies, and selfhood alongside their commentary and experiences regarding race and gender reveals that they, in great contrast to the Chinese women, were extremely opposed to and uncomfortable with any association between bodies and *group* identities, which they saw as the foundation for categorical oppression and inequality. They were highly critical of not just the beauty ideals they encountered in the city but also the way that race and gender held undue significance in their lives. All the ways that race and gender seemed to matter in Shanghai provided a powerful backdrop to the Western women's overtly critical attitudes toward Chinese women pursuing seemingly white traits—to them it was further evidence of the inappropriate gendered and racialized hierarchy between Asian bodies and Western bodies to which they were subject and in which they were forced to play a part.

Contrasting the Western women's ideas about race with how the Chinese women viewed body-based differences and identities enables an intervention into the critical studies of both whiteness and Han-ness. The assumed unmodifiable materiality of bodies/selves informed how the white women experienced and sought to undermine "race" as a social category, an approach drastically different from how the Han Chinese women experienced and pursued a national identity. This illuminates the extent to which the white women rejected whiteness as a central aspect of their identity, while the Chinese women were actively (and thoughtfully) trying to "be Chinese." Moreover, these women's ideas about bodies, selves, and race/nation highlight culturally particular kinds of individualisms that enable further reflection about the relevance of (neo)liberalism as a framework for understanding post-reform-era China.

What is the relationship between the Western women's clear liberal tendencies (such as their desire for individuals to interact as "individuals"), their ideas about bodily-selves, and how they conceptualized race? More pointedly, how and why did they view categories "based on the body" as the source of the most nefarious forms of social inequality?

BIG EYES, WHITE SKIN, AND RACIAL DIFFERENCE

When the Western women discussed the traits of big eyes and white skin, they, too, invoked "racial" categories, although they were slightly different from those used by the Chinese women. In particular, they typically used "Asian" (never "yellow") when discussing the eye shape of Chinese people, which they compared to either "Western" or "Caucasian" eyes. When discussing white skin, they would sometimes invoke the categories "white" or "black," but again always in contrast to "Asians"; to them, *yellow*, given its racist roots in the United States, was an inappropriate term to use in discussions about physical appearance (on rare occasions when someone would use *yellow* as a descriptor, they were quickly rebuked: "Uh, I don't think we should be using that term"). Although *white* and *Western* were used, the women clearly favored the term *Caucasian* in these discussions because, according to them, (1) it did not conflate geography with race ("There are plenty of non-white people in the West") and (2) it seemed to incorporate more diverse body types (and a range of skin colors) than was implied by the category "white."[3]

In addition to using somewhat different terms, the two groups of women had dissimilar ideas about what "race" was in relation to physical traits and its significance for identity. For the Chinese women, race (*zhongzu*) was typically attributed to some of the "surface"-level, appearance-based differences that could change given the right kinds of (perhaps drastic) procedures. Whether seeking the "Asian" version of big eyes and white skin, or modifying one's "race" by pursuing the white versions of them, the Chinese women were not especially troubled about such changes. To them, modifying what some considered "racial" features through products and cosmetic surgery was not categorically more problematic than the kinds of body-based changes that came from daily life. However, they did view such features as *easier* to change than the historically produced body-based differences that came from eating particular kinds of foods, to which they attributed a fundamental aspect of selfhood and being Chinese (and which they often contrasted with the bodies of Westerners).

The Western women, however, at least in their discussions about big eyes and white skin, conceptualized "race" and "racial" features in quite different ways. First, although they employed large categorical terms such as *Asian* and *Caucasian*, they adamantly rejected "race" as a viable or legitimate social category. In great contrast to the Chinese women's notions of the bodily nature of their identities, the Western women were steadfast that "their bodies" should not inform any aspect of their social life. This was especially the case regarding race (and gender), which, as they described, was a problematic extension of Western colonialism and imperialism that sought to *naturalize* differences as a way of establishing (and justifying) a body-based hierarchy.

Second, the Western women typically presumed that the significance of racial features was limited to individual identity and selfhood. They thought facial features and skin color, much like individual tastes and wants, were to be recognized as a part of selfhood and celebrated as what made each person unique. According to them, one's "racial" makeup was a "natural" part of "who one was" that was linked to enduring physical traits. In fact, for the Western women, race was something that fundamentally *could not change*; regardless of how many or what kinds of cosmetic procedures one underwent, the Western women were certain that one's race remained the same. They thus opposed the idea that people in China were changing their race by undergoing (even drastic) kinds of cosmetic surgery. The same was true for the performer Michael Jackson, they argued: no matter how much he altered his "look," he was still black. In this way, then, "race" for them went "deeper" than just external, physical appearance; it was a natural part of selfhood that endured regardless of surface-level changes one made to the body.

The Western women, then, understood racial differences as being significant only for individual identity insofar as they created unique selves; the same categories they employed to describe such individual traits became deeply problematic when imputed to group difference that went beyond such physical descriptors. Thus, although they were highly invested in deciphering the physical attributes of selfhood (such as cravings), to them what "kind" of body one had should not, in any way, define one's identity outside of unique selfhood. Unfortunately for them, however, there were aspects of living in Shanghai that forced them to continually confront the fact that they were indeed racialized and gendered subjects.

(GENDERED) WHITENESS IN SHANGHAI

Much like the frequent comments the Western women heard about body size and being overweight that made them self-conscious about their appearance, two overt and defining aspects of their day-to-day lives reminded them that they could not escape their race and gender: explicit (or "felt") white privilege and limited (gendered) opportunities for romance. Together, these social pressures elicited much critical commentary from the women, who, as very much in line with their discussions about beauty, were adamant that bodies "shouldn't matter," a fundamental premise of their identity ideology.

In expat communities across China, stories abound about the privileges that whiteness affords. As in most parts of the contemporary world, in China there are plenty of benefits to being white that white people do not necessarily experience as such. For example, most white foreigners in a study conducted in Guangzhou reported that an important part of their experiences abroad was to "find themselves," oftentimes by developing their careers through a variety of (fairly easy) opportunities based on their English-language skills and, more often than not, their whiteness. In contrast, many of the immigrants from African countries were in China to escape extreme poverty and "get a financial foothold in life" (Mathews, Lin, and Yang 2017, 31). Unlike the white foreigners who moved in and out of their expat communities with relative ease, black foreigners in Guangzhou were in constant danger of police raids; they were the subject of much state suspicion and struggled to retain legal visas as they sought out business deals and economic opportunities. In the worst-case scenarios, they were deported without any financial success to show for their time abroad. Like the Guangzhou expats, the Western women I knew in Shanghai all narrated their time in Shanghai as one of personal discovery, which sometimes (but not always) included career development. They were not stressed about their visas (the slight exception might be an "annoying" but necessary trip to Hong Kong for a renewal). They felt safe and secure as they moved throughout the city, sometimes even safer than they felt back home.

While these implicit white privileges were clearly a defining feature of these women's lives in Shanghai, and should not be overlooked, of concern here are the conversations the women had as they dealt with the *explicit* ways that race seemed to matter in Shanghai. Indeed, in addition to many of the implicit and unfelt benefits of being white Westerners, for these women there was an overt and problematic way their whiteness informed what they could and could not do in the city. On the one hand, being a white Westerner in Shanghai seemed to bring undue privilege. As Kate put it, "Having white skin means you can do just about anything you want." In certain moments (which I, too, experienced), it felt as if there were "no rules" that applied to those who were white. Getting past security to wander into a residential lane, for example, was as easy as "looking the other way and ignoring the gatekeeper as he tried to shoo you away," Sophie explained to me on an evening walk. Or walking down the street between bars with an open container was "fine, no one will bother you," she said on another occasion. White foreigners were also afforded privileges and showered with benefits as people vied for their attention and patronage. Stories abound about white foreigners being able to bypass long lines at clubs, forgo entrance fees, and get served free beverages all night long just because the bars wanted them to stay. It was not unusual to be quickly seated at a "full" restaurant when others had to wait hours for a table. Many dinners at nice restaurants began with free drinks and appetizers as a gesture to their "foreign friends." Visiting a touristy part of the city typically meant at least a couple of requests by strangers to be in photographs.

Although seemingly small, these activities, day in and day out, had a clear impact on white foreigners in Shanghai and elicited a variety of reactions. For some (most notoriously young white men), the privileges were often assumed to be a recognition of well-deserved individual achievement and translated into an unbearable arrogance. For others, like the women

I knew who were dedicated to an anti-racist ideology common among white liberals, the (explicit) white privilege they experienced made them highly uncomfortable, as it indicated to them a clear mapping of the global hierarchy of Western hegemony onto local hierarchies of privilege. They were frustrated by the extent to which race mattered, even as they moved back and forth between taking advantage of their privilege and working to critique and undermine it.

In addition, there were more problematic aspects of having white skin in Shanghai that also informed aspects of daily life and the conversations the women had about race and racism. Perhaps the most explicit example was the growing industry of "renting" white people. In 2011, when I was conducting research for this book, one of the newly emerging "markets" for white foreigners in Shanghai (as well as in other parts of China) was being hired by a Chinese company that was looking to boost its image. For the most part, these companies sought white men who were willing to wear suits and white women who would act either as important business leaders or as the wives or girlfriends of top executives of the Chinese company; typically, a basic requirement was the ability to speak English, or at least not Chinese (they did not want them speaking with the other employees). Gigs for those who were hired included attending banquets, traveling with the company on business trips, and sometimes giving speeches or toasts in English. For some, it was a quite lucrative career.

Not surprisingly, interpretations of these practices varied, from seeing them as an innocuous and "interesting" aspect of "Chinese culture" to viewing them as "racist" and dishonest. Those who saw the practice as indicating something unique about "Chinese" culture were typically the ones participating in the industry; they were often aspiring actors and actresses who used the opportunities to hone their acting skills. They enjoyed the opportunities to work and were, for the most part, comfortable with their roles. On the other side, as among most of the women I knew, there were those who saw renting white people as a highly problematic enterprise that was insincere, essentializing, and a reproduction (again) of globalized racial hierarchies. They contended that it was not *actually* acting (where the audience is in on the fiction) but fraud; it was real life, and the companies were using white people to further their corporate interests and connec-tions. Moreover, the fact that white people were there only to be seen—and not actually work—was just blatant racism. The differing interpretations of these practices, it should be noted, demonstrate once again that there is not a unified "Western" approach to these topics; indeed, "situating" the Western women I knew in Shanghai and their style of feminism must take into account how their critiques differed from how other Westerners (in this case) thought about race and racism.

At the same time, as white heterosexual *women*, they encountered diffi-culties that their white male counterparts did not. Indeed, their experiences as white women were starkly different from the experiences of white men in China, particularly when it came to opportunities for dating or finding romantic partners in the city. Many of the Western women complained—or at least noticed—that they were not especially desired by either Western or Chinese "local" men. In fact, many of the women spent their time in Shanghai single or with long-distance boyfriends back home. Very few had partners in Shanghai (Emily and Rob were the only couple, besides me and Adam, that stayed together during their time in Shanghai), and almost no woman I knew started dating anyone while there (though not for a lack of trying). As Sophie bemoaned, "No one even looks at me on the streets." White women abandoned by their boyfriends or husbands for Chinese women was such a common phenomenon that support groups sprang up around the city to provide emotional help and encouragement to the women who experienced it. There were plenty of stories circulating about white women being much more demanding, and power hungry, than Chinese women. Thus, while Shanghai provided ample opportunities for the women to "find themselves" and advance their careers, time in the city typically put a "pause" on their love lives. This added to the women's frus-tration with having to contend with beauty ideals in the city and provided fodder for their criticisms of the (global) male-dominated power structure.

Taken together, these two aspects of life in Shanghai—white privilege coupled with romantic frustration—compelled the women to talk at length about race, gender, and the problems of organizing society on the basis of bodily differences, talk that provides insight into their culturally particular ideas about the relationship between the materiality of bodies and social inequality. As they insisted again and again, they did not want their race or gender to inform how they were treated or the kinds of opportunities open to them; for them, the ideal world was when selves could "just be"—just be themselves, just be equal, just be treated the same.

Ideas about race, gender, and bodies were epitomized in a dinner conversation one evening at the house of Marie, a relatively new friend in town who also knew Emily. Over a home-cooked meal of multiple courses, Emily told us about her yoga class that afternoon, which had a male teacher and both male and female students. During one of the poses, the instructor told the class that women who were on their periods should abstain from doing the pose and instead stay in the previous position longer. Frustrated by this attitude, Emily, who had indeed been on her period, said, "I wasn't going to let my body get in the way of my ability to do yoga. I figured, if men can do it, I can do it too."

Marie, fully in support of Emily's frustration, bemoaned her experience that morning when she took a cab with a white male colleague to a business meeting at a nearby hotel. Her colleague made the cab driver enter a pedestrian area clearly marked "no cars." When she explained they could not go that way, her colleague condescendingly told her: "It's fine. We're white. No one will care." She went on to describe how a security guard approached the cab angrily but, on seeing the two of them in the back, sighed and let them through. Both women were furious at the colleague's unapologetic attitude and at the security guard for letting them in. They agreed that the extent to which bodies mattered in Shanghai was an indication that China, just like the West, was a racist and sexist place.

They spent the rest of dinner co-producing a vision of what an ideal world would look like: they described a future that was almost all virtual, where there were "no bodies" and everyone, through their virtual frames, could just "be themselves." Or, if people wanted to live embodied lives, they had to experience life as a multitude of kinds of bodies before they could join society. "Yeah, in order to be considered a full citizen you would have to pass certain trainings, without which you couldn't interact with others," Marie suggested. Emily picked up the theme: "Exactly. And the trainings would consist of living life as a woman if you're a man, and as a variety of races, so that everyone could experience all kinds of bodies." This was the only way for equality to happen, they argued. A space needed to be created where either there were no bodies, so that everyone could live without the judgment or gaze of others, or, to eliminate bias, one had to occupy a variety of bodies to experience racial and gender difference before reverting to one's original (and unmodified) body.

BEAUTY, RACE, AND NATURE

The black sociologist Tressie McMillan Cottom (2013) wrote a piece for *Slate* about Miley Cyrus's performance at the 2013 MTV Music Awards show, in which she argued that the way Cyrus incorporated black women dancers into her performance enabled Cyrus to present herself as a "sexually free" woman while "maintaining a hierarchy of female bodies from which white women benefit materially." While her analysis received much praise, Cottom heard overwhelmingly negative responses to an offhand comment she made about herself in the piece—that she was "unattractive" and therefore had a particular experience with racism and the white gaze. In a more fully developed essay, Cottom (2019) reflected on those responses to demonstrate the way that beauty standards are as much about race as they are about gender. For many of the black women who wrote to her, Cottom's comment indicated an internalization of a white notion of what was beautiful (and what was not). For the white women who responded, her claim just could not be true: they passionately argued that she was indeed beautiful (many of whom had never seen her). According to Cottom, the white women "need me to believe beauty is both achievable and individual, because the alternative makes them vulnerable" (2019, 60). Cottom responded, "What those white women did not know or could not admit to knowing is that I cannot, by definition, ever be that kind of beautiful. In the way that gender has so structured how we move through the intersecting planes of class and status and income and wealth that shape our world and our selves, so does race. Rather, I should say, so does blackness, because everyone—including white women—have 'race.' It is actually blackness, as it has been created through the history of colonization, imperialism, and domination, that excludes me from the forces of beauty" (64–65).

Cottom's insights about the need for white women to see beauty as democratic are relevant to the conceptual link between race and beauty for the women I knew in Shanghai. The Western women were especially troubled by beauty ideals because they saw them as *creating* an unequal world, especially regarding gendered and racialized hierarchies. Indeed, in their logic, much as in that of the white women who pushed back on Cottom's negative self-assessment, all "selves" are equally beautiful "just as they are"; it is beauty ideals that make one think otherwise. A central tenet underlying their claim that all selves are equally beautiful was a particular understanding of "nature" and its assumed structural relationship to the social world.

Just as with their desire to know which "wants" were "naturally" part of the self and which were being *created* by advertising and flavor manipulation, the Western women had an intense desire to decipher what was and was not "natural" about the social world. But why was the distinction between what was and was not natural important to their ideas about social inequality? And how did the women know that something was or was not "natural"?

The Western women took "race" to be a defining aspect of unique selves, yet at the same time they rejected racial *categories* as a meaningful way of grouping people together. As they sought to undermine the use of race as a socially defining aspect of life, they almost always invoked the fact that the categories were not natural as a means for legitimizing their critiques. For example, according to Emily, "There's nothing biological or natural about whiteness. It's a social construct. I mean, when the Irish first arrived in the United States, they weren't seen as white. Now they are. Their biology hasn't changed—it's just who counts as white that's changed. Race isn't biological. It's not natural. It's just a social construction meant to justify discrimination." In a similar fashion, their evaluations of beauty standards relied on—and typically evoked—the fact that such standards were not natural. As Sophie pointed out to me one day: "There's nothing naturally more beautiful about big eyes or white skin. In fact, beauty ideals have been changing throughout history. It used to be that fat was beautiful.

Everyone wanted big hips and big breasts. Now skinny's in. Who knows what's coming next. I hope we go back to big butts soon. Ha." Throughout my time in the city I heard critiques in this vein repeated by almost all the Western women I knew.

Explicating the ways the women mobilized the concept of nature in their critiques reveals three interconnected assumptions they held about it and its relationship to the social world. First, they had a working definition of nature as the stuff that *did not change*. As such, to demonstrate that something was not in fact natural, they often gave examples of how it changed through time. Emily noted that racial categories cannot be natural (which she conflates with the biological) because who counts as what race has changed through time. Similarly, Sophie gave examples of how beauty standards have historically been different and therefore are not "natural." In short, for all the women I knew, invoking *historical change* was the way to demonstrate that something was not, in fact, natural.

Second, in addition to their understanding that nature was something that did not change, the women's preoccupation with what was or was not natural was central to their ideas about power and inequality. For them, individual identity was predicated on an understanding of authentic natural selves and unmodified bodies. When in the social world a category or hierarchy was portrayed as or assumed to be natural and, hence, fundamentally unchangeable, it held undue power over people and produced the worst kinds of inequalities. That is why, according to the Western women, racialized beauty ideals were especially dangerous: they made certain bodies seem "naturally" superior to others. As such, adding to the oppressive nature of beauty ideals (in general) was the way the powerful imposed their particular and naturalized standards on the rest of the world, which then became taken for granted by others: globalizing beauty ideals of Caucasian bodies illustrated this influence explicitly. Racial categories and beauty ideals, the Western women assumed, then, derived their power from the presumption that they were "natural" and unchangeable.

Given this framework, it is not surprising that the Western women sought to demonstrate how race was not "natural" as the first step in creating a deracialized, and thus more equitable, social world. However, as they critiqued the ideals of big eyes and white skin—and as they sought to make sense of their experiences as white women in Shanghai—they went a step further in their third assumption: to insinuate that *because* "race" did not exist in nature, it therefore *should not* be a part of social life. Indeed, they assumed unvarnished Nature (devoid of cultural construction) to be the principle on which social life should be based in creating a more equitable world, because, as they saw it, the social world's or "society's" organizing of people according to non-natural but naturalized body-based differences hinders the ability of individuals to interact as equals.

The bundling together of these three assumptions about nature provides insight into not only the women's ideas about white (liberal) identity but also its conceptual overlap with the scholarly project of denaturalizing categories. In particular, they assumed that "nature" does not change; that hierarchies and inequalities come from people presuming that categorical differences are natural when, in fact, they are not; and that in order for there to be equality, the social world should be based on what is "natural," without the imposition of "society," so "selves" can just "be themselves."

BODIES AND NATURALIZED DIFFERENCE

The idea that "naturalized" bodily differences (unrecognized as cultural constructions) are more "dangerous" than other kinds of difference because of their ability to produce and maintain social inequality is an assumption that runs throughout much anthropological literature. It certainly informs a substantial part of the critiques in studies of race and gender. While these comparisons are not meant to demonstrate overarching "Western" approaches to and critiques about beauty, they do show how the liberal tendencies of the Western women I knew in Shanghai, who were particularly situated in terms of class, generation, and race, are also informing much critical scholarship about beauty and power, particularly in its propensity to "denaturalize" categories and body-based differences.

For many scholars, ethnographic accounts of beauty present a dilemma of agency: women pursuing beauty often see it as an empowering practice. Scholars, however, cannot divorce their analysis from the sexist and racist context in which such ideals exist and therefore must navigate both sides in their research. Many such scholars, whether employing the Foucauldian framework of bodily discipline or the Gramscian notion of hegemony, conclude that the women are "internalizing" certain norms, which makes such norms appear as "natural" desires of the self, instead of problematic influences of society. The scholarly goal in these accounts is to "make visible" how power is "operating" through such desires in order to undermine the influence of the ideals. In short, they seek to "denaturalize" the desires as well as the ideals.

Importantly for this discussion, there are other beauty-related practices that at first glance seem to present a radically different picture: body modifications that aim to undermine traditional beauty ideals. A well-known case is that of the French performance artist Orlan, who elected to undergo a variety of surgeries "that destabilized male-defined notions of idealized female beauty" (Negrin 2002, 31; see also Hirschhorn 1996). Scholars writing about Orlan typically position her modifications as a means of empowerment, by which they mean she was able to demonstrate that what was taken for granted as "natural" could in fact change (which would thereby undermine its "naturalness"). Similarly, some think that any use of cosmetic surgery undermines neoromantic conceptions of the body as "natural" and illustrates the body as changeable and artificial, which is empowering to women (Balsamo 1996). Both sides, then—those who see body modifications as oppressive and those who deem it empowering—share a propensity to view power as that which naturalizes, either "bodies" or the desire to pursue certain norms. Then when differences or categories are problematically "naturalized," critics attack them conceptually by redefining them as "constructed," not natural, and simultaneously endorse violating them in practice in order to undo (or change) their bodily effects.

Connecting this literature back to Shanghai shows important parallels between ideas about nature and bodies that are directly linked to the Western women's understandings of bodily-selves; indeed, the assumption found throughout almost all of this literature—that "naturalized" bodily differences are more prone to perpetuating hierarchies and more difficult to overcome than socially produced difference—is central to the Western women's ideas about nature and power. The way many scholars are engaging in critiques about beauty, then, is clearly based on a culturally particular model of nature, bodies, and power that the liberal white Western women I knew in Shanghai shared; both advocate a particular *democratic* notion of "equality," which necessitates the dual initiatives of (1) undermining body-based distinctions for identity and (2) mobilizing "historical change" as a means to open up "naturalized" difference (such as standards of beauty) to future change.

Comparisons with the Chinese women in Shanghai accentuate the shared framework between the Western women and scholarship about bodies, nature, and power. The Chinese women understood their body-based attributes, as well as the power of beauty ideals, in quite different ways. Beauty ideals mattered not because they were natural but because of *social* reasons—class, history, cultural difference—and the most significant aspects of their bodily identities were those cultivated through time. Unlike their "racial" features, which were given (if one wants to label them in such a way) yet liable to be modified, their Chineseness was something they actively sought to produce in their bodies through their daily practices. Indeed, for them, the most drastic and significant differences between Chinese and Western peoples were both bodily and historically produced. They were not at all concerned with legitimizing racial or national categories by mobilizing the concept of nature; whether something was "natural" or not held no significance if it was appropriate or useful for social life.

GENDER, WHITENESS STUDIES, AND ANTHROPOLOGICAL ENGAGEMENTS WITH RACE

What is at stake in examining "culturally" variant ideas about race? According to Dikötter (1992), it allows a better understanding of (without overlooking) how racial prejudice has operated in other times and in other places. While I agree that understanding how social inequality operates in other places should be central to the anthropological project, in this case I suggest the opposite: comparing the Chinese and Western women's ideas about race and the body reveals the ways that liberal whiteness shapes anthropological interests in racial categories and their relationship to social life and inequality. It raises important questions: What assumptions do defining theories in (North American) cultural anthropology share with liberal white notions about race? How do such theories inform approaches to undermining racism?

This ethnographic example, in which the Western women understood race as an inherent and unique part of the "natural self" has important implications in that it draws attention to how *in practice* the Western women drew parallels between race and gender, in ways that the Chinese women did not. Indeed, quite unlike the Chinese women, who rarely discussed gender in their commentary on big eyes and white skin or in their comparisons of China and the West, the Western women more often than not linked race and gender together because they saw them as similarly problematic in their assumed link to essentialized body-based categories.[4] Put another way, they saw race and gender as *the same*: social categories that acquired their problematic power by using inaccurate portrayals of what was "natural" to justify inequalities.

The Western women were all college educated, considered themselves "feminists," and took courses at school about gender and empowerment. In short, they were all familiar with the gender theorist Judith Butler's view that gender was not about the body and instead was "performance" based. What they recalled from Butler-style critiques, and put into practice in Shanghai, was a rejection of the notion that body-based gender identity "existed." This, at least in part, was informing their desire to denaturalize categories and separate their social identity from the body, very much aligned with white female academics who understood Butler's (1990, 1993) work as liberating, especially for those who felt "trapped" within their bodies (see, for example, Zito and Barlow 1994, 4; see also Ortner 2006, 441). And yet, interestingly, at the same time, quite unlike Butler and her theories that *critiqued* the notion of a natural "inner self," the women I knew assumed that gender and racial categories were problematic because they attempted to make a problematic *social* identity out of unique traits of the self, which they assumed were indeed "natural."[5] In short, the Western women were operating with a sense that unmodified bodies (that is, selves) were natural, but individualized, and should not be used to create artificial categories. This is perhaps why their visions of utopia included body-less selves interacting in a virtual world. Performing gender, to these women, then, as a critical approach, meant rejecting restrictive categories that were not "natural" as they sought to be their "natural selves."

What does it mean to assume, as these women did, that race is conceptually akin to gender? What kinds of insights about *whiteness* and white liberal identity does this pairing generate? And, finally, how does that pairing shape not just the politics of these women's bodies but their visions of how to make a better world? Because the women recognized that both race and gender are body-based categories on which hierarchies have relied in the Western world, they presumed the same critique could be applied to both. Indeed, they assumed that denaturalizing the categories of race would have the same liberating effect for marginalized racial groups that denaturalizing gender did for themselves. This not only provides insight into their culturally particular understandings of race but also highlights their particular notion of "equality" as democratic in nature: as being *the same.*

Parallels between the Western women's ideas about empowerment and certain North American anthropological approaches to race and racism have the unintended consequence of preventing the ability to take seriously racial identity as anything other than something that should (eventually) be overcome (Visweswaran 1998). North American anthropology, at least since Franz Boas's work in the early twentieth century, has tended to interrogate the relationship between racial categories and nature as part of the political project to undermine racism. Although, admittedly, somewhat of a detour from the main arguments in this book, the following discussion is an essential part of the "situating feminisms" approach employed here, especially regarding race, identity, and bodily politics. This analysis builds on the critiques posited by (mostly) black and brown scholars about the limitations of the culture concept for understanding racial identities, especially in the context of the United States. However, the focus moves away from "culture" to the link between the project of denaturalizing categories and liberal ideas about whiteness and race more generally. Of particular interest is the Western women's aspiration to undermine the power of gender and race (that is, body-based categories) by demonstrating that they are not "natural" and this effort's conceptual linkage to the long-standing tradition in liberal white North American anthropology of assuming that the more fluid categories are, the less severe social discrimination will be.

Of note is the way that the Western women in Shanghai shared with many contemporary anthropologists (as well as scholars in other disciplines) the notion that denaturalizing racial categories is essential for undermining racism. Indeed, rejecting "race" as a viable "social" category *because it does not exist in nature* has a long conceptual history in anthropology that continues to this day. For example, the current anthropological statement on race, drafted at the end of the twentieth century, *begins*, tellingly, with the fact that racial categories are not natural/biological: "In the United States both scholars and the general public have been conditioned to viewing human races as natural and separate divisions within the human species based on visible physical differences. With the vast expansion of scientific knowledge in this century, however, it has become clear that human populations are not unambiguous, clearly demarcated, biologically distinct groups."[6] Then, after describing how physical variations occur (gradually and independently from one another) and giving a historical overview of how naturalized racial categories were used to justify racist ideology, the statement continues: "At the end of the 20th century, we now understand that human cultural behavior is learned, conditioned into infants beginning at birth, and always subject to modification. No human is born with a built-in culture or language. Our temperaments, dispositions, and personalities, regardless of genetic propensities, are developed within sets of meanings and values that we call 'culture.'"

What is notable here is the race/culture division, where culture, and not race, is positioned as the most important and defining aspect of human life. Indeed, "race" in this account is just a problematic category of difference standing in the way of understanding cultural or "learned" behavior. The document concludes with a strong statement de-linking any "natural" affiliation between racial inequalities and biological difference. The history of justifying racial discrimination through the mobilization of race-as-biology in the United States renders this a powerful political statement. Indeed, that is exactly how this statement is framed: "As a result of public confusion about the meaning of 'race,' claims as to major biological differences among 'races' continue to be advanced. Stemming from past AAA [American Anthropological Association] actions designed to address public misconceptions on race and intelligence, the need was apparent for a clear AAA statement on the biology and politics of race that would be educational and informational."[7]

In (relatively) recent accounts, scholars have begun unpacking the way that liberal whiteness has informed anthropological theories about race, particularly within the Boasian tradition in the United States (see, for example, Visweswaran 1998; Trouillot 2003; M. Anderson 2019; Baker 2010). For some, the conceptual divide between race and culture that is informing the anthropological statement about race can be traced to Boas, who rendered culture, not race, the central focus of the discipline. This, they suggest, "produced a legacy in which cultural anthropologists came to avoid racism, particularly as a structural feature of contemporary society" (M. Anderson 2019, 9; see also Trouillot 2003; Visweswaran 1998).

Whereas these scholars are concerned with how the concept of "culture" in anthropology hindered the discipline's ability to take seriously race and racism, the more poignant point is how efforts to undermine racism in the discipline, typically framed in opposition to mainstream white, explicitly racist theories, did not, actually, have the same "liberating" effect for brown and black scholars that performance-based theories of gender did for white women. Indeed, it was not that anthropologists were not tackling issues of race and racism but that they were doing so in a way that presumed that racial categories—and the essentialization of them—were the problem. Indeed, Boas himself was actually quite active in trying to undermine the racism of his time and went to great lengths in his scholarship and personal life to take on the most problematic racist theories in circulation during his time. However, because many such theories were based on essentialist renderings of a static hierarchy of race, Boas saw demonstrating *change through time* as central to the project of destabilizing racial categories (see, for example, Boas 1912). This same move informed many of the conversations within the discipline about the problems of anthropological othering, particularly in regard to producing or reproducing essentialized categories of difference (see, for example, Chakrabarty 2000; Fabian 1983). Indeed, most theorizing about undermining racial *and cultural* inequality has been about de-essentializing categories. In this way, then, such disciplinary efforts to undermine racism presuppose many of the same things that the Western women did in Shanghai. It is this legacy, and not one of a race/culture divide, I think, that informs the problem, as stated by the anthropologist Kamala Visweswaran, that "the modern anthropological concept of culture has lost any descriptive ability with regard to the construction of racial identities" (1998, 77).

What this particular ethnographic case in Shanghai demonstrates and adds to this conversation is the way that the denaturalizing critical approach to racism is entangled with particularly situated ideas and experiences of the materiality of self. Indeed, for the Western women I knew in Shanghai, the race-as-not-biology framework had the same effect on their visions of racial equality that gender-as-not-biology had on their utopian ideas about gender equality: equality could only exist when racial and gender categories went away and individuals could be seen as just "themselves."[8] For the Western women I knew in Shanghai, this generated a form of political engagement that made it difficult for them to fully account for the enduring significance of race—or any body-based identity—as anything more than what "shouldn't be there." Thus, although the standard anthropological approach is to say "race is a biological fiction but a social fact," this ethnographic case demonstrates how that approach, when coupled with the Western women's unspoken assumption that "self" was the natural unit on which social life *should* be based, excludes the possibility of racial categories existing in an "equal" world.

For example, the Chinese women I knew understood both selfhood and "Chineseness" to be body-based identities that they cultivated through time, at least partially through the foods they ate. They were conscientious and focused on creating "Chinese" versions of things and ways of being in the world. As the Western women encountered Chinese colleagues and friends who were actively trying to "be Chinese," the Western women were critical of their attempts. They thought Chinese people, rather than working so hard to produce "Chinese" versions of things, should just "be themselves" and then, by default, what they produced would "be Chinese." Their logic, then, presumed that whatever one did, if one was truly being oneself, could be representative of the nation to which one belonged, because that nation provided the context in which that self emerged. Empowerment meant being able to "be oneself" in the face of oppressive ideals and naturalized categories. Thus, as the Western women sought out a global cosmopolitanism where selves could interact with other authentic selves, they critiqued naturalized social categories (including the nation) and beauty ideals as *getting in the way* of selves being valorized as unique individuals. The scholarly preoccupation with "denaturalizing" categories, especially those related to the body, has a similar effect. Namely, it renders the scholarly position as less than well suited to address the significance of body-based categories as social concepts and meaningful identities and informs a particular kind of anti-racist politics that is not necessarily experienced as "liberating" by those who are racially marginalized.

The different attitudes of these Western women and the Chinese women I knew in Shanghai regarding what they saw as racialized or national beauty ideals demonstrate that their understandings of the nature of body-based differences informed their commentary and ideals about equality, in effect nuancing recent accounts of social categories becoming "racialized" in contemporary China. Because of its structural dominance in relation to minority nationalities and its perceived unmarkedness, the category "Han" appears, to some (see, for example, Blum 2001), similar to the category of "whiteness." Indeed, studying the "unmarked" and "dominant" group is what draws many scholars to engage whiteness literature when studying Han in China. However, the two groups of women I knew were clearly operating with different ideas about the nature and significance of body-based identities. This is significant because, for the particularly situated white Western women in Shanghai, whiteness was a highly problematic aspect of their identities that they were committed to undermining, much as they were for all racial/national categories that presupposed a "natural" affiliation between body-based categories and social life, a view they share with much anthropological work about race. For the Han women, however, their "Chineseness" was a body-based identity that they were actively trying to cultivate. They saw the cultivation of this body-based identity as an essential part of their ability to be empowered against the hegemony of the West, a viewpoint that would be (de)constructed as problematic in denaturalizing approaches to race. Using the model of "whiteness studies" to study the Han assumes a conceptual similarity between the two contexts that did not exist for the particularly situated Western and Chinese women I knew in Shanghai and thus actually hinders the ability, in this case, to understand aspects of national and racial identity in China.

CONCLUSION

For the two groups of women in Shanghai profiled in this book, different ideas about the materiality of selfhood informed their body politics and the extent to which they were willing to modify their bodies in pursuit of the beauty ideals they encountered in the city. The political significance the women attached to modifying (or not modifying) their bodies through dieting, for example, was a direct result of their different understandings and experiences of the relationship between "body" and "self" and the varying temporal dimensions they attributed to selfhood. And their different ideas about what "race" was, especially in relationship to self, shaped their attitudes toward the ideals of white skin and big eyes—ideals that were consistently assumed by them to be either racialized or of national interest. The way the women understood the materiality of bodily-selves, then, directly informed their ideas about identities, particularly those that were presumed to be body based. The ethnographic approach of "situated feminisms," rather than taking for granted the agentive nature of certain body politics, demonstrates that the practices through which the women pursued empowerment in Shanghai, at least in regard to beauty, cannot be divorced from their culturally informed and context-dependent understandings and experiences of embodied selfhood.

Comparison of the cravings of the expat women I knew to my Chinese informants' notions of *tizhi* and *xiguan* reveals that embodied experiences were not naturalized as part of inner selfhood to the same degree for these two groups of women. Neither group assumed that their pleasures were "natural" or that they were able to authentically represent selfhood in a consumerist context. But the Western women did seem to rely on an essen-tialized (unchanging and deriving its virtue from being authentic) reading of selfhood through their embodied cravings. For them, bodies were the site of the "really real" because they were viewed as outside the influence of humans and society. Even if something changed—for instance, Sophie's newfound like of Indian food—it was assumed to be indicative not of his-torically and socially produced selfhood but of the ability to find out who one "really is" apart from social influences. And while other cravings come and go—Emily's iron craving or Kate's comfort foods, for example—and are thus "historical," these are typically understood to be reflecting changes that are "biological" and body based, not socially determined. In short, the Western women I knew had an enduring-through-time experience of selfhood, which they authenticated in bodily experiences they deemed outside of society's influence.

However, for the Chinese women I knew, the embodied sensations they associated with selfhood were assumed to be created through continued and habitual eating of certain foods. And, furthermore, although this was seen as an important indicator of who one is, it was never assumed to be essential or unchanging. I am not suggesting that selfhood was less "inner" in nature; it was just less essentialized by being located in an ever-changing bodily-self. Thus, for Mei and Dandan, for example, balancing one's *tizhi* had nothing to do with figuring out or returning to their original or authen-tic state of bodily-self, but instead hinged on their being able to read the body's signals (reflecting its current state and context) correctly and then to eat accordingly. For my friends, the bodily experience of "feeling full," for example, was not solely based on one's stomach sending "natural" signals when it had had enough; instead, it had to do with the relationship one had with the food one was eating (*and* those with whom one was sharing the meal). In fact, feeling full before one had eaten a sufficient amount was often *the* indicator that one's stomach was not used to a food. Thus, on the one hand, subjective sensations such as feeling satiated and being able to work immediately after a meal were indicators that one was used to a food. On the other hand, the bodily sensation of being full could not be trusted on its own, as it did not necessarily correspond with the amount of food consumed. For the Chinese women, then, bodily experiences of feeling full and being satiated were "historically" contingent (on a lifetime of experience): these were based on what one had been eating throughout one's life. And, accordingly, this said something about a person.

In short, then, the differences between the two groups of women shows cultural variability in the degree to which embodied experiences were understood as an essential part of an immutable and authentic "inner self." Comparisons are productive, however, not just between the two groups of women but also between their differing ideas and the theoretical/political approaches scholars have taken when addressing similar topics. Much academic literature about beauty, bodies, and power, for example, assumes that certain economic transformations (often referred to as "neoliberalism" or "late capitalism") produce a particular kind of inner selfhood that is naturalized in the body. Once naturalized, power operates through such selves through the mechanism of internalization, producing certain desires that are assumed to originate in the self. Ethnographically, in this case, that theory is actually aligned with a culturally particular rendering of embodied selfhood, as found among the expat women I knew, but not the Chinese women.

Culturally particular experiences of the materiality of selfhood are in turn linked to ideas about body-based identities of race and nation. Although both groups of women discussed the ideals of big eyes and white skin in terms of race/nation, they had drastically different ideas about what race was and the implications of modifying racialized traits. For the Chinese women, "race" was mostly appearance-based attributes that were modifiable, given the right kinds of (sometimes drastic) cosmetic surgery. However, they were adamant that they were not trying to look more Western—or change their race—through modifying their eyes and skin; the version of big eyes and white skin that they sought was "Asian" in nature and based on *Chinese* beauty ideals. Moreover, running counter to the Chinese Communist Party's discourse about the genetic unity of "Chineseness," the Shanghai Chinese women I knew theorized that the most important differences between Chinese and Westerners were produced through time and daily practices. They were invested in creating, producing, and determining

"Chinese" versions of things in the contemporary moment. Indeed, the emphasis they placed on the ideals of big eyes and white skin being "Chinese" was in no way an isolated example. In fact, from art and movies to academic theories and political systems, the women actively discussed—and disagreed about—what the "Chinese" contributions to such fields should be. In sharp contrast to the Western women, they did not think Chinese people could just "be themselves" and call what they produced "Chinese."

The Shanghai Western women, however, understood racial differences as being significant only for *individual* identity insofar as they created *unique selves*; the same categories the women employed to describe such individual traits became deeply problematic when imputed to group identity. Moreover, they thought race was an enduring trait of the self regardless of the kinds of modifications made to the body. They were highly critical of the ideals they encountered in Shanghai and the way their bodies (that is, gender and race) seemed to have undue importance for their lives in Shanghai.

Their critiques about inequalities linked to body-based identities merit examination. Pitting of the "social" world against the "natural" world through a logic that distinguishes the changeable from the unchangeable informed how the Western women I knew in Shanghai understood not just themselves and their cravings but also the beauty ideals and racial and gendered experiences they had in Shanghai. A common theme of their critiques of the beauty ideals, race, and gender was that they were not "natural," sharing a conceptual framework with the scholarly project of denaturalizing categories, which can be linked to a particular white liberal entanglement between bodies, nature, and power. The Shanghai Western women's particular version of feminism, then, which is often mobilized in political interventions about beauty, is similar to recent work on anthropology of the body that typically assumes that power everywhere has a propensity to *naturalize*. To counter the power of naturalization, scholars have employed a well-worn theoretical approach that seeks to reveal that what is assumed to be "natural" is actually "cultural" in order to "open it up" for change. The Shanghai Western women also sought to undermine the efficacy of beauty ideals and categories by invoking their historical variability to demonstrate that they were not "natural." At the same time, they assumed that the "truest" aspects of self/body were those most impervious to change (that is, "natural").

An important goal of this book has been to explore the portability of the "denaturalizing" project as a means for undermining body-based inequalities in the context of China, especially in the post-reform era. The Chinese women I knew were not at all preoccupied with what was or was not "natural"; in fact, they pursued identities without regard to their "naturalness," but with regard to their desirability in the social and historical present. For them, as they sought ways to improve the self, "natural" bodily traits were actually *easier to change* than socially or historically produced expectations about bodily differences. In other words, "history" and "process"—far from being the tools through which to undermine the current world order— were what made the current social world so powerful. Not only were the Chinese women operating with a different cultural framework, but, even more importantly, their framework rendered the "denaturalizing" critique ineffective.[1] For them, improving the body involved both balancing *tizhi* and modifying appearances, both of which would increase their ability to influence others. Unlike the Western women, who wanted to challenge social norms and be themselves (an enterprise the Chinese women thought was sure to fail), the Chinese women sought ways to take advantage of them.

However, far from presuming that the overlap between the Shanghai Western women and scholarly approaches to denaturalizing bodies somehow points to a general "Western" approach to beauty that can then be compared to a general "Chinese" approach, this ethnographic account of "situated feminisms" locates such differences within particularly positioned groups of women in Shanghai. For the Western women, their approach to denaturalizing racial categories was informed by certain aspects of Judith Butler–style critiques about gender that they found liberating as liberal white women. In Shanghai, this approach hindered their ability to take seriously racial or national identity, which was made explicit in their critique of how the Chinese women actively sought out ways to "be Chinese." Recognizing how the cultural framework of liberal whiteness informed the denaturalizing approach in this ethnographic context also shows how similar approaches to race in anthropology have hindered the ability to understand other racial identities in the United States as well. It also mattered that the Chinese women were all Han and from rural areas. They were college educated and worked in corporate jobs in Shanghai, indicating a high degree of social mobility that was very much linked to their relatively well-off status. Far from representing all of "China," then, these were clearly particularly located Chinese women who were focused on pursuing certain kinds of identities and empowerment that were not available to everyone. More situated feminist ethnographies are needed to generate further insight into the variety of ways that culturally particular notions of the materiality of selfhood (among other things) inform practices of empowerment in the contemporary milieu.

●   The way the women understood the materiality of bodily-selves, then, directly informed their ideas about identities, particularly those that were presumed to be body based. In contrast to the Chinese women and their focus on *cultivating* a "Chinese" identity/selfhood, the Western women were determined to "be themselves." Indeed, for the Western women I knew, "self" was the natural unit on which social life *should* be based. This framework created two problems for them in Shanghai. First, what "self" was, exactly, especially in relation to "body" was not always clear, creating an unending tension as they navigated their lives in the city. They firmly believed that bodies should not matter (they rejected gender, race, and beauty ideals) but also thought bodies were the site of authentic selfhood (such as cravings or skin color and eye shape). Second, because they understood empowerment as being able to "be oneself" in the face of oppressive ideals and naturalized categories, they had to sift through which "wants" were coming from the self and which ones were being produced by the social world around them. And, as they sought out a global cosmopolitanism where selves could interact with other authentic selves, they critiqued naturalized social categories (including the nation) and beauty ideals as *getting in the way* of selves being valorized as unique individuals.

In great contrast, the Chinese women I knew understood both selfhood and "Chineseness" to be body-based identities that they cultivated through time, at least partially through the foods they ate. They, too, were interested in consuming global products and being cosmopolitan, but they wanted to do so in ways that were explicitly Chinese. Indeed, they were conscientious and focused on creating "Chinese" versions of things and ways of being in the world. For them, an important part of cultivating this identity was not being "too Western," which included rejecting the idea of "doing something for the self." During the luncheon I attended with Mei, the women in the room actively resisted the speaker's advice that they pursue beauty for themselves. According to Mei, they stopped listening to the speaker when he made that argument because, to them, this was a "Western" orientation to selfhood and empowerment; she argued that Chinese people know that beauty should be done for the gaze of "others," since the point of a healthy self is to *influence others*.

The comparisons in this book inform understandings of culturally particular forms of individualism, especially regarding forms of "governance" assumed to be at work in shaping modern subjectivities. As has been described by many, one of the most profound changes in social life in the reform and post-reform eras in China has been the emergence of the "individual" as a legitimate social unit. Inextricably linked to changing family dynamics and the shift away from the political class struggle that was central to social life in Maoist China, scholars have demonstrated, is a focus now on consumer-based self-cultivation and realization in the post-reform era, especially for the urban middle class. Rather than assume that these changes merely duplicated the way that individualization emerged in the Western world, recent China/West comparisons have demonstrated the uniqueness of the "rise of the individual" in the Chinese context—particularly the way that the individual emerged as the unlikely and unanticipated outcome of party-state efforts to create loyal socialist citizens (see, for example, Y. Yan 2003, 2009). Or, pushing back against the commonly held idea that a market-driven economy would lead to political democracy, the anthropologists Li Zhang and Aihwa Ong (2008) show that neoliberal policies can be utilized by an authoritarian government to maintain control.

As scholars seek to better understand the individual in China, some have taken an interest in the mechanisms of state power through which such individuals are governed. Drawing on the insights of Michel Foucault (and

Émile Durkheim, in some cases), they show the ways in which individuals in contemporary China are subject to the same kinds of social controls central to modernity in the West. The self, in these accounts, is typically assumed to be the site of such social governance through bodily and self discipline. Harking back to a Maussian conflation of the modern person/self, then, in this literature *selves* and *individuals* are typically assumed to be synonyms.

For example, Lisa Rofel (2007), in her work on desire in "neoliberal" China, is interested in how certain embodied traits are attributed—by locals in the post-socialist milieu—to a universal human nature. She begins her book with an account of a Chinese person treating their embodied desires of sexuality, and the ability to express them, as a universal (and thus noncultural) "natural" trait of humanity. Rofel contends that the narratives she describes are of an emancipatory nature, where her informants believe that "to the extent that the state recedes, people will be free to 'have' their human natures" (1999, 217–18). Rofel (2007, 3) sees this shift to self-as-naturalized-desire as part of a globalizing neoliberal capitalism; instead of taking this kind of selfhood for granted, she interrogates how it is actually a product of state efforts to create modern subjects. Rofel, then, views her work as making visible what is invisible to her informants: the way that embodied desires are made, not given. And, by doing so, she is able to illustrate that what appears and is experienced as "natural" to her Chinese informants is a means through which post-socialist power operates. Rofel's theorizing of selves, power, and naturalization resonated with the Western women I knew in Shanghai, but not the Chinese women.

At first glance, the anthropologist Andrew Kipnis's (2012a) edited volume about individualism in contemporary China seems to align with Rofel's theorizing about state power and the self/individual. In Kipnis's introduction, he explains how the scholars contributing to the volume seek to unsettle the presumed linear relationship between modernity and individualism that is take for granted in the West. Attempting to disrupt what they call the myth of individualization, he writes: "The liberation of the individual is simultaneously her or his enslavement to wider social forces; differentiation is often accompanied by conformity, and estrangement or alienation by freedom. Premodern people were individuals as well and modern people remain socially constructed" (Kipnis 2012b, 7). Like Rofel, then, they theorize that what people experience as "freedoms" of the individual are *actually* mechanisms by the state to create proper subjects, which points to the impossibility of pure individualism: "If a person's psyche is being governed by others, how can 'individualism' exist?" (Kipnis 2012b, 9). Both books, then, in certain ways assume that the way individuals experience something (as freeing or as natural, in these two cases) actually hinders their ability to see or contest power-at-work by the state.

However, Kipnis contends that one way to investigate different kinds of individualisms is to interrogate the relationship between different modernities and "the individual psyche" (2012b, 9). He insists that (1) there has always been and will always be a tension between individuals and society and (2) to treat this as a new social phenomenon, as part of "modernity," is misleading. Instead, "what changes are the particular social relationships, discourses, and tensions that constitute the social environment and, consequently, the structures of the individual psyche that are immersed therein" (8).

In some ways, then, what Kipnis et al. are calling the "individual psyche" is akin to my theorizing of the "materiality of self," especially in how they contend that individual psyches are produced in certain ways in certain contexts. However, where they presume a universal tension between the self and society, that tension was actually part of a culturally particular rendering of (dis)empowerment that the Western women I knew in Shanghai actively sought to overcome. Indeed, for the Western women, the individual/natural self had to guard itself against the influences of "society" so that all selves could be equal and unique (and therefore, ironically, the same). This, perhaps, is why the Western women were comfortable applying the same critique to race that they did to gender: what worked (at least in theory) to "free" them from their body-based discrimination should work for all. The Chinese women did not experience a tension between the individual and society in the same way. Indeed, empowerment for them was not about rejecting the influence of society, nor was it about their ability to influence "society" per se; it was about their ability to influence *other people*. Thus, they were actively trying to situate their practices as historically and socially important, for them as *Chinese* individuals, and not on behalf of all marginalized peoples.

As Alexis de Tocqueville pointed out long ago, the presumption that there is a universal tension between the individual and society was unique, at the time of his writings in the nineteenth century, to democracies (see Handler 2005, 31–34). One of the main concerns in this book is the presumption in much current literature about beauty and inequality that power operates on and through bodies everywhere the same way. As these Shanghai case studies show, through a situated feminisms approach, denaturalizing approaches to body-based inequalities are informed by a particular kind of power, which is linked to democratic theories of empowerment, where individuals are meant to have equal amounts of power over "society" in general but operate as autonomous selves in daily life. In China, however, where an authoritarian state legitimizes itself through promises of bringing prosperity to its people as it maintains social order, individuals such as the Chinese women I knew do not expect to have equal power over "society" and do not see the ideal world as one in which they can just "be themselves."

There is little doubt that the contemporary Chinese Communist Party is fully invested in managing the Chinese population. But much of that work is *explicit*—and experienced as such. At least it was by the Chinese women I knew in Shanghai. This raises questions about the effectiveness of the scholarly preoccupation with making *visible* power by denaturalizing what is "taken for granted." Different ideas about bodies and materiality not only shape experiences of embodied selfhood but also inform the political significance attributed to body-based identities in the context of late capitalism and the pursuit of particular kinds of empowerment. This sheds light on the different kinds of experiences and expectations held by individuals in the two groups of women as they navigated their appearances and identities in Shanghai. In addition, explicit comparisons show that there is much work to be done to understand the full range of embodied experiences of modernity and how those influence or inform ideas and orientations to power. In particular, these comparisons raise important questions about the effectiveness of the denaturalizing approach to revealing and contesting "power" when working in contexts where people are not insistent that "nature" serve as the basis for what social life should be.

NOTES

INTRODUCTION

All translations, unless otherwise noted, are mine.

1. For these women, "success" had everything to do with financial stability and very little to do with personal happiness. Ideally, of course, one could have both, but they unanimously prioritized the former over the latter. For example, many of my Chinese friends found it quite confounding that I chose to marry a musician, whom I clearly liked (they jokingly called him my "hobby") but who could provide me very little financial support.

2. For scholarly accounts of how beauty ideals have become sites for ideological investment, see, for example, Lee 2006; J. Yang 2011.

3. The comedian Lamu Yangzi and the singer Jike Junyi are well-known examples.

4. See, for example, Bourdieu 1984; Featherstone 1982, 1991; Witz 2000; Black 2004. See also Kroker and Kroker (1987) for a discussion of how commodification and bombardment of images of body parts has destabilized the notion of "a body."

5. For descriptions of the beauty economy and its relevance for understanding the marginalization of women in post-reform-era China, see Osburg 2013, 144; Jha 2016, 73–89; Wen 2013; Otis 2012; Hanser 2005, 2008; T. Zheng 2009, 21–22.

6. See also Edwards (2006) for an account of how a notion of physicality and beauty is enabling (or forcing) female politicians (for example, Wu Yi) to negotiate their essential femaleness within the traditionally male realm of politics.

7. Jieyu Liu (2017) also worked with white-collar women, but she focuses on sales departments in state-run companies, and thus the women she knew often had to network as part of their jobs. In important ways (for example, the sexualization of the workplace), then, their experiences aligned with those

of the female entrepreneurs with whom Osburg worked, which were quite different from the experiences of the women I knew.

8. Such economic arguments are typically linked to the emerging markets of late capitalism in which "the essence of entrepreneurialism [is] generating wealth out of the bare minimum of capital, one's own body" (Osburg 2013, 181) and is seen as an arguably adequate lens for understanding all of those pursuing beautification—or bodily based consumerism—in China. The literature on *suzhi* (quality) provides an interesting contrast here, detailing how bodies of urbanites are the sites of cultivation of certain qualities peasants are assumed to lack (see, for example, Anagnost 2004; H. Yan 2003).

9. In this book, then, *culture* is not meant to indicate one half of a nature/culture divide (for a discussion of how that divide was really a way for anthropologists to think about sameness/difference, see Geertz 1973a) but is instead a broad term that takes as its inquiry the different possible configurations of how sameness/difference exists in the world.

10. As Lynn M. Thomas (2020) points out, cosmetic companies are fully invested in cultivating and selling desire, which is another reason scholars have focused their attention on how beauty-based desires come to be.

11. See also Jarrín (2017) and Thomas (2020) for a discussion about the politics of beauty and emotions.

12. These imported ideas also had a profound impact on ideas about race and nation, which I discuss in depth in part 2 of this book.

13. Tani E. Barlow (1994) makes a similar argument based on an analysis of the terms for "woman"; she describes how with the emergence of the term *nüxing* (female sex) during the republican era, bodies became the basis for new conceptualizations of gender difference. John Zou (2006) makes a similar argument for masculinity in the republican period, in which a concept of "maleness" emerged, predicated on an essential understanding of gender. This emergence of "the unclothed and essentially male body" contrasted markedly with the masculine subject of imperial times, who was often constructed through his clothing (Zou 2006, 83).

14. For work discussing the importance of the cosmos in relation to bodies in CM, see, for example, Brownell 1995; Kuriyama 1994; Zito 1994; Farquhar 1994b, 2010; Farquhar and Zhang 2012.

15. Discussions about bare life are based on Giorgio Agamben's (1995) theorizing of how the biological aspect of "life" is prioritized in the modern concept over "how one lives."

16. An interesting counterexample is Yanhua Zhang's (2007) suggestion that in emotion-related disorders, doctors in CM engage in "thought" work that is laden with power. But her discussion merely touches on the subject and moves on before developing any critique.

17. There is a difference, then, between situated comparisons and what Thomas (2020) and others (see, for example, Tsing 2005) call *connective comparison*, which "entails attending to developments in multiple places, and then determining when those developments are linked and when they diverge" (Thomas 2020, 12).

18. This strategic comparison also enables an engagement with Chinese feminists who reject how "the local" is often a stand-in for essentialized differences between China and the West (see J. Liu 2017, 44–46).

19. This project, then, is in some ways informed by what many call the "ontological turn" in anthropology in its propensity to interrogate differences in the material or "natural" world (see, for example, Heywood 2017; for a discussion about ontology and politics, see also Holbraad, Pedersen, and Viveiros de Castro 2014).

20. For work on new materialism, see, for example, Coole and Frost 2010; Grosz 2011. For discussions about material feminisms, see Alaimo and Hekman 2008.

21. Although Mei's spoken English was good, I only ever heard her use it when Charlie was in town or when she wanted to say something directly to Adam. Otherwise, I would translate her standard Chinese into English.

22. These separate meetings were mainly due to a language barrier. Most of my Western friends did not speak Chinese, and many of the Chinese women were not comfortable speaking English in social situations.

ONE SELF

1. *Pang* is the term typically used to describe people who are overweight in Chinese, although it often carries the connotation of chubby rather than fat.

2. This first wave of scholarship came out of mainland China after it opened its doors to foreign scholars beginning in the 1970s. The work on relational selves has overlaps with discussions about holism and relational ethics in China (see, for example, Ji, Lee, and Guo 2010).

3. For work comparing Chinese and Western selves, see, for example, G. Chu 1985; Fei (1947) 1992; F. Hsu 1948; Fiske et al. 1998; Nisbett 2003; Markus and

Kitayama 1998. See also Shi-xu (2002) for a critique of the Western ethnocentrism inherent in this work.

4. See Mark Elvin (1993) for a critique of conflating "China" with a "Confucian" tradition.

5. The exception is a focus on bodily selves in Chinese medicine.

6. For scholarship exploring new notions of self in contemporary China, especially in regard to self-expression, feelings, and sexual preference, see Kipnis 2012a; X. Liu 2002; Kleinman et al. 2011; Morris 2002; Rofel 2007; Y. Yan 2003, 2008, 2009. For scholarship about self-as-desires in the United States, see, for example, Lancaster 2003.

7. See also H. Yan (2003), Woronov (2003), Thøgersen (2003), and Bakken (2000) for similar critiques about neoliberalism, bodies, and the cultivation of *suzhi*.

8. It is important to note that there are strong critiques of the thesis that *suzhi* is an inherently neoliberal concept. See Andrew Kipnis (2007) for a discussion of the overuse of the term *neoliberal*, and the problems of employing the term to describe *suzhi*, in which not all individuals have the same potential for development, a central assumption of neoliberalism. Also, Carolyn Hsu (2007) addresses a similar problem in her ethnographic account of market socialism in Harbin and offers compelling critiques of the ways that scholars conflate *suzhi* with neoliberalism. According to Hsu, it is not just that *suzhi* discourse is not necessarily neoliberal; it is that *suzhi* discourse also serves as a "resistance against neoliberalism, by emphasizing the importance of social structures and by positing a moral vision of status based on contribution and culture rather than money" (2007, 188). Even though Kipnis and Hsu offer compelling critiques, they do not address the fact that "body" is a taken-for-granted concept in discussions of *suzhi*. Kipnis (2006) hints at it when he suggests that *suzhi* is no longer conceptualized as the nature side of the nature/nurture divide, but in his critiques he moves the discussion about *suzhi* away from the body, to the realm of the "social."

TWO *TIZHI*

1. An example of a popular media post about regional cuisines and their link to personalities can be found at Zhihu.com, posted by Stevejoy, accessed January 10, 2023, https://zhuanlan.zhihu.com/p/85538006.

2. For another scholarly discussion about *tizhi* and food, see Farquhar 2002, 47–77.

3. 阴虚体质，内热体质，脾湿体质。

4. The original reads:

> 为什么我总是游离与人群之外，总是觉被孤立？
>
> 为什么他（她）总是不懂我的心，他（她）的意见总是和我向左？
>
> 我已经没有力气和他（她）继续争吵了。
>
> 我已经很努力，为什么在工作上还是业绩平平呢？
>
> 最近老板对我的态度似乎有点儿不对劲，是我什么地方做错了吗？
>
> 不要再怀疑自己，是你对自己缺乏正确的认知，对他人缺乏真正的了解。
>
> 真是每个人的不同体质决定了形形色色的性格，最终决定了每个人的处事方式。
>
> 不是习惯决定命运，不是性格决定命运，而是体质决定命运！

5. In this chapter, I rely heavily on *Nine Types of Tizhi: A Nutrition Plan* to describe what *tizhi* is and how it is related to self and food. I use this book because it resonated with my friends' ideas about *tizhi* and thus is a good indicator of their understandings and experiences of the concept.

6. The original reads:

> 我们通常说的体质，是指人群中的个体由于先天禀赋，后天生说方式，生存环境等多种因素的影响，在生长发育和衰老过程中，在机体形态结构，功能活动，物质代谢，心理活动等方面固有的相对稳定的特征。先天禀赋是体质形成的基础，后天因素测决定着体制的形成和转变。生活环境，生活习惯，饮食，疾病，药物等因素都属于后天因素，其中饮食对于体质的形成和转变有着重要的影响。

7. The original reads:

> 众所周知身体发肤受之父母。其实，人的体质基础也同样来自于父母的遗传，但研究发现，除了先天因素对于体质的形成响外，人们日常的饮食，所处环境，情绪，药物，疾病等都是改变和影响体制的因素。

8. The original reads: 1 = 没有；2 = 很少；3 = 有时；4 = 经常；5 = 总是。

9. The original reads:

1. 您手脚发凉吗？
2. 您胃脘部，背部或腰膝部怕冷吗？
3. 您感到怕冷，衣服比别人穿得多吗？
4. 您比一般的人不耐寒冷（冬天的寒冷，夏天的冷空调，电扇，等）吗？
5. 您比别人容易患感冒吗？
6. 您吃（喝）凉的东西会感到不舒服或者怕吃（喝）凉东西吗？
7. 您受凉或吃（喝）凉的东西后，容易腹泻（拉肚子）吗？

10. The original reads:

1. 您感到胸闷或腹部胀满吗？
2. 你感到身体不轻松或不爽快吗？
3. 您腹部肥厚松软吗？
4. 您有额部油脂分泌多的现象吗？
5. 您上眼睑比别人肿（轻微隆起）吗？
6. 您嘴里有黏黏的感觉吗？
7. 您平时痰多，特别是咽喉部总感到有痰堵着吗？
8. 您舌苔厚腻或有舌苔厚厚的感觉吗？

11. The original reads:
   1. 您容易疲乏吗？
   2. 您容易气短（呼吸短促，接不上气）吗？
   3. 您容易心慌吗？
   4. 您容易头晕或站起时晕眩吗？
   5. 您比别人容易患感冒吗？
   6. 您喜欢安静，懒得说话吗？
   7. 您说话声音无力吗？
   8. 您稍增加活动量就容易出虚汗吗？

12. The word for sun in Chinese includes the word *yang*, which people with this kind of *tizhi* are lacking.

13. The original reads:
   3. 阳虚体质：中医讲究"阴阳平衡"，如果我们身体阳气不足，体质就会偏颇成阳虚体质，这种体质以身体出现虚寒现象为主要特征。常言道"万物生长靠太阳"，人类作为自然界中的一员当然也不能例外，如果我们的身体里阳气不够，就会怕冷，手脚冰凉，贪睡，吃点凉的东西就腹胀，腹痛，腹泻，脸色很差，也不喜欢运动，给人懒洋洋的感觉，小陈的感觉。曾经遇到一个患者，小姑娘人很漂亮，就是总怕冷，据她对我讲，她到了夏天还会穿毛衣，就这样还不敢吹风扇，开空调，看着街头别人穿着轻盈飘逸的连衣裙，火辣时尚的短裙，自己只有美慕嫉妒的份儿，独自在角落里"望裙兴叹"。其实，这个小姑娘就是典型的阳虚体质，如果不进行仔细调理，体质会更加偏颇。

14. The original reads:
   4. 气虚体质：如果人身体内的元气不足了，就会出现气息低弱，机体和脏腑功能低下等症状，这就是我们所说的气虚体质.大家一起爬楼梯，有的朋友气定神闲地到了楼顶，有的朋友则爬得上气不接下气，到了楼上好像半条命都丢了。同样是加班，别人回家好好睡一觉，第二天照样精神百倍，有些朋友却不行，几天都恢复不了，给人感觉他每天都疲惫不堪。这种总是感觉很累，气不够用的朋友就是典型的气虚体质，他们还很容易出汗，甚至连吃个饭都可以汗流夹背，经常搞得自己狼狈不堪，耐力也差，还总是被感冒折腾。

15. Descriptions of the other kinds of *tizhi* were as follows (Ji 2012, 29):

1. Balanced *tizhi*: People with a balanced *tizhi* glow with health. They are not too skinny and not too fat. Although many people in today's world suffer from insomnia and anxiety, these afflictions do not affect people with balanced *tizhi*. They eat well, sleep well, have a positive outlook on life, rarely get sick, and, when they catch a cold, drinking hot water is enough to cure them. They have a positive outlook on life, are easygoing and open-minded. These lucky people need to be careful, as many of those with balanced *tizhi* act too audaciously; they stay awake late at night, drink, smoke, work too hard, and, as time passes, they end up turning their healthy *tizhi* into an unbalanced one. (1. 平和体质: 生活中我们会遇到这样一些朋友，他们不胖不瘦，神采奕奕，强壮有力，一看就是个健康的人。现代人常有失眠，焦虑在他们身上完全看不到，吃得好，睡得香，每天都乐观向上，还很少生病，一年也就得点感冒，有的人多喝点白开水，感冒就好了，连药都不用吃。拥有这样体质的朋友实在是幸运儿，因为他们属于最健康的平和体质。不过这种幸运也要靠自己珍惜，很多平和体质的朋友任性妄为，熬夜，酗酒，吸烟，劳累过度，久而久之就毁掉了自己的健康体质，转化成了偏颇体质。)

2. Weak yin: Those with a weak yin *tizhi* are lacking fluids in the body. These people are typically thin but also have a "hot fire" burning inside them: their hands, feet, and hearts are always hot; their faces are flushed; their mouths, throats, and noses are dry. It is as if all the fluids in their bodies have evaporated. These people are typically anxious and, although they understand that "Rome was not built in a day," they cannot help but try to accomplish everything they do as quickly as possible. These characteristics will appear in people with this kind of *tizhi*, which is the result of their bodies lacking water, the foundation for life. Without enough water, bodies will have all kinds of problems, eventually leading to a weak yin *tizhi*. (2. 阴虚体质: 由于体内的津液精血等物质亏少，出现了以相关组织器官失养和身体内热为主要症状的体质状态，就是我们所说的阴虚体质。很多朋友长得很瘦，却是个"火热"的人，手脚心热，脸上烘热，口干，咽干，鼻子干，仿佛身体里德水分被过多地蒸发出丢了。这类朋友性格也很有特点，说话办事容易着急，做什么事情总希望能一蹴而就，吃饭恨不能一口吃完，工作恨不得一口气全做完，"罗马不是一天建成的"他们明白，但是就是做不到心平气和，有条不紊地境界，无论做什么都喜欢

风风火火。这类朋友之所以会出现这些特征，就是因为身体里缺水了，水是生命之源，缺少了之后身体自然会表现出这样那样的问题，最后把自己弄成了阴虚体质。）

The text continues (Ji 2012, 30–32):

5. Wet phlegm: When the liquids in the body are restricted in movement this causes one's phlegm and moisture to cohere, leading to a sticky and heavy condition. "Phlegm" is the body's water, liquid, and saliva. "Wet" includes both inner and outer moisture. Outer wetness is the humidity and moisture from one's living environment. Inner wetness is a result of poor digestion, causing one's saliva and fluids to stagnate. People with this kind of *tizhi* are typically overweight with oily and shiny complexions. They are often afflicted with "rich people sicknesses," including high blood pressure. Most people with diabetes have wet phlegm *tizhi*. You could say that this kind of *tizhi* is a hotbed for "rich people sicknesses." (5. 痰湿体质：身体里的水液滞留，导致了痰和湿凝聚在一起，由此形成的黏滞重浊体质状态就是我们所说的痰湿体质。"痰"是身体里水，液，津代谢障碍所形成的病理产物，"湿"则分为外湿和内湿，生活居住环境的潮湿属于外湿，内湿是由于消化系统运作不良导致体内津液停滞不化而形成的，"痰"和"湿"一起发力，就导致了痰湿体质的形成。痰湿体质很容易辨认，属于这类体质的人给人的第一印象是腹大腰圆，油光满面，痰湿体质多见于胖人。不仅如此，痰湿体质也是"富贵病"的重灾区，高血压，高血脂，糖尿病患者多是痰湿体质，可以这样说，痰湿体质为"富贵病"提供了土壤和温床。）

6. Stasis blood *tizhi*: Stasis blood *tizhi* points to a condition where blood is not able to flow freely throughout the body, causing numerous ailments, including many external symptoms and signs. There is a saying in Chinese medicine: "When things are flowing freely there is no pain; when there is pain things aren't flowing freely." Thus for those people with a stasis blood *tizhi*, where blood is not able to flow properly through the body, they will encounter all kinds of problems. If you are not careful, bumping into hard objects will leave a big mark; deep lines will form on your face; your tongue will be a dark color; sometimes you will have large bruises; you often have acne; women afflicted with this kind of *tizhi* will have problems with their menstrual cycle. All of these symptoms are ways the body communicates that it has a stasis blood *tizhi*. (6. 血瘀体质：血瘀体质指的是体内有血液运行不畅的潜在倾向或者淤血内阻的病理基础，并表现出一系列外在征象的体质状态。中医里有句话："通则不痛，痛则不通"，血液

淤滞住，不畅通了，我们的身体就会表现出各种不适。不小心撞到硬物上会出现"鬼拧青"，脸上出现"钞票纹"，舌头颜色偏暗，有时候还有淤斑，脸上容易长斑，女性朋友则会被痛经折磨得心神不宁，这些都是身体在用自己的话言告诉我们血瘀体质已经找上门了。）

7. Wet hot *tizhi*: Acne is a staple of youth. But nowadays, when you look around, you can see that more and more middle-aged people are also struggling with acne. This is because of having a wet hot *tizhi*. When we see their acne, this is a just a symptom of something else. These people are also often afflicted with oral ulcers and sores. Even though they take medicine and vitamins and apply topical creams, nothing has too much of an effect on their bodies. (7. 湿热体质：青春痘本来是年经人的专利，长痘痘是青春无敌的标志，不过现在却不是这么回事了，放眼看看身边的人，很多四五十岁得朋友液长着"青春洋溢"的痘痘，战"痘"的队伍里出现了越来越多中年朋友的身影。年经人处于特殊的生理时期，长痘痘是正常的生理现象，可是大龄朋友也摆脱不了痘痘的纠缠是怎么回事呢？这都是湿热体质在作怪，它以湿热内蕴为主要特征，我们看到的就是满脸痘痘，口舌生疮。很多朋友长年累月被口腔溃疡折磨，吃药，敷药，吃维生素，作用都不大，这其实也是温热体质在
捣鬼。）

8. Gloomy *qi tizhi*: As the name implies, gloomy *qi tizhi* is a result of enduring emotions that are inhibited, which eventually influences a person's personality. The quintessential example of a person with a gloomy *tizhi* is the beautiful Lin Daiyu from *Dream of the Red Chamber*. She is troubled, prone to mood swings, and always sad and crying. To put it in a more modern way, her personality lacks sunshine. This is typical of a person with a gloomy *qi tizhi*. They do not have much of an appetite, have trouble sleeping, are absent-minded, are pessimistic, and are prone to hysteria and the feeling of having a lump in their throat. (8. 气郁体质：顾名思义，气郁体质就是因为长期情志不畅，气机郁滞而形成的以性格内向，情绪不稳定，忧郁脆弱，多疑为主要表现的体质状态。忧郁之美，美则美矣，却美得很病态，美得让人心伤。就拿忧郁之美的巅峰人物林黛玉来说吧，自《红楼梦》问世以来，这位"态生两届之愁，娇袭一身之病。泪光点点，娇喘微微"的林妹妹不知赚了多少痴男怨女的眼泪。她心眼儿小，生性多疑，动不动就生闷气，痛哭，用现在时髦的话来说就是心理不阳光，这就是典型的气郁体质。气郁久不了不仅胃口不好，失眠，健忘，悲观，失落，还会与百合病，脏躁，梅核气等疾病纠缠不清。）

9. Special endowments *tizhi*: Those with a special endowment *tizhi* are a

unique group of people. In general, we encourage people to eat a balanced diet and discourage people from choosing foods based on their likes and dislikes or being picky about what they eat. But for this group of people, we actually suggest being selective about what they eat. That is because this group of people has a unique *tizhi*, based on the fact that they are lacking certain things that did not get passed on to them through inheritance, manifested in the fact that they are plagued by allergies. So in the springtime, when everyone is out enjoying the flowers, these people have to stay inside due to their allergies of flower pollen. And when their friends are busy eating seafood, these people are not able to even get close to the table. There is only one option available for these people if they want to rid themselves of their allergies: work hard to change your *tizhi*. If you change your *tizhi*, the conditions necessary for allergies will disappear, naturally alleviating your ailments. (9. 特禀体质：特禀体质的朋友属于"特殊"的人裙，我们讲究科学饮食的时候都会提倡大家不偏食，不挑食，可是对于具有特禀体质的这类"特殊"朋友，我们则会建议吃东西要合理"挑食"。这是因为特禀体质表现一种特异性体质，是由于先天禀赋不足，禀赋遗传等因素造成的一种体质缺陷，最常见的特禀体质是过敏体质。春天百花争艳，大家争着赏花踏青，特禀体质的朋友却唯恐避之不及，因为他们对花粉过敏；海鲜味道一绝，大家大快朵颐的时候特禀体质的朋友碰也不敢碰，因为海鲜也是他们的过敏原。过敏原防不胜防，要想改变被动挨打的局面，特禀体质的朋友只有一个方法可以以不变应万变，那就是努力改变自己的体质，过敏的土壤消失了，过敏自然不会盯上你。)

16. This categorization schema correlates with the CM concern for balanced bodies, based on a yin/yang cosmic ordering, where too much cold (yin) or hot (yang) can wreak havoc on a person's health. Foods that are cool or cold are associated with yin and are important for those with too much yang; warm and hot foods are yang and are essential for those with too much yin (for a historical account of these properties, see E. Anderson 1988). The Chinese women I knew in Shanghai were especially concerned with the hot/cold distinction when they were menstruating, an extremely cooling activity, throughout which time they would avoid all cold foods and diligently police their friends' food choices.

In addition to the internal properties of hot and cold food, CM also categorizes herbal medicines according to the five flavors (sour, bitter, sweet, pungent, and salty), which correspond to the five elements (wood, fire, earth, metal, and water). The efficacy of the medicine depends on the subjective experience of those flavors, which then causes certain physiological activities (sour: contrasting and constricting; bitter: draining and drying; sweet: replenishing and supplementing; pungent: spreading and disseminating; salty: softening and dispersing) (see Farquhar 2002, 62–66).

17. Not all personality traits were linked to *tizhi*. For example, the terms *introvert* (内向) and *extrovert* (外向) are common in China for describing people and their habits. In my experience, these terms were most frequently used by academics when explaining why they or their children liked to study. For my Chinese friends whom I am describing in this chapter, being too introverted was a sign that something was amiss with a person's body.

18. *Dianping* 点评 means "to advise" or "to offer comment" on a topic.

19. It is worth noting that in my conversations with people about McDonald's, they complained not that they did not "like" the food but that they were not "used to" it. They were hungry again, quite quickly, and thus thought of the food as more of a snack than a meal.

20.This observation parallels Farquhar's (1994b, 1996, 2010) discussion of *yang-sheng* cultivation and bodiliness and Brownell's (1995) and Y. Zhang's (2007) work on culturally particular models of bodies and health.

THREE CRAVINGS

1. This discussion is restricted to the Puxi side of Shanghai; I am less familiar with the foreign clusters on the east side/bank of Shanghai in Pudong.

2. To ensure the anonymity of these women, I have changed some of the details of their stories. These descriptions, then, while "composites," remain as true as possible to how I understood the women's experiences in the city and their attitudes toward food.

3. Some notable examples of food scares that made the news were fake eggs, watermelons pumped full of dirty water, reused cooking oil, and cardboard used as a supplement in steamed buns. The culprits were almost always street vendors, making Kate, and many other expats, wary of street food (see, for example, Tam and Yang 2005; Veeck, Yu, and Burns 2010; Y. Yan 2012; Klein 2013).

4. This kind of scene can also be found at more touristy sites, including Xintiandi, a newly renovated district of stone gatehouses (*shikumen*) on narrow alleyways. The houses have been converted into boutiques and Western restaurants and bars, catering mostly to a foreign population. The narrow streets are always

jammed full of people, including foreigners there for the international experience (often snapping photos of the few locals still living in the houses on the
alleyways) and Chinese tourists who are curious about foreigners (and thus
snapping pictures of the foreigners eating pizza or drinking beer or wine).

5. This observation is consistent with recent critiques of scholars working in
the context of the United States who are demonstrating that the commodification of selfhood, in various kinds of labor, is leading to an explosion of
problems associated with what is now called "mental health." For example, in
many kinds of service labor, emotions must be "faked" for the sake of customers, which, over the long term, creates situations where it is difficult to "know"
if a feeling is genuine or not (see, for example, Arlie Hochschild's [(1983) 2012]
work on airline attendants). Or, for other kinds of "corporate" labor, individuals have to work to "brand" the self, creating an image of something that is
unique but consistent (see, for example, Gershon 2014).

6. See Scrinis (2008) for an explication of "nutritionism," an ideology of food
with direct parallels to biological notions of the body.

7. Given the temporal notion of self that was important for these women, one
possible direction of future research would be to compare ideas and experiences of aging to see how or if it influences women's anxiety about their
appearance.

FOUR RACE

1. This paradox is described most explicitly in Hunter (2005, 57–67), following
Morgan's (1991) model of identifying paradoxes in cosmetic surgery.

2. For scholars working on Orientalism and beauty, see Mohanty 1984; Kim
2012, also cited in Elias, Gill, and Scharff 2017. For works about race and
beauty, see, for example, Burke 1996; Hall 2005; Kawashima 2002; Glenn
2008; Thomas 2020.

FIVE "CHINESE" IDEALS

1. This topic is also common in the West, especially in the context of cosmetic
surgery.

2. This form of "dissent" echoes Martin Schoenhals's (1993, 97–98) account of
students demonstrating dissatisfaction with teachers by having private conversations during lectures.

3. However, see Waltner (1990) for a discussion of the notion of "pure" patrilineal *qi*, which is not affected by maternal inheritance.

4. It is important to note that Ebrey and Dikötter were discussing different contexts for understanding the Han. Dikötter was mostly concerned with the relationship between Han and non-Han, whereas Ebrey focused on Han identity. Nevertheless, they disagreed about whether or not *race* was an appropriate term for understanding the category Han.

5. This question has clear conceptual linkage to David Schneider's (1984) critique of kinship studies. In fact, given that race in the West is clearly informed by biology, as much as kinship is, I see these questions as parallel inquiries.

6. My concern is with contemporary attitudes and understandings about race, not in determining which historical interpretation is correct. For more on race in China's history, see, for example, Wyatt 2010; Abramson 2008.

7. For a somewhat technical account of these surgical procedures, see, for example, Fakhro et al. 2015; Gao et al. 2018.

8. For similar accounts in mainstream media, see Hooi 2009; Yuan 1989.

9. For a general and historical account of cosmetic surgery in China, see Wen 2013.

10. Pamela Crossley (1999) agrees with Dikötter that racial taxonomies were already in place when Chinese nationalists encountered Western racial theories in the nineteenth century; however, instead of rooting such racial categories in "traditional" Chinese othering, Crossley shows how it emerged in the conquest dynasty of the Qing. Moreover, she demonstrates that the nationalists of the nineteenth century pulled from seventeenth- and eighteenth-century Chinese sources—as much as they did from Western theories—to create a racial ordering of the world.

11. Lan cites Lufrano (1994), Sullivan (1994), and Crane (1994).

12. The women were not necessarily concerned with or consistent in comparing geographical versus color-based categories. Thus they would sometimes compare "Asian" with "Western" and sometimes would use "white" instead. They used "yellow" the least, and, more often than not, "yellow" would be compared with "white," although sometimes they would use "Western" instead.

13. An important follow-up to this research would be to determine if the kinds of racial distinctions the women made between "Asian" and "white" would also be applied to blackness. As Daniel Segal (2000) showed for the United States, race as a concept is not applied in the same ways to all bodies (for example, harking back to slavery and property ownership, blackness in the United

States is determined by the "one-drop" rule, whereas Native American-ness is often divided into fractions or small portions). Similar comparisons in China would greatly enhance the understanding of the consistency with which the concept is applied to different groups.

14. Over time, the state-assigned ethnic minority labels of the 1950s have become much more than the government's way of categorizing its peoples (Gladney 1990, 1994, 2004; Rudelson 1997; Schein 2000). Besides serving to legitimize the PRC as a modern state, the labeling of groups has also had the effect of solidifying ethnic identities that had been much more fluid during traditional and imperial times (Gladney 1990, 2004). Thus, although often viewed (at least by Western scholars) as grouping people together in problematic ways, the groups have begun to be used by the minorities as a marker of identity and as vehicles for political and economic development. Recently, in an attempt to counter separatist sentiments in some groups, Chinese scholars have suggested getting rid of the term *minzu* (which could imply "national" status) and replacing it with the politically more neutral *zuqun* (cultural groups) (R. Ma 2010). Therefore, minority groups could be seen less as separate nations and more as cultural groups within a nation.

15. What the terms *minzu* and *zhongzu* share is the character *zu*, one of the words Dikötter (1992) translated as "race" in his account.

16. Some scholarly and state discourse in the PRC has gone so far as to use the discovery of Peking Man to support theories of human polygenesis that claim the "Chinese" are an identifiable line of humans beginning as far back as *Homo erectus* (see Sautman 1994; Cheng 2017). It should be noted that not everyone in China is convinced that Chinese are a separate group of humans, and many scholars, scientists, and laypeople support the "Out of Africa" theory of human origins. Some attribute the desire to assert a genetic basis for Chineseness to the importation of a Western notion of race (see Lan 2016).

17. Loss of blood and *qi* during childbirth has a cooling effect on the body and weakens it. Drinking something cold right afterward is considered especially dangerous and causes imbalance.

18. It is important to note that this account is very much in line with state discourse about China's "peaceful" history, denying any expansionist disposition, although many historians point out that China's territory today owes much to Qing expansion, for example, the Qianlong emperor's ten great campaigns (see, for example, Rowe 2010; Rawski 1996).

SIX "RACIALIZED" IDEALS

1. Clearly, body modification practices are not limited to the context of China. In general, the Western women I knew were also dismayed by women in the Western world who sought to change their appearance, although they did not typically discuss beauty ideals in the West as racialized. Women who do undergo cosmetic surgery in the United States often find themselves in a bind narrating selfhood: on the one hand, modifying their body undermines the authenticity of selfhood. On the other hand, their improved appearance is often described as a better indicator of self (see Gimlin 2000). What is of interest here is that these studies rarely explore the relationship between how the women who are modifying their bodies are situated (by class, race, generation) and their ideas about the politics of their bodies. In this case, it is also worth noting that the Western women I knew in Shanghai never questioned body modification practices such as orthodontics, which typically extend across races and genders, suggesting that it is racial and gender issues that are driving their discourse. Much could be added to these discussions, I think, if more "situated feminist" ethnographic research were done exploring the relationship between body politics and cultural frameworks for understanding the relationship between bodies and identities.

2. It is noteworthy that this framing of self in relation to aging enables the possibility of future modifications in the name of self-preservation, rather than self-modification. I thank Bonnie Urciuoli for pointing this out to me.

3. Of course, "Caucasian" is a geographic category, and it originally did conflate geography and race; see, for example, Moses (2017).

4. Because the Chinese women rarely raised issues of gender inequality in conjunction with China/West comparisons, I have not included an explication of the body-based nature of gender for them. I think such a project would be an invaluable contribution to this line of research.

5. Many thanks to one of the reviewers, who pointed out this important difference.

6. American Anthropological Association, "AAA Statement on Race," accessed January 11, 2021, www.americananthro.org/ConnectWithAAA/Content.aspx?ItemNumber=2583.

7. American Anthropological Association, "AAA Statement on Race."

8. See M. Anderson (2019, 60–89) for an account of Boas's solution to the problem of race in the United States: miscegenation.

CONCLUSION

1. The ineffectiveness of the denaturalizing critique resonates with social media accounts in China of women complaining about those trying to "empower" them to "be themselves" and reject beauty ideals.

BIBLIOGRAPHY

Abramson, Marc S. 2008. *Ethnic Identity in Tang China*. Philadelphia: University of Pennsylvania Press.

Agamben, Giorgio. 1995. *Homo Sacer: Sovereign Power and Bare Life*. Stanford, CA: Stanford University Press.

Alaimo, Stacy, and Susan Hekman, eds. 2008. *Material Feminisms*. Bloomington: Indiana University Press.

Anagnost, Ann. 2004. "The Corporeal Politics of Quality (*Suzhi*)." *Public Culture* 16, no. 2: 189–208.

Anderson, Eugene. 1988. *The Food of China*. New Haven, CT: Yale University Press.

Anderson, Mark. 2019. *From Boas to Black Power: Racism, Liberalism, and American Anthropology*. Stanford, CA: Stanford University Press.

Baker, Lee. 2010. *Anthropology and the Racial Politics of Culture*. Durham, NC: Duke University Press.

Bakken, Børge. 2000. *The Exemplary Society: Human Improvement, Social Control, and the Dangers of Modernity in China*. Oxford: Oxford University Press.

Balsamo, Ann. 1992. "On the Cutting Edge: Cosmetic Surgery and the Technological Production of the Gendered Body." *Camera Obscura* 10, no. 1: 206–37.

———. 1996. *Technologies of the Gendered Body: Reading Cyborg Women*. Durham, NC: Duke University Press.

Banet-Weiser, Sarah. 1999. *The Most Beautiful Girl in the World: Beauty Pageants and National Identity*. Berkeley: University of California Press.

Barlow, Tani E. 1994. "Theorizing Woman: *Funü, Guojia, Jiating*." In *Body, Subject & Power in China*, edited by Angela Zito and Tani E. Barlow, 253–90. Chicago: University of Chicago Press.

Bashkow, Ira. 2006. *The Meaning of Whitemen: Race and Modernity in the Orokaiva Cultural World*. Chicago: University of Chicago Press.

Black, Paula. 2004. *The Beauty Industry: Gender, Culture, Pleasure*. New York: Routledge.

Blum, Susan. 2001. *Portraits of "Primitives": Ordering Human Kinds in the Chinese Nation*. Lanham, MD: Rowman & Littlefield.

Blumenthal, David, and William Hsiao. 2005. "Privatization and Its Discontents: The Evolving Chinese Health Care System." *New England Journal of Medicine* 353, no. 11: 1165–70.

Boas, Franz. 1912. "Changes in the Bodily Forms of Descendants of Immigrants." *American Anthropologist*, n.s., 14, no. 3: 530–62.

Bonilla-Silva, Eduardo. 2003. *Racism without Racists: Color-Blind Racism and the Persistence of Racial Inequality in the United States*. Lanham, MD: Rowman & Littlefield.

Bordo, Susan. 1993. *Unbearable Weight: Feminism, Western Culture, and the Body*. Berkeley: University of California Press.

Bourdieu, Pierre. 1977. *Outline of a Theory of Practice*. Cambridge: Cambridge University Press.

———. 1984. *Distinction: A Social Critique of the Judgement of Taste*. London: Routledge.

Brownell, Susan. 1995. *Training the Body for China: Sports in the Moral Order of the People's Republic*. Chicago: University of Chicago Press.

———. 1999. "The Body and the Beautiful in Chinese Nationalism: Sportswomen and Fashion Models in the Reform Era." *China Information* 13, no. 2–3: 36–58.

Burke, Timothy. 1996. *Lifebuoy Men, Lux Women: Commodification, Consumption, and Cleanliness in Modern Zimbabwe*. Durham, NC: Duke University Press.

Butler, Judith. 1990. *Gender Trouble: Feminism and the Subversion of Identity*. New York: Routledge.

———. 1993. *Bodies That Matter: On the Discursive Limits of "Sex."* New York: Routledge.

Carolan, Michael. 2005. "The Conspicuous Body: Capitalism, Consumerism, Class, and Consumption." *Worldviews: Global Religions, Culture, and Ecology* 9, no. 1: 82–111.

Carrithers, Michael, Steven Collins, and Steven Lukes, eds. 1985. *The Category of the Person: Anthropology, Philosophy, History*. Cambridge: Cambridge University Press.

Cederström, Carl, and André Spicer. 2015. *The Wellness Syndrome*. Malden, MA: Polity Press.

Chakrabarty, Dipesh. 2000. *Provincializing Europe: Postcolonial Thought and Historical Difference*. Princeton, NJ: Princeton University Press.

Chang, Kwang-chih, ed. 1977. *Food in Chinese Culture: Anthropological and Historical Perspectives*. New Haven, CT: Yale University Press.

Chao, Emily. 1996. "Hegemony, Agency, and Re-presenting the Past: The Invention of Dongba Culture among the Naxi of Southwest China." In *Negotiating Ethnicities in China and Taiwan*, edited by Melissa J. Brown, 208–39. Berkeley: Institute of East Asian Studies, University of California, Berkeley.

Chen, Nancy. 2002. "Embodying *Qi* and Masculinities in Post-Mao China." In *Chinese Femininities / Chinese Masculinities: A Reader*, edited by Susan Brownell and Jeffrey Wasserstrom, 315–29. Berkeley: University of California Press.

———. 2008. "Consuming Medicine and Biotechnology in China." In *Privatizing China: Socialism from Afar*, edited by Li Zhang and Aihwa Ong, 123–32. Ithaca, NY: Cornell University Press.

Cheng, Yinghong. 2011. "From Campus Racism to Cyber Racism: Discourse of Race and Chinese Nationalism." *China Quarterly*, no. 207: 561–79.

———. 2017. "'Is Peking Man Still Our Ancestor?'—Genetics, Anthropology, and the Politics of Racial Nationalism in China." *Journal of Asian Studies* 76, no. 3: 575–602.

Chow, Rey. 1991. *Woman and Chinese Modernity: The Politics of Reading between West and East*. Minneapolis: University of Minnesota Press.

Chu, Godwin. 1985. "The Changing Concept of Self in Contemporary China." In *Culture and Self: Asian and Western Perspectives*, edited by Anthony J. Marsella, George A. De Vos, and Francis L. K. Hsu, 252–77. New York: Tavistock.

Chu, Julie. 2010. *Cosmologies of Credit: Transnational Mobility and the Politics of Destination in China*. Durham, NC: Duke University Press.

Collier, Jane, and Sylvia Yanagisako. 1987. "Toward a Unified Analysis of Gender and Kinship." In *Gender and Kinship: Essays toward a Unified Analysis*, edited by Jane Collier and Sylvia Yanagisako, 14–50. Stanford, CA: Stanford University Press.

Coole, Diana, and Samantha Frost, eds. 2010. *New Materialisms: Ontology, Agency, and Politics*. Durham, NC: Duke University Press.

Cottom, Tressie McMillan. 2013. "Brown Body, White Wonderland." *Slate*, August 29, 2013.

———. 2019. *Thick, and Other Essays*. New York: New Press.

Counihan, Carole M. 1999. *The Anthropology of Food and Body: Gender, Meaning, and Power*. New York: Routledge.

Crane, George T. 1994. "Collective Identity, Symbolic Mobilization, and Student Protest in Nanjing, China, 1988–1989." *Comparative Politics* 26, no. 4: 395–413.

Crawford, Robert. 2004. "A Cultural Account of 'Health': Control, Release, and the Social Body." In *The Body: Critical Concepts in Sociology*, vol. 4, *Living and Dying Bodies*, edited by Andrew Blaikie, Mike Hepworth, Mary Holmes, Alexandra Howson, David Inglis, and Sheree Sartain, 275–308. New York: Routledge.

Croll, Elisabeth J. 2006. "Conjuring Goods, Identities, and Cultures." In *Consuming China: Approaches to Cultural Change in Contemporary China*, edited by Kevin Latham, Stuart Thompson, and Jakob Klein, 22–41. New York: Routledge.

Crossley, Pamela. 1999. *A Translucent Mirror: History and Identity in Qing Imperial Ideology*. Berkeley: University of California Press.

Csordas, Thomas J. 1999. "The Body's Career in Anthropology." In *Anthropological Theory Today*, edited by Henrietta L. Moore, 172–205. Cambridge, UK: Polity Press.

Davis, Deborah S., ed. 2000. *The Consumer Revolution in Urban China*. Berkeley: University of California Press.

Davis, Kathy. 1995. *Reshaping the Female Body: The Dilemma of Cosmetic Surgery*. New York: Routledge.

Delgado, Richard, and Jean Stefancic. 2001. *Critical Race Theory: An Introduction*. New York: New York University Press.

de Solier, Isabelle. 2013a. *Food and the Self: Consumption, Production, and Material Culture*. New York: Bloomsbury.

——. 2013b. "Food Culture: Introduction." *Cultural Studies Review* 19, no. 1: 4–8.

Dikötter, Frank. 1992. *The Discourse of Race in Modern China*. Stanford, CA: Stanford University Press.

——. 1994. "Racial Identities in China: Context and Meaning." *China Quarterly*, no. 138: 404–12.

——. 1995. *Sex, Culture and Modernity in China: Medical Science and the Construction of Sexual Identities in the Early Republican Period*. Honolulu: University of Hawai'i Press.

——. 1998. *Imperfect Conditions: Medical Knowledge, Birth Defects, and Eugenics in China*. New York: Columbia University Press.

——. 2008. *The Age of Openness: China before Mao*. Berkeley: University of California Press.

——. 2015. *The Discourse of Race in Modern China*. 2nd ed. Oxford: Oxford University Press.

Dirlik, Arif. 1993. "Review Article: The Discourse of Race in Modern China." *China Information* 7, no. 4: 68–71.

Dreyer, June. 1976. *China's Forty Millions: Minority Nationalities and National*

Integration in the People's Republic of China. Cambridge, MA: Harvard University Press.

——. 2006. *China's Political System: Modernization and Tradition.* New York: Pearson/Longman.

Duara, Prasenjit. 1995. *Rescuing History from the Nation.* Chicago: University of Chicago Press.

Du Bois, W. E. B. 1940. *Dusk of Dawn: An Essay toward an Autobiography of a Race Concept.* New Brunswick, NJ: Transaction Publishers.

Dumont, Louis. 1970. *Homo Hierarchicus: the caste system and its implications.* University of Chicago Press: Chicago.

Ebrey, Patricia. 1996. "Surnames and Han Chinese Identity." In *Negotiating Ethnicities in China and Taiwan,* edited by Melissa J. Brown, 19–36. Berkeley: Institute of East Asian Studies, University of California, Berkeley.

Edmonds, Alexander. 2007. "'The Poor Have the Right to Be Beautiful': Cosmetic Surgery in Neoliberal Brazil." *Journal of the Royal Anthropological Institute* 13, no. 2: 363–81.

Edwards, Louise. 2006. "Sport, Fashion, and Beauty: New Incarnations of the Female Politician in Contemporary China." In *Embodied Modernities: Corporeality, Representation, and Chinese Cultures,* edited by Fran Martin and Larissa Heinrich, 146–62. Honolulu: University of Hawai'i Press.

Elias, Ana Sofia, Rosalind Gill, and Christina Scharff, eds. 2017. *Aesthetic Labour: Rethinking Beauty Politics in Neoliberalism.* London: Palgrave Macmillan.

Elvin, Mark. 1985. "Between the Earth and Heaven: Conceptions of the Self in China." In *The Category of the Person: Anthropology, Philosophy, History,* edited by Michael Carrithers, Steven Collins, and Steven Lukes, 156–89. Cambridge: Cambridge University Press.

——. 1993. "Tales of *Shen* and *Xin*: Body-Person and Heart-Mind in China during the Last 150 Years." In *Self as Body in Asian Theory and Practice,* edited by Thomas Kasulis, Roger Ames, and Wimal Dissanayake, 213–94. Albany: State University of New York Press.

Evans, Harriet. 1997. *Women and Sexuality in China: Dominant Discourses of Female Sexuality and Gender since 1949.* London: Blackwell.

——. 2006. "Fashions and Feminine Consumption." In *Consuming China: Approaches to Cultural Change in Contemporary China,* edited by Kevin Latham, Stuart Thompson, and Jakob Klein, 173–89. New York: Routledge.

Fabian, Johannes. 1983. *Time and the Other: How Anthropology Makes Its Object.* New York: Columbia University Press.

Fakhro, Abdullah, Hyung Woo Yim, Yong Kyu Kim, and Anh H. Nguyen. 2015. "The Evolution of Looks and Expectations of Asian Eyelid and Eye Appearance." *Seminars in Plastic Surgery* 29, no. 3: 135–44.

Farquhar, Judith. 1987. "Problems of Knowledge in Contemporary Chinese Medical Discourse." *Social Science and Medicine* 24, no. 12: 1013–21.

———. 1994a. "Eating Chinese Medicine." *Cultural Anthropology* 9, no. 4: 471–97.

———. 1994b. "Multiplicity, Point of View, and Responsibility in Traditional Chinese Healing." In *Body, Subject & Power in China*, edited by Angela Zito and Tani E. Barlow, 78–99. Chicago: University of Chicago Press.

———. 1996. *Knowing Practice: The Clinical Encounter of Chinese Medicine*. Boulder, CO: Westview Press, 1996.

———. 2002. *Appetites: Food and Sex in Post-Socialist China*. Durham, NC: Duke University Press.

———. 2010. "Rising and Resting: Being and Time in Beijing's Neighborhoods." Paper presented at the University of Virginia.

Farquhar, Judith, and Qicheng Zhang. 2012. *Ten Thousand Things: Nurturing Life in Contemporary Beijing*. New York: Zone Books.

Farrer, James. 2002. *Opening Up: Youth Sex Culture and Market Reform in Shanghai*. Chicago: University of Chicago Press.

Fausto-Sterling, Anne. 2000. *Sexing the Body: Gender Politics and the Construction of Sexuality*. New York: Basic Books.

Featherstone, Mike. 1982. "The Body in Consumer Culture." *Theory, Culture & Society* 1, no. 2: 18–33.

———. 1991. *Consumer Culture and Postmodernism*. London: Sage.

———. 2010. "Body, Image, and Affect in Consumer Culture." *Body & Society* 16, no. 1: 193–221.

Fei, Xiaotong. (1947) 1992. *From the Soil: The Foundations of Chinese Society*. Berkeley: University of California Press.

Fennell, Vera L. 2013. "Race: China's Question and Problem." *Review of Black Political Economy* 40, no. 3: 245–75.

Fiske, Alan P., Shinobu Kitayama, Hazel R. Markus, and Richard E. Nisbett. 1998. "The Cultural Matrix of Social Psychology." In *The Handbook of Social Psychology*, edited by Daniel T. Gilbert, Susan T. Fiske, and Gardner Lindzey, 915–81. Boston: McGraw-Hill.

Flood, David, and Julie E. Starr. 2019. "Situated Comparison: A Methodological Response to an Epistemological Dilemma." *Ethos* 47, no. 2: 211–32.

Fong, Vanessa. 2004. "Filial Nationalism among Chinese Teenagers with Global Identities." *American Ethnologist* 31, no. 4: 631–48.

Foucault, Michel. 1973. *The Birth of the Clinic: An Archaeology of Medical Perception.* New York: Pantheon Books.

———. 1978. *The History of Sexuality.* Vol. 1, *An Introduction.* London: Allen Lane.

———. 1979. *Discipline and Punish: The Birth of the Prison.* New York: Vintage Books.

Frankenberg, Ruth. 1993. *White Women, Race Matters: The Social Construction of Whiteness.* Minneapolis: University of Minnesota Press.

French, Howard. 2006. "Wealth Grows, but Health Care Withers in China." *New York Times,* January 14, 2006.

Furth, Charlotte. 1999. *A Flourishing Yin: Gender in China's Medical History, 960–1665.* Berkeley: University of California Press.

Gagné, Patricia, and Deanna McGaughey. 2002. "Designing Women: Cultural Hegemony and the Exercise of Power among Women Who Have Undergone Elective Mammoplasty." *Gender & Society* 16, no. 6: 814–38.

Gao, Yuan, Jeremy Niddam, Warren Noel, Barbara Hersant, and Jean-Paul Meningaud. 2018. "Comparison of Aesthetic Facial Criteria between Caucasian and East Asian Female Populations: An Esthetic Surgeon's Perspective." *Asian Journal of Surgery* 41, no. 1: 4–11.

Geertz, Clifford. 1973a. "The Impact of the Concept of Culture on the Concept of Man." In *The Interpretation of Cultures: Selected Essays,* 33–54. New York: Basic Books.

———. 1973b. *The Interpretation of Cultures: Selected Essays.* New York: Basic Books.

Gershon, Ilana. 2014. "Selling Your Self in the United States." *Ethos* 37, no. 2: 281–95.

Giddens, Anthony. 1991. *Modernity and Self-Identity: Self and Society in the Late Modern Age.* Cambridge, UK: Polity Press.

Gimlin, Debra. 2000. "Cosmetic Surgery: Beauty as Commodity." *Qualitative Sociology* 23, no. 1: 77–98.

Gladney, Dru. 1990. "The Ethnogenesis of the Uighur." *Central Asian Survey* 9, no. 1: 1–28.

———. 1994. "Representing Nationality in China: Refiguring Majority/Minority Identities." *Journal of Asian Studies* 53, no. 1: 92–123.

———. 1996. *Muslim Chinese: Ethnic Nationalism in the People's Republic.* Cambridge, MA: Council on East Asian Studies, Harvard University.

———. 2004. *Dislocating China: Muslims, Minorities, and Other Subaltern Subjects*. Chicago: University of Chicago Press.

Glenn, Evelyn Nakano, ed. 2008. *Shades of Difference: Why Skin Color Matters*. Stanford, CA: Stanford University Press.

Grosz, Elizabeth. 2004. *Nick of Time: Politics, Evolution, and the Untimely*. Durham, NC: Duke University Press.

———. 2011. *Becoming Undone: Darwinian Reflections on Life, Politics, and Art*. Durham, NC: Duke University Press.

Gupta, Akhil, and James Ferguson. 1992. "Beyond 'Culture': Space, Identity, and the Politics of Difference." *Cultural Anthropology* 7, no. 1: 6–23.

———, eds. 1997. *Culture, Power, Place: Explorations in Critical Anthropology*. Durham, NC: Duke University Press.

Hall, Ronald. 2005. "The Euro-Americanization of Race: Alien Perspective of African Americans vis-à-vis Trivialization of Skin Color." *Journal of Black Studies* 36, no. 1: 116–29.

Handler, Richard. 1988. *Nationalism and the Politics of Culture in Quebec*. Madison: University of Wisconsin Press.

———. 2005. *Critics against Culture: Anthropological Observers of Mass Society*. Madison: University of Wisconsin Press.

———. 2009. "The Uses of Incommensurability in Anthropology." *New Literary History* 40, no. 3: 627–47.

Hansen, Mette Halskov, and Cuiming Pang. 2008. "Me and My Family: Perceptions of Individual and Collective among Young Rural Chinese." *European Journal of East Asian Studies* 7, no. 1: 75–99.

Hansen, Mette Halskov, and Rune Svarverud, eds. 2010. *iChina: The Rise of the Individual in Modern Chinese Society*. Copenhagen: Nordic Institute of Asian Studies.

Hanser, Amy. 2002. "The Chinese Enterprising Self: Young, Educated Urbanites and the Search for Work." In *Popular China: Unofficial Culture in a Globalizing Society*, edited by Perry Link, Richard P. Madsen, and Paul Pickowicz, 189–206. Lanham, MD: Rowman & Littlefield.

———. 2005. "The Gendered Rice Bowl: The Sexual Politics of Service Work in Urban China." *Gender & Society* 19, no. 5: 581–600.

———. 2008. *Service Encounters: Class, Gender, and the Market for Social Distinction in Urban China*. Stanford, CA: Stanford University Press, 2008.

Hanser, Amy, and Jialin Camille Li. 2015. "Opting Out? Gated Consumption, Infant Formula and China's Affluent Urban Consumers." *China Journal*, no. 74: 110–28.

Haraway, Donna. 1988. "Situated Knowledges: The Science Question in Feminism and the Privilege of Partial Perspective." *Feminist Studies* 14, no. 3 (1988): 575–99.

Harrell, Stevan. 1985. "Why Do the Chinese Work So Hard? Reflections on an Entrepreneurial Ethic." *Modern China* 11, no. 2: 203–26.

———. 1995a. *Cultural Encounters on China's Ethnic Frontiers*. Seattle: University of Washington Press.

———. 1995b. "Introduction: Civilizing Projects and the Reaction to Them." In *Cultural Encounters on China's Ethnic Frontiers*, edited by Stevan Harrell, 3–36. Seattle: University of Washington Press.

Hartigan, John. 1997. "Establishing the Fact of Whiteness." *American Anthropologist*, n.s., 99, no. 3: 495–505.

He Qinglian. 2005. "Huse nuxing ji Qita: Yuanshi jilei shiqi de zhongshengxiang" (Gray woman and others: The social creatures produced by the period of primitive accumulation). *Zhongguo baogao zhoukan* (China report weekly), January 8, 2005. www.china-week.com/html/2358.htm.

Herzfeld, Michael. 2001. "Performing Comparisons: Ethnography, Globetrotting, and the Spaces of Social Knowledge." *Journal of Anthropological Research* 57, no. 3: 259–76.

Heywood, Paolo. 2017. "The Ontological Turn." In *The Cambridge Encyclopedia of Anthropology*, edited by Felix Stein, Sian Lazar, Matei Candea, Hildegard Diemberger, Joel Robbins, Andrew Sanchez, and Rupert Stasch. Cambridge: Cambridge University Press. http://doi.org/10.29164/17ontology.

Hirschhorn, Michelle. 1996. "Orlan: Artist in the Post-Human Age of Mechanical Reincarnation: Body as Ready (to Be Re-) Made." In *Generations and Geographies in the Visual Arts: Feminist Readings*, edited by Griselda Pollock, 110–34. New York: Routledge.

Hochschild, Arlie. (1983) 2012. *The Managed Heart: Commercialization of Human Feeling*. Berkeley: University of California Press.

Holbraad, Martin, Morten Axel Pedersen, and Eduardo Viveiros de Castro. 2014. "The Politics of Ontology: Anthropological Positions." *Fieldsites*, January 13, 2014. https://culanth.org/fieldsights/the-politics-of-ontology-anthropological -positions.

Hollan, Douglas. 1997. "The Relevance of Person-Centered Ethnography to Cross-Cultural Psychiatry." *Transcultural Psychiatry* 34, no. 2: 219–34.

———. 2001. "Developments in Person-Centered Ethnography." In *The Psychology of Cultural Experience*, edited by Carmella Moore and Holly Mathews, 48–67. Cambridge: Cambridge University Press.

Holland, Dorothy, and Andrew Kipnis. 1994. "Metaphors of Embarrassment and Stories of Exposures: The Not-So-Egocentric Self in American Culture." *Ethos* 22, no. 3: 316–42.

Hooi, Alexis. 2009. "The Disunited Colors of Prejudice." *China Daily*, July 31, 2009.

Hsu, Carolyn. 2007. *Creating Market Socialism: How Ordinary People Are Shaping Class and Status in China.* Durham, NC: Duke University Press.

Hsu, Elisabeth. 1999. *The Transmission of Chinese Medicine.* Cambridge: Cambridge University Press.

Hsu, Francis L. K. 1948. *Under the Ancestor's Shadow: Chinese Culture and Personality.* New York: Columbia University Press.

Hunter, Margaret. 2005. *Race, Gender, and the Politics of Skin Tone.* New York: Routledge.

Jarrín, Alvaro. 2017. *The Biopolitics of Beauty: Cosmetic Citizenship and Affective Capital in Brazil.* Durham, NC: Duke University Press.

Jha, Meeta Rani. 2016. *The Global Beauty Industry: Colorism, Racism, and the National Body.* New York: Routledge.

Ji Jun (吉军). 2012. *Jiuzhong tizhi: Yingyang fangan*, 九种体质：营养方案 (Nine types of *tizhi*: A nutrition plan). Beijing: Publishing House of Electronics Industry.

Ji, Li-Jun, Albert Lee, and Tieyuan Guo. 2010. "The Thinking Styles of Chinese People." In *The Oxford Handbook of Chinese Psychology*, edited by Michael Harris Bond, 155–67. Oxford: Oxford University Press.

Johansson, Perry. 1998. "White Skin, Large Breasts: Chinese Beauty Product Advertising as Cultural Discourse." *China Information* 13, no. 2–3: 59–84.

Juvin, Hervé. 2010. *The Coming of the Body.* London: Verso.

Kapferer, Bruce. 1988. *Legends of People, Myths of State: Violence, Intolerance, and Political Culture in Sri Lanka and Australia.* Washington, DC: Smithsonian Institution Press.

———. 1989. "Nationalist Ideology and a Comparative Anthropology." *Ethnos* 54, no. 3–4: 161–99.

Kaw, Eugenia. 1993. "Medicalization of Racial Features: Asian American Women and Cosmetic Surgery." *Medical Anthropology Quarterly* 7, no. 1: 74–89.

Kawashima, Terry. 2002. "Seeing Faces, Making Races: Challenging Visual Tropes of Racial Difference." *Meridians* 3, no. 1: 161–90.

Kim, Jongmi. 2012. *Women in South Korea: New Femininities and Consumption.* New York: Routledge.

Kipnis, Andrew. 1997. *Producing Guanxi: Sentiment, Self, and Subculture in a North China Village*. Durham, NC: Duke University Press.

——. 2002. "Practices of *Guanxi* Production and Practices of *Ganqing* Avoidance." In *Social Connections in China: Institutions, Culture, and the Changing Nature of* Guanxi, edited by Thomas Gold, Doug Guthrie, and David Wank, 21–34. Cambridge: Cambridge University Press.

——. 2006. "*Suzhi*: A Keyword Approach." *China Quarterly*, no. 186: 295–313.

——. 2007. "Neoliberalism Reified: *Suzhi* Discourse and Tropes of Neoliberalism in the People's Republic of China." *Journal of the Royal Anthropological Institute* 13, no. 2: 383–400.

——, ed. 2012a. *Chinese Modernity and the Individual Psyche*. New York: Palgrave Macmillan.

——. 2012b. "Introduction: Chinese Modernity and the Individual Psyche." In *Chinese Modernity and the Individual Psyche*, edited by Andrew Kipnis, 1–16. New York: Palgrave Macmillan.

Klein, Jacob. 2013. "Everyday Approaches to Food Safety in Kunming." *China Quarterly*, no. 214: 376–93.

Kleinman, Arthur. 1981. *Patients and Healers in the Context of Culture: An Exploration of the Borderland between Anthropology, Medicine, and Psychiatry*. Berkeley: University of California Press.

——. 1999. "Experience and Its Moral Modes: Culture, Human Conditions, and Disorder." In *The Tanner Lectures on Human Values*, vol. 20, edited by Grethe B. Peterson, 355–420. Salt Lake City: University of Utah Press.

Kleinman, Arthur, and Joan Kleinman. 1991. "Suffering and Its Professional Transformation: Toward an Ethnography of Interpersonal Experience." *Culture, Medicine, and Psychiatry* 15, no. 3: 275–301.

Kleinman, Arthur, Yunxiang Yan, Jing Jun, Sing Lee, Everett Zhang, Pan Tianshu, Wu Fei, and Guo Jinhua. 2011. *Deep China: The Moral Life of the Person; What Anthropology and Psychiatry Tell Us about China Today*. Berkeley: University of California Press.

Kolchin, Peter. 2002. "Whiteness Studies: The New History of Race in America." *Journal of American History* 89, no. 1: 154–73.

Kondo, Dorinne. 1990. *Crafting Selves: Power, Gender, and Discourses of Identity in a Japanese Workplace*. Chicago: University of Chicago Press.

Kroker, Arthur, and Marilouise Kroker, eds. 1987. *Body Invaders: Sexuality and the Postmodern Condition*. New York: Macmillan Education.

Kulick, Don, and Anne Meneley, eds. 2005. *Fat: The Anthropology of an Obsession*. New York: Penguin Group.

Kuriyama, Shigehisa. 1994. "The Imagination of Winds and the Development of the Chinese Conception of the Body." In *Body, Subject & Power in China*, edited by Angela Zito and Tani E. Barlow, 23–41. Chicago: University of Chicago Press.

———. 2002. *The Expressiveness of the Body and the Divergence of Greek and Chinese Medicine*. New York: Zone Books.

Lan, Shanshan. 2016. "The Shifting Meanings of Race in China: A Case Study of the African Diaspora Communities in Guangzhou." *City and Society* 28, no. 3: 298–318.

Lancaster, Roger N. 2003. *The Trouble with Nature: Sex in Science and Popular Culture*. Berkeley: University of California Press.

Latham, Kevin, Stuart Thompson, and Jakob Klein, eds. 2006. *Consuming China: Approaches to Cultural Change in Contemporary China*. London and New York: Routledge

Laurel, Brenda. 1993. *Computers as Theatre*. Reading, MA: Addison-Wesley.

Lee, Haiyan. 2006. "Governmentality and the Aesthetic State: A Chinese Fantasia." *Positions: East Asia Cultures Critique* 14, no. 1: 99–129.

Lewis, Amanda. 2004. "'What Group?' Studying Whites and Whiteness in the Era of 'Color-Blindness.'" *Sociological Theory* 22, no. 4: 623–46.

Lindholm, Charles. 2008. *Culture and Authenticity*. Malden, MA: Blackwell.

Litzinger, Ralph. 1995. Review of *The Discourse of Race in Modern China*, by Frank Dikötter. H-World, H-Net Reviews, August. www.hartford-hwp.com /archives/55/043.html.

Liu, Jieyu. 2017. *Gender, Sexuality and Power in Chinese Corporations: Beauties at Work*. London: Palgrave Macmillan.

Liu, Xin. 2002. *The Otherness of Self: A Genealogy of the Self in Contemporary China*. Ann Arbor: University of Michigan Press.

Liu, Y. 2012. "The Analysis of the Current Needs and Education in Chinese Medical Cosmetology." www.xahtxy.cn/2012/xsyj_0416/1338.html.

Lock, Margaret. 1993. *Encounters with Aging: Mythologies of Menopause in Japan and North America*. Berkeley: University of California Press.

Lock, Margaret, and Judith Farquhar, eds. 2007. *Beyond the Body Proper: Reading the Anthropology of Material Life*. Durham, NC: Duke University Press.

Lock, Margaret, and Vinh-Kim Nguyen. 2010. *An Anthropology of Biomedicine*. Oxford, UK: Wiley-Blackwell.

Lufrano, Richard. 1994. "The 1988 Nanjing Incident: Notes on Race and Politics in Contemporary China." *Bulletin of Concerned Asian Scholars* 26, no. 1–2: 83–92.

Ma, Rong. 2010. "'Culturalism' and 'Nationalism' in Modern China." In *The Ethnicity Reader: Nationalism, Multiculturalism and Migration*, edited by Montserrat Guibernau and John Rex, 299–307. 2nd ed. Cambridge, UK: Polity Press.

Ma, Zhiying. 2012. "Psychiatric Subjectivity and Cultural Resistance: Experience and Explanations of Schizophrenia in Contemporary China." In *Chinese Modernity and the Individual Psyche*, edited by Andrew Kipnis, 203–28. New York: Palgrave Macmillan.

Markus, Hazel R., and Shinobu Kitayama. 1998. "The Cultural Psychology of Personality." *Journal of Cross-Cultural Psychology* 29, no. 1: 63–87.

Mathews, Gordon, Linessa Dan Lin, and Yang Yang. 2017. *The World in Guangzhou: Africans and Other Foreigners in South China's Global Marketplace*. Chicago: University of Chicago Press.

Mauss, Marcel. (1938) 1985. "A Category of the Human Mind: The Notion of Person; the Notion of Self." Translated by W. D. Halls. In *The Category of the Person: Anthropology, Philosophy, History*, edited by Michael Carrithers, Steven Collins, and Steven Lukes, 1–25. Cambridge: Cambridge University Press.

McClaurin, Irma. 2001. "Theorizing a Black Feminist Self in Anthropology: Toward an Autoethnographic Approach." In *Black Feminist Anthropology: Theory, Politics, Praxis, and Poetics*, edited by Irma McClaurin, 49–76. New Brunswick, NJ: Rutgers University Press.

McCrum, Kirstie. 2015. "Shakespeare Superfan Blows £150K on Extreme Plastic Surgery to Make Himself Look like the Bard." *Mirror*, April 3, 2015. www .mirror.co.uk/news/world-news/shakespeare-superfan-blows-150k-extreme -5452241.

McKhann, Charles F. 1995. "The Naxi and the Nationalities Question." In *Cultural Encounters on China's Ethnic Frontiers*, edited by Stevan Harrell, 39–62. Seattle: University of Washington Press.

Mercer, Kobena. 1990. "Black Hair/Style Politics." In *Out There: Marginalization and Contemporary Culture*, edited by Russell Ferguson, Marsha Gever, Trinh T. Minh-ha, and Cornel West, 247–64. New York: New Museum of Contemporary Art; Cambridge, MA: MIT Press.

Miller, Laura. 2006. *Beauty Up: Exploring Contemporary Japanese Body Aesthetics*. Berkeley: University of California Press.

Millman, Marcia. 1980. *Such a Pretty Face: Being Fat in America*. New York: Norton.

Mohanty, Chandra. 1984. "Under Western Eyes: Feminist Scholarship and Colonial Discourses." *Boundary 2* 12, no. 3; 13, no. 1: 333–58.

Morgan, Kathryn Pauly. 1991. "Women and the Knife: Cosmetic Surgery and the Colonization of Women's Bodies." *Hypatia* 6, no. 3: 25–53.

Morris, Andrew. 2002. "'I Believe You Can Fly': Basketball Culture in Postsocialist China." In *Popular China: Unofficial Culture in a Globalizing Society*, edited by Perry Link, Richard P. Madsen, and Paul Pickowicz, 9–38. Lanham, MD: Rowman & Littlefield.

Moses, Yolanda. 2017. "Why Do We Keep Using the Word 'Caucasian'?" *SAPIENS*, February 1, 2017. www.sapiens.org/column/race/caucasian-terminology-origin.

Munro, Donald J. 1977. *The Concept of Man in Contemporary China*. Ann Arbor: University of Michigan Press.

Negrin, Llewellyn. 2002. "Cosmetic Surgery and the Eclipse of Identity." *Body & Society* 8, no. 4: 21–42.

Nisbett, Richard E. 2003. *The Geography of Thought: How Asians and Westerners Think Differently—and Why*. New York: Free Press.

Ong, Aihwa. 1997. "Chinese Modernities: Narratives of Nation and of Capitalism." In *Ungrounded Empires: The Cultural Politics of Modern Chinese Transnationalism*, edited by Aihwa Ong and Donald Nonini, 171–202. New York: Routledge.

——. 2007. *Neoliberalism as Exception: Mutations of Citizenship and Sovereignty*. Durham, NC: Duke University Press.

Ortner, Sherry B. 2006. *Anthropology and Social Theory: Culture, Power, and the Acting Subject*. Durham, NC: Duke University Press.

Osburg, John. 2013. *Anxious Wealth: Money and Morality among China's New Rich*. Stanford, CA: Stanford University Press.

Otis, Eileen. 2012. *Markets and Bodies: Women, Service Work, and the Making of Inequality in China*. Stanford, CA: Stanford University Press.

Ots, Thomas. 1990. "The Angry Liver, the Anxious Heart, and the Melancholy Spleen: The Phenomenology of Perceptions in Chinese Culture." *Culture, Medicine, and Psychiatry* 14: 21–58.

Oxfeld, Ellen. 2017. *Bitter and Sweet: Food, Meaning, and Modernity in Rural China*. Berkeley: University of California Press.

Oyewumi, Oyeronke. 1997. *The Invention of Women: Making an African Sense of Western Gender Discourse*. Minneapolis: University of Minnesota Press.

Page, Helán. 1995. North American Dialogue. Interview by Sam Beck. *Anthropology Newsletter* 36, no. 1: 21–22.

Pels, Peter. 2008. "What Has Anthropology Learned from the Anthropology of Colonialism?" *Social Anthropology* 16, no. 3: 280–99.

Popenoe, Rebecca. 2005. "Ideal." In *Fat: The Anthropology of an Obsession*, edited by Don Kulick and Anne Meneley, 9–28. New York: Penguin Group.

Potter, Sulamith Heins. 1988. "The Cultural Construction of Emotion in Rural Chinese Social Life." *Ethos* 16, no. 2: 181–208.

Pow, Choon-Piew. 2009. *Gated Communities in China: Class, Privilege and the Moral Politics of the Good Life*. London: Routledge.

Rawski, Evelyn. 1996. "Reenvisioning the Qing: The Significance of the Qing Period in Chinese History." *Journal of Asian Studies* 55, no. 4: 829–50.

Reischer, Erica, and Kathryn S. Koo. 2004. "The Body Beautiful: Symbolism and Agency in the Social World." *Annual Review of Anthropology* 33: 297–317.

Rofel, Lisa. 1999. *Other Modernities: Gendered Yearnings in China after Socialism*. Berkeley: University of California Press.

———. 2007. *Desiring China: Experiments in Neoliberalism, Sexuality, and Public Culture*. Annotated ed. Durham, NC: Duke University Press.

Rossabi, Morris. 2004. Introduction to *Governing China's Multiethnic Frontiers*, edited by Morris Rossabi, 3–18. Seattle: University of Washington Press.

Rowe, William T. 2010. *China's Last Empire: The Great Qing*. Cambridge, MA: Belknap Press of Harvard University Press.

Rudelson, Justin. 1997. *Oasis Identities: Uyghur Nationalism along China's Silk Road*. New York: Columbia University Press.

Said, Edward. 1978. *Orientalism*. New York: Vintage Books.

Saraswati, L. Ayu. 2010. "Cosmopolitan Whiteness: The Effects and Affects of Skin-Whitening Advertisements in a Transnational Women's Magazine in Indonesia." *Meridians* 10, no. 2: 15–41.

———. 2013. *Seeing Beauty, Sending Race in Transnational Indonesia*. Honolulu: University of Hawai'i Press.

Sautman, Barry. 1994. "Anti-Black Racism in Post-Mao China." *China Quarterly*, no. 138: 413–37.

Scheid, Volker. 2002. *Chinese Medicine in Contemporary China: Plurality and Synthesis*. Durham, NC: Duke University Press.

Schein, Louisa. 1994. "The Consumption of Color and the Politics of White Skin in Post-Mao China." *Social Text*, no. 41: 141–64.

———. 2000. *Minority Rules: The Miao and the Feminine in China's Cultural Politics*. Durham, NC: Duke University Press.

Schneider, David. 1984. *A Critique of the Study of Kinship.* Ann Arbor: University of Michigan Press.

Schoenhals, Martin. 1993. *The Paradox of Power in a People's Republic of China Middle School.* Armonk, NY: M. E. Sharpe.

Scott, David. 1999. *Refashioning Futures: Criticism after Postcoloniality.* Princeton, NJ: Princeton University Press.

Scrinis, Gyorgy. 2008. "On the Ideology of Nutritionism." *Gastronomica* 8, no. 1: 39–48.

Segal, Daniel. 2000. "'Western Civ' and the Staging of History in American Higher Education." *American Historical Review* 105, no. 3: 770–805.

Segal, Daniel, and Richard Handler. 2006. "Cultural Approaches to Nationalism." In *The Sage Handbook of Nations and Nationalism*, edited by Gerard Delanty and Krishan Kumar, 57–65. London: Sage.

Shepherd, John R. 1993. *Statecraft and Political Economy on the Taiwan Frontier, 1600–1800.* Stanford, CA: Stanford University Press.

———. 2003. "Rethinking Sinicization: Process of Acculturation and Assimilation." In *Papers from the Third International Conference on Sinology: State, Market and Ethnic Groups Contextualized.* Taipei: Institute of Ethnology, Academia Sinica.

Shilling, Chris. 2005. *The Body in Culture, Technology and Society.* London: Sage.

Shi-xu. 2002. "The Discourse of Cultural Psychology: Transforming the Discourses of Self, Memory, Narrative and Culture." *Culture & Psychology* 8, no. 1: 65–78.

Sivin, Nathan. 1987. *Traditional Medicine in Contemporary China.* Ann Arbor: Center for Chinese Studies, University of Michigan.

Sökefeld, Martin. 1999. "Debating Self, Identity, and Culture in Anthropology." *Current Anthropology* 40, no. 4: 417–47.

Spiro, Melford E. 1993. "Is the Western Conception of the Self 'Peculiar' within the Context of the World Cultures?" *Ethos* 21, no. 2: 107–53.

Spivak, Gayatri Chakravorty. 1988. "Subaltern Studies: Deconstructing Historiography." In *Selected Subaltern Studies*, edited by Ranajit Guha and Gayatri Chakravorty Spivak, 3–32. New York: Oxford University Press.

Stafford, Charles. 1993. Review of *The Discourse of Race in Modern China*, by Frank Dikötter. *Man: The Journal of the Royal Anthropological Institute*, n.s., 28, no. 3: 609.

Stasch, Rupert. 2009. *Society of Others: Kinship and Mourning in a West Papuan Place.* Berkeley: University of California Press.

Stocking, George W., Jr. 1966. "Franz Boas and the Culture Concept in Historical

Perspective." *American Anthropologist*, n.s., 68, no. 4: 867–82.

———. 1992. *The Ethnographer's Magic, and Other Essays in the History of Anthropology*. Madison: Univeristy of Wisconsin Press.

Sullivan, Michael J. 1994. "The 1988–89 Nanjing Anti-African Protests: Racial Nationalism or National Racism?" *China Quarterly*, no. 138: 438–57.

Tam, Waikeung, and Dali Yang. 2005. "Food Safety and the Development of Regulatory Institutions in China." *Asian Perspective* 29, no. 4: 5–36.

Thøgersen, Stig. 2003. "Parasites or Civilizers: The Legitimacy of the Chinese Communist Party in Rural Areas." *China: An International Journal* 1, no. 2: 200–223.

Thomas, Lynn M. 2020. *Beneath the Surface: A Transnational History of Skin Lighteners*. Durham, NC: Duke University Press.

Tomba, Luigi. 2004. "Creating an Urban Middle Class: Social Engineering in Beijing." *China Journal*, no. 51: 1–26.

———. 2009. "Of Quality, Harmony, and Community: Civilization and the Middle Class in Urban China." *Positions: East Asia Cultures Critique* 17, no. 3: 591–616.

———. 2010. "Gating Urban Spaces in China: Inclusion, Exclusion and Government." In *Gated Communities: Social Sustainability in Contemporary and Historical Gated Developments*, edited by Samer Bagaeen and Ola Uduku, 27–37. London: Earthscan.

Trouillot, Michel-Rolph. 2003. *Global Transformations: Anthropology and the Modern World*. New York: Macmillan Education.

Tsing, Anna. 2005. *Friction: An Ethnography of Global Connection*. Princeton, NJ: Princeton University Press.

Tu, Wei-Ming. 1985. *Confucian Thought: Selfhood as Creative Transformation*. Albany: State University of New York Press.

Tung, May P. M. 1994. "Symbolic Meanings of the Body in Chinese Culture and 'Somatization.'" *Culture, Medicine, and Psychiatry* 18: 483–92.

Veeck, Ann, Hongyan Yu, and Alvin Burns. 2010. "Consumer Risks and New Food Systems in Urban China." *Journal of Macromarketing* 30, no. 3: 222–37.

Visweswaran, Kamala. 1998. "Race and the Culture of Anthropology." *American Anthropologist*, n.s., 100, no. 1: 70–83.

Wagley, Charles, and Marvin Harris. 1958. *Minorities in the New World: Six Case Studies*. New York: Columbia University Press.

Walsh, Eileen. 2009. "Anthropology of China's Frontier: From the Periphery to the Centre." In "Anthropology of Contemporary China." Special issue, *Social Anthropology* 17, no. 1: 109–14.

Waltner, Ann. 1990. *Getting an Heir: Adoption and the Construction of Kinship in Late Imperial China*. Honolulu: University of Hawai'i Press.

Wang, Qi, and Jens Brockmeier. 2002. "Autobiographical Remembering as Cultural Practice: Understanding the Interplay between Memory, Self and Culture." *Culture & Psychology* 8, no. 1: 45–64.

Wang Yong (王永). 2012. *Sixing renge: Sixiang tizhide rensheng shuomingshu*, 四型人格：四象体质的人生说明书 (Four types of people: A book describing the four essential types of *tizhi*). Nanjing: Yilin Publishing.

Weitz, Rose. 2001. "Women and Their Hair: Seeking Power through Resistance and Accommodation." *Gender & Society* 15, no. 6: 667–86.

Wen, Hua. 2009. "'Being Good-Looking Is Capital': Cosmetic Surgery in China Today." *Asian Anthropology* 8, no. 1: 89–107.

———. 2013. *Buying Beauty: Cosmetic Surgery in China*. Hong Kong: Hong Kong University Press.

Wilk, Richard. 2004. "Morals and Metaphors: The Meaning of Consumption." In *Elusive Consumption*, edited by Karin Ekström and Helene Brembeck, 11–26. New York: Berg.

Willis, William. 1972. "Skeletons in the Anthropological Closet." In *Reinventing Anthropology*, edited by Dell Hymes, 121–52. New York: Pantheon Books.

Witz, Anne 2000. "Whose Body Matters? Feminist Sociology and the Corporeal Turn in Sociology and Feminism." *Body & Society* 6, no. 2: 1–24.

Wolf, Margery. 1972. *Women and the Family in Rural Taiwan*. Stanford, CA: Stanford University Press.

Wolf, Margery, and Roxane Witke, eds. 1975. *Women in Chinese Society*. Stanford, CA: Stanford University Press.

Wolf, Naomi. 1990. *The Beauty Myth: How Images of Beauty Are Used against Women*. New York: William Morrow.

Woronov, Terry. 2003. "Transforming the Future: 'Quality' Children and the Chinese Nation." PhD diss., University of Chicago.

Wyatt, Don J. 2010. *The Blacks of Premodern China*. Philadelphia: University of Pennsylvania Press.

Yan, Hairong. 2003. "Neoliberal Governmentality and Neohumanism: Organizing Suzhi/Value Flow through Labor Recruitment Networks." *Cultural Anthropology* 18, no. 4: 493–523.

Yan, Yunxiang. 1996. *The Flow of Gifts: Reciprocity and Social Networks in a Chinese Village*. Stanford, CA: Stanford University Press.

———. 1997. "McDonald's in Beijing: The Localization of Americana." In *Golden Arches East: McDonald's in East Asia*, edited by James L. Watson, 39–76. Stanford, CA: Stanford University Press.

———. 2003. *Private Life under Socialism: Love, Intimacy, and Family Change in a Chinese Village, 1949–1999*. Stanford, CA: Stanford University Press.

———. 2008. "Introduction: Understanding the Rise of the Chinese Individual." *European Journal of Asian Studies* 7, no. 1: 1–9.

———. 2009. *The Individualization of Chinese Society*. New York: Berg.

———. 2012. "Food Safety and Social Risk in Contemporary China." *Journal of Asian Studies* 71, no. 3: 705–29.

Yanagisako, Sylvia. 2002. *Producing Culture and Capital: Family Firms in Italy*. Princeton, NJ: Princeton University Press.

Yanagisako, Sylvia, and Carole Delaney, eds. 1994. *Naturalizing Power: Essays in Feminist Cultural Analysis*. New York: Routledge.

Yang, Jie. 2011. "*Nennu* and *Shunu*: Gender, Body Politics, and the Beauty Economy in China." *Signs: Journal of Women in Culture and Society* 36, no. 2: 333–57.

———. 2013. "'Fake Happiness': Counseling, Potentiality, and Psycho-Politics in China." *Ethos* 41, no. 3: 292–312.

———. 2017. "Holistic Labor: Gender, Body and the Beauty and Wellness Industry in China." In *Aesthetic Labour: Rethinking Beauty Politics in Neoliberalism*, edited by Ana Sofia Elias, Rosalind Gill, and Christina Scharff, 117–31. London: Palgrave Macmillan.

Yang, Mayfair. 1994. *Gifts, Favors, and Banquets: The Art of Social Relationships in China*. Ithaca, NY: Cornell University Press.

Yuan, Gao. 1989. "In China, Black Isn't Beautiful." *New York Times*, January 25, 1989.

Zhan, Mei. 2009. *Other-Worldly: Making Chinese Medicine through Transnational Frames*. Durham, NC: Duke University Press.

Zhang, Li. 2002. "Urban Experiences and Social Belonging among Chinese Rural Migrants." In *Popular China: Unofficial Culture in a Globalizing Society*, edited by Perry Link, Richard P. Madsen, and Paul Pickowicz, 275–300. Lanham, MD: Rowman & Littlefield.

———. 2008. "Private Homes, Distinct Lifestyles: Performing a New Middle Class." In *Privatizing China: Socialism from Afar*, edited by Li Zhang and Aihwa Ong, 23–40. Ithaca, NY: Cornell University Press.

———. 2010. *In Search of Paradise: Middle-Class Living in a Chinese Metropolis*. Ithaca, NY: Cornell University Press.

Zhang, Li, and Aihwa Ong, eds. 2008. *Privatizing China: Socialism from Afar.* Ithaca, NY: Cornell University Press.

Zhang, Yanhua. 2007. *Transforming Emotions with Chinese Medicine: An Ethnographic Account from Contemporary China.* Albany: State University of New York Press.

Zhen, Zhang. 2000. "Mediating Time: The 'Rice Bowl of Youth' in Fin de Siècle Urban China." *Public Culture* 12, no. 1: 93–113.

Zheng, Tiantian. 2009. *Red Lights: The Lives of Sex Workers in Postsocialist China.* Minneapolis: University of Minnesota Press.

Zheng, Wang. 2001. "Call Me 'Qingnian' but Not 'Funü': A Maoist Youth in Retrospect." In *Some of Us: Chinese Women Growing Up in the Mao Era*, edited by Xueping Zhong, Wang Zheng, and Bai Di, 27–52. New Brunswick, NJ: Rutgers University Press.

Zheng, Wenwen, Qian Yang , Kaiping Peng, and Feng Yu. 2016. "What's in the Chinese Babyface? Cultural Differences in Understanding the Babyface." *Frontiers in Psychology* 7: 819. https://doi.org/10.3389/fpsyg.2016.00819.

Zhong, Xueping, Wang Zheng, and Bai Di, eds. 2001. *Some of Us: Chinese Women Growing Up in the Mao Era.* New Brunswick, NJ: Rutgers University Press.

Zhou, Minglang. 2003. *Multilingualism in China: The Politics of Writing Reforms for Minority Languages, 1949–2002.* Berlin: Mouton de Gruyter.

———. 2008. "Models of Nation-State Building and the Meaning of Being Chinese in Contemporary China." Paper presented at the Critical Han Studies Conference and Workshop, Stanford University, April 25–27, 2008.

Zhou, Viola. 2015. "Why Double Eyelid Surgery Is on the Rise in Asia: Rising Incomes and Acceptance, and Star Power of Fan Bingbing, Angelababy." *South China Morning Post*, May 15, 2015. www.scmp.com/lifestyle/health-beauty /article/2093921/why-double-eyelid-surgery-rise-asia-rising-incomes-and.

Zito, Angela. 1994. "Silk and Skin: Significant Boundaries." In *Body, Subject & Power in China*, edited by Angela Zito and Tani E. Barlow, 103–30. Chicago: University of Chicago Press.

Zito, Angela, and Tani E. Barlow, eds. 1994. *Body, Subject & Power in China.* Chicago: University of Chicago Press.

Zou, John. 2006. "Cross-Dressed Nation: Mei Lanfang and the Clothing of Modern Chinese Men." In *Embodied Modernities: Corporeality, Representation, and Chinese Cultures*, edited by Fran Martin and Larissa Heinrich, 79–97. Honolulu: University of Hawai'i Press.

INDEX

Page numbers in *italic* indicate illustrations.

food choices (*cont.*)
and character traits, 66; Chinese women's, 178n16; and identity, 72, 86; and necessity, 88; and personalities, 51–54; and self, 44, 73, 87, 89; and *tizhi*, 64, 68, 69–70; Western women's, 73, 81, 83, 89
foodies, 78, 87; foodie cosmopolitanism, 84
Foucault, Michel: bodily discipline, 14, 48, 149; economic system, 16; power, 15, 91; scholars disrupting cultural discourses, 29; scholars on social controls, 164–65
friendships, 35–36
fullness, feeling of, 93, 159–60

Gagné, Patricia, 15
Geertz, Clifford, 28, 36
gender: categories, 124; Chinese women, 137, 151; "construction," 108; critiques about, 162, 166; denaturalizing, 152; denial, 10; difference, 20, 23, 27, 30–31, 145, 170n13; discrimination, 19, 20, 24; equality, 155; hierarchies, 13, 17, 20, 28, 106, 108; inequality, 5, 13, 24; life in Shanghai, 143–44; oppression, 106; performance-based theories of, 154; theorist, 30; Western women, 109, 137, 140, 151–53, 183n1
golden ratio, 113
Gramsci, Antonio, 15
"gray women" (*huise nüren*), 11, 12

Han ethnicity, 32, 118, 129, 163; as category, 156; identity, 133–34, 137, 156–57; as majority, 131; women, 6
Haraway, Donna, 29
hegemony: of biomedicine, 4; common sense, 15; cultural norms, 15; Gramsci, 15, 17, 149; maintaining cultural, 16; naturalization, 17; of the Western world, 9, 18, 142, 157; of whiteness, 106
Herzfeld, Michael, 27
Hollan, Douglas, 36
homesickness, Kate's, 81
Hsu, Carolyn, 172n8

ideals. *See* beauty ideals; body ideals
identity: aesthetics of bodies, 7; bodily-selves, 31, 127; body-based, 150, 151, 155, 157; Chinese ideas about, 124; diversity, 129; and equality, 150; ethnic, 118, 182n14; food choices, 72, 86; gender, 151; group, 161; Han, 133–34, 137, 156–57; historically produced bodily differences, 109; ideology, 140; individual, 139, 147, 161; national, 130, 137, 162; nationalist narrative, 123; physical differences, 120; politics, 125; race, 108, 118; racial, 110, 115, 120, 152, 157, 162; racial features, 139; selfhood, 133, 135, 139–40; situated feminisms, 152; social, 151; static, 116; traits, 122, 138; Western women, 132, 135, 161; white liberal, 148, 152. *See also* Chinese identity
internalization, 106, 160

Jackson, Michael, 139
Juvin, Hervé, 88

power (*cont.*)

and internalization, 16, 104, 106, 160; of the market, 21; materiality of selfhood, 38, 95; mechanisms of, 17; model of, 17; and naturalization, 31, 149, 160, 161; and nature, 147, 150; operation of, 29, 91; post-socialist, 165; of racial categories, 109, 110; of social categories, 151; state, 164, 165, 166; structure, 135; struggles, 14; and *suzhi,* 46; white women and, 143; women gaining, 15; zero-sum entity, 15. *See also* theorizations of power

qi, 22, 24, 30, 62–63, 130
Qi, Wang, 56
Qin, Jiang (Avocado Lady), 76–78
Qinglian, He, 11
quality (*suzhi*), 46–47

race, 104–6, 108–10, 124, 126, 128, 137–40
racial categories, 115–16, 117–19, 125–26; hierarchies, 116–17; and othering, 115–16, 117
racial identities, 152
racialization, 120, 130; of traits, 104, 105
racism, 109–10; anthropologists avoiding, 154; anti-, 110; and Cottom, 145; daily life in Shanghai, 142; and feminism, 143; problem of the West, 109; and racial hierarchies, 116; social inequalities, 24; undermining, 151, 152–53, 154, 155; white people, 143
"real" bodies, 108
resistance, 14–15
restaurants, 67, 73, 74, 78, 83

Roberts, Julia, 102
Rofel, Lisa, 46, 47, 165, 166

Said, Edward, 131
salons, beauty, 33–34
Saraswati, L. Ayu, 16–17, 106–8
satiety. *See* feeling full
Scheid, Volker, 22
Schein, Louisa, 124–25
selfhood: autonomous, 37; beauty ideals, 70; bodies in relation to, 10, 22, 111, 120; in China, 44, 45, 47, 54, 93, 163; Chinese identity, 132, 163; "Chineseness," 132, 155, 163; Chinese women, 47–48, 160; commodification of, 180n5; cravings, 84, 86, 88, 93, 135–36, 140; desires, 46, 47; and dieting, 37, 73, 87, 91, 102, 158; differences between China and the West, 133, 137, 139–40; through disciplinary practices, 16; experiences of, 6, 93; food choices, 69, 73; forms of, 44; identity, 133, 135, 139–40; inner, 159–60; physical traits, 135; preserving, 136; quality (*suzhi*), 46; race, 38; significance for, 122; skin color, 135, 139, 163; social influences, 159; society, 31, 166; struggling with, 9; taking for granted, 165; in the West, 45, 47, 139; Western orientation to, 164; Western women, 47–48, 86–87. *See also* authentic selfhood; embodiment of selfhood; materiality of selfhood
Shakespeare, William, 126
single eyelids, 120–21
situated comparison, 26–29, 119

Western women (*cont.*)
  and eating, 85; race, 137, 150–57;
  selfhood, 47–48, 86–87; taking Chinese women's desires for granted,
  38; thinness, 48, 85
"white-collar" women, 12
whiteness: affinity with yellowness,
  123; Asian whiteness, 121, 126;
  category of, 156; construct, 146;
  conversations about, 110; cosmopolitan, 106–7, 108; critical studies, 137;
  denaturalizing categories about, 152;
  liberal, 154, 162; preference for, 16;
  privileges, 140, 141; problematic for
  Western women in Shanghai, 156;
  products enhancing, 122; racial hierarchies, 108; shapes anthropological
  interests, 150–51; trait of Caucasian
  bodies, 106–7; in the United States,
  134; Western whiteness, 126; Western women rejecting, 134, 137; and

white liberal identity, 152; whiteness
  studies, 157
whitening agents, 99–101, 112, 136
white privilege, 141–42, 143
Wilk, Richard, 87
Wolf, Naomi, 7

xiguan (used to), 49–51, 158
xihuan (liking), 49–51
Xueping (author's friend), 131, 133

Yan, Yunxiang, 36
Yang, Yang, 124
Yiyi, Zhang, 126

Zengxiu, Sheng, 56
Zhan, Mei, 30
Zhang, Li, 55–56, 164
Zheng, Tiantian, 21
Zito, Angela, 23–24, 30
Zou, John, 170n13

CPSIA information can be obtained
at www.ICGtesting.com
Printed in the USA
JSHW020951020723
44031JS00010B/1